Current Issues in Turkish Economy

Çağlar Yurtseven / Mahmut Tekçe (eds.)

Current Issues in Turkish Economy

Problems and Policy Suggestions

PETER LANG

Bibliographic Information published by the Deutsche Nationalbibliothek
The Deutsche Nationalbibliothek lists this publication in the Deutsche Nationalbibliografie; detailed bibliographic data is available online at http://dnb.d-nb.de.

Library of Congress Cataloging-in-Publication Data
A CIP catalog record for this book has been applied for at the Library of Congress.

The chapters in this book are first reviewed by the independent reviewers and then proof-read and edited by the editors. The opinions and views expressed in the articles are not necessarily those of the editors. All the views expressed in the book are purely that of the authors themselves and may not in any circumstances be regarded as stating an official position of Bahçeşehir University nor that of the editors of the book.

BAU Publications

Cover Design: © Olaf Gloeckler, Atelier Platen, Friedberg
Cover Image: © istock/peshkov

ISBN 978-3-631-78279-8 (Print)
E-ISBN 978-3-631-78438-9 (E-PDF)
E-ISBN 978-3-631-78439-6 (EPUB)
E-ISBN 978-3-631-78440-2 (MOBI)
DOI 10.3726/b15390

Peter Lang – Berlin · Bern · Bruxelles · New York · Oxford · Warszawa · Wien

This publication has been peer reviewed.

www.peterlang.com

Foreword

Turkey, the world's 17th largest economy, has several distinctive features, where the study of the characteristics and challenges of Turkish economy bears great importance for anyone who is interested in the economic performances of developing countries. Turkey is a dynamic economy with a strong economic infrastructure, well-developed financial market and competitive work force. Its strategic geographical and political position at the crossroads of the world trade and energy routes makes Turkey an economy of utmost importance for Europe.

However, despite its potential and several advantages, Turkey remains trapped in middle-income status. Turkey has experienced repetitious economic crisis and has shown episodes of remarkable economic growth since the 1980s. This makes the curious case of Turkey worth examining.

This book covers a wide range of issues in Turkish economy and aims to discuss the problems, challenges and potential of Turkey in various sectors. The topics covered in the book include areas related to macroeconomics and monetary economics (inflation expectations, determinants and conduct of monetary policy), labor economics (earning differences, overeducation in labor markets), health economics (adult obesity), tourism economics (tourism response to disruptive events) and energy economics (solar energy systems). The individual chapters are valuable not only for the scholars interested in Turkish economy, but also for the ones interested in following the applications of the most recent econometric techniques in micro and macroeconomic issues. The book as a whole, on the other hand, draws a very clear picture of the Turkish economy and sheds light on the current and future challenges of Turkey.

Editors Mahmut Tekçe, Çağlar Yurtseven

Contents

List of Contributors

Barış Soybilgen
Istanbul Bilgi University, Department of Economics,
Adress: Eski Silahtarağa Elektrik Santralı Kazım Karabekir Cad. No: 2/13 34060 Eyüpsultan / Istanbul / Turkey
email: baris.soybilgen@bilgi.edu.tr

Bilge Eriş Dereli
Marmara University, Department of Economics
e-mail: bilge.eris@marmara.edu.tr

Burak Alparslan Eroğlu
Istanbul Bilgi University, Department of Economics,
Adress: Eski Silahtarağa Elektrik Santralı Kazım Karabekir Cad. No: 2/13 34060 Eyüpsultan / Istanbul / Turkey
email: burak.eroglu@bilgi.edu.tr

Burcu Düzgün Öncel
Marmara University, Department of Economics
e-mail: burcu.duzgun@marmara.edu.tr

Çağlar Yurtseven
Bahcesehir University, Department of Economics
Adress: Çırağan Caddesi, Osmanpaşa Mektebi Sokak, No: 4 - 6
34353 Beşiktaş, Istanbul / Turkey
e-mail: caglar.yurtseven@eas.bau.edu.tr

Dinçer Dedeoğlu
Bahcesehir University, Department of Economics
Adress: Çırağan Caddesi, Osmanpaşa Mektebi Sokak, No: 4 - 6
34353 Beşiktaş, Istanbul / Turkey,
e-mail: dincer.dedeoglu@eas.bahcesehir.edu.tr

Deniz Karaoğlan
Bahcesehir University, Department of Economics
Adress: Çırağan Caddesi, Osmanpaşa Mektebi Sokak, No: 4 - 6
34353 Beşiktaş, Istanbul / Turkey
e-mail: hanifedeniz.karaoglan@eas.bau.edu.tr

Erhan Aslanoğlu
Piri Reis University, Department of Economics and Finance,
e-mail: easlanoglu@pirireis.edu.tr

Hakan Acaroğlu
Department of Economics, Eskisehir Osmangazi University
Adress: 26480 Eskisehir / Turkey
e-mail address: hacaroglu@ogu.edu.tr

Haluk Yener
Istanbul Bilgi University, Department of Economics
Adress: Eski Silahtarağa Elektrik Santralı Kazım Karabekir Cad. No: 2/13 34060 Eyüpsultan / Istanbul / Turkey
email: haluk.yener@bilgi.edu.tr

Hüseyin Kaya
Istanbul Medeniyet University, Department of Economics
Adress: 34000 Kadikoy / Istanbul / Turkey
e-mail: huseyin.kaya@medeniyet.edu.tr

Kaan Öğüt
Bahcesehir University, Department of Economics
Adress: Çırağan Caddesi, Osmanpaşa Mektebi Sokak, No: 4 - 6
34353 Beşiktaş, Istanbul / Turkey
e-mail: kaan.ogut@eas.bahcesehir.edu.tr

Kıvanç Karaman
Bogazici University, Department of Economics.
e-mail:kivanc.karaman@boun.edu.tr

Mahmut Tekçe
Department of Economics, Marmara University
e-mail: mtekce@marmara.edu.tr

M. Celalettin Baykul
Department of Metallurgical and Materials Engineering, Faculty of Engineering and Architecture, Eskisehir Osmangazi University
Adress: 26480 Eskisehir / Turkey.
e-mail address: cbaykul@ogu.edu.tr

Özer Selçuk
Department of Economics, Istanbul Medeniyet University
Adress: 34000 Kadikoy, Istanbul / Turkey,
e-mail: ozer.selcuk@medeniyet.edu.tr

Pınar Deniz
Marmara University, Department of Economics
e-mail: pinar.deniz@marmara.edu.tr

Seçil Yıldırım-Karaman
Altınbaş University, Department of Economics.

Serkan Yeşilyurt
Bahcesehir University, Department of Economics and Finance
Adress: Çırağan Caddesi, Osmanpaşa Mektebi Sokak, No: 4 - 6
34353 Beşiktaş / Istanbul / Turkey
e-mail: serkan.yesilyurt@eas.bau.edu.tr

Barış Soybilgen, Burak Alparslan Eroğlu and Haluk Yener

Taylor Rule for Turkey under Multiple Structural Breaks

Estimating the Forward-Looking Taylor Rule for Turkey under Multiple Structural Breaks

Abstract: We estimate a forward-looking Taylor rule for Turkey covering both implicit and explicit inflation-targeting periods. In this analysis, we also consider the presence of structural breaks in the policy coefficients. Even though the Turkish economy has been undergoing several structural changes since 2002, the previous studies that estimate the monetary policy rule for Turkey disregard structural breaks, while fitting a policy reaction function. In this study, we examine a Taylor rule for Turkey using a two-stage least square regression that is coupled with the analysis of multiple structural breaks with unknown dates. By using this methodology, we show that the monetary policy function of the Central Bank of the Republic of Turkey exhibits four different periods. This result demonstrates that it is crucial to take account of structural breaks, while estimating monetary policy rules.

Keywords: Taylor rule, monetary policy, structural breaks

JEL: E43, E58, E52

1 Introduction

During the 90s, Turkey suffered from high inflation and frequent economic crises due to a weak banking system, systematic high budget deficits and a central bank under political control. At the end of 1999, Turkey adopted an IMF-backed stabilization program with a crawling peg exchange rate regime to re-balance its macroeconomic indicators. However, the crawling peg exchange rate regime collapsed due to the considerable decline in foreign exchange reserves of the Central Bank of the Republic of Turkey (CBRT) and the CBRT allowed the exchange rate to float freely in February 2001. Afterwards, Turkey adopted another IMF-backed programme called "the Transition to the Strong Economy Programme" in May 2001, and in the meantime, the Central Bank Law was revised to ensure the success of it. According to this revised law, maintaining price stability became the primary objective of the CBRT; the CBRT obtained authority to implement monetary policy in Turkey, and it gained instrument independence while conducting the monetary policy. To maintain price stability and reduce inflation, the CBRT first adopted implicit inflation targeting between

2002 and 2005[1] as Turkey did not satisfy technical and macroeconomic preconditions for explicit inflation targeting at that time. After three years of successful monetary policy, which reduced inflation from 70 percent to single-digit numbers, the CBRT implemented the full-fledged inflation-targeting regime in 2006. In this study, we analyze the monetary policy function of the CBRT since the beginning of implicit inflation targeting[2] by using a forward-looking Taylor (1993) rule. This helps us to determine the monetary policy reaction of the CBRT in respect to the deviation of inflation expectations from the official inflation target and the output gap.

There are a few studies that analyze the policy reaction function of the CBRT since the implementation of the implicit inflation-targeting regime. Yapraklı (2011) uses the bounds test approach of Paseran et al. (2001) to model the policy rate of the CBRT using the inflation gap, the output gap and the real effective exchange rate between 2001:08 and 2009:09. They show that, in addition to the output gap and the inflation gap, the real effective exchange rate affects the policy rate of the CBRT during the investigated period. In addition to Yapraklı (2011), Demirbaş and Kaya (2012) and Zortuk (2007) also use a bounds test approach to model the policy reaction function using similar variables during the inflation-targeting period, and their findings are in line with the results of Yapraklı (2011). However, these studies ignore the endogeneity problem of forward-looking monetary policy rules. By following Clarida et al. (1998, 1999, 2000), Yazgan and Yılmazkuday (2007) estimate forward-looking Taylor rules covering the period between 2001:08 and 2004:04 by using a generalized method of moments (GMM) estimation to get rid of the endogeneity problem. Yazgan and Yılmazkuday (2007) show that forward-looking Taylor rules capture the CBRT's policy function quite successfully. In addition to forward-looking Taylor rule as in Yazgan and Yılmazkuday (2007), Aklan and Nargelecekenler (2008) also estimate a backward-looking Taylor rule covering the period between 2001:08 and 2006:09. Aklan and Nargelecekenler (2008) show that both forward-looking and backward-looking equations explain the CBRT's monetary policy function, but coefficients of the inflation gap and the output gap are more significant in forward-looking models compared to backward-looking models. Since 2002, Turkey has undergone several different periods, and the CBRT may

1 For more detailed information about implicit inflation targeting adopted by the CBRT, see Kara (2008).

2 We don't analyze the period before 2002 because there would be no consistent monetary policy rule in an economy without a flexible exchange rate and an inflation-targeting regime.

adopt various monetary policy stances during these periods. However, previous studies mainly ignore the possibility of parameter changes in monetary policy rules. In an attempt to include various monetary policy stances of the CBRT, Kayhan et al. (2013) use a two-state Markov switching model following the approach of King (1996) to investigate the monetary policy function of the CBRT between 2002:02 and 2011:02. They show that during expansionary periods, the CBRT puts more emphasis on the inflation gap for the adjusting monetary policy function, and during recession periods, the CBRT puts more emphasis on the output gap.

Even though Kayhan et al.'s (2013) study is an exceptional attempt to model the different monetary policy stances of the CBRT, the evolution of Turkish economy is highly complicated to be only captured by two states. From 2002 until the mid of 2004, Turkey experienced a very rapid decline in the inflation rate; it declined from 70 percent to 7 percent within two and a half years. After the mid-2004 until the global crisis, Turkish inflation fluctuated between 7 and 11 percent. During this period, the CBRT pursued a monetary policy with a high real interest rate. Fig. 1 shows the two-year benchmark interest rate, one-year ahead inflation expectations and the real interest rate as the difference between them. We may observe that the real interest rate was above 10 percent between 2002 and 2008. During the global crisis, the CBRT quickly decreased the policy rate to support the economy. However, inflation also declined sharply due to the

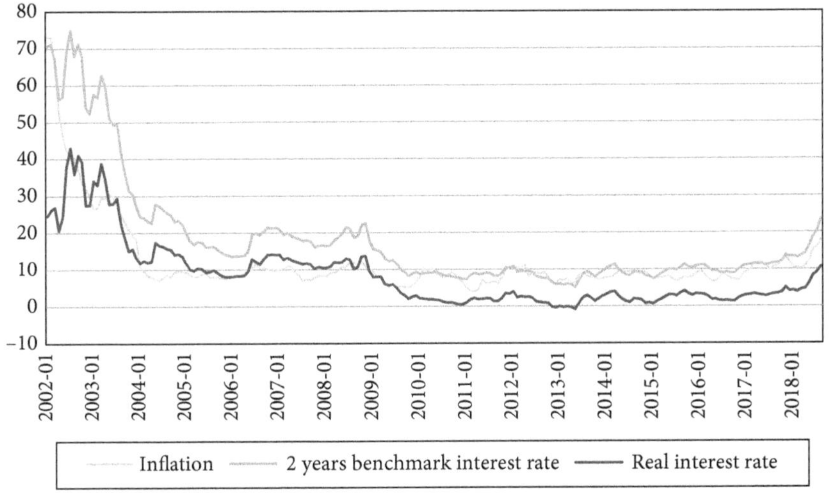

Fig. 1: Inflation, the two-year benchmark interest rate and the real interest rate

low demand. After 2009, the CBRT did not increase the policy rate back to the pre-2008 period so Turkey entered a low real interest rate period after the global crisis as it can be seen in Fig. 1. Due to the low-interest rate and high-capital flows, Turkey experienced a very rapid growth in 2010 and 2011, but this caused a massive spike in the current account deficit. At the end of 2011, it is evident that high growth accompanied by a large account deficit was unsustainable, so the CBRT adopted a non-orthodox monetary policy to curb the current account deficit while maintaining low real interest rates.

In this study, to capture different monetary policy reaction functions of the CBRT since 2002, we adopt the Bai and Perron's (2003) structural break-testing procedure. We also employ a Two-Stage Least Squares (2SLS) method to deal with the endogeneity problem of the forward-looking monetary policy rule estimation. In this testing strategy, we do not determine the number of structural periods or dates of structural periods in advance. According to our methodology, we show that there are four different monetary policy periods in Turkey. These are the periods between 2002:03–2004:08, 2004:09–2008:11, 2008:12–2011:10 and 2011:11–2018:08. These periods coincide with our narrative of the Turkish monetary policy. First period between 2002:03 and 2004:08 is the rapid disinflation period. The second period between 2004:09 and 2008:11 is the stable inflation period with high real interest rates. The third period between 2008:12 and 2011:10 covers the crisis and the recovery period, and finally, the last period is the unorthodox policy mix period of the CBRT. Our results clearly show that modeling the policy function the CBRT will yield flawed results, if parameter instability is not taken into account.

The rest of the study is organized as follows: In Section 2, we introduce the methodology and data. In Section 3, we present the empirical results, and in Section 4 we conclude by summarizing our findings.

2 The Model and Data

2.1 The Theoretical and Empirical Model

In this study, we consider the model for the monetary policy rule that is proposed by Taylor (1993) and improved by Clarida et al. (1998, 2000). This model is given as follows:

$$i_t^* = r + \pi_{t-k}^* + \beta\left[\mathbb{E}\left(\pi_{t+k} \mid \Omega_t\right) - \pi_{t+k}^*\right] + \gamma\mathbb{E}\left(x_t \mid \Omega_t\right) \tag{1}$$

where i_t^* is the target nominal interest rate at period t, π_{t+k} is the inflation rate between the periods t and $t+k$, π_{t+k}^* is the target inflation rate between periods t and $t+k$ and x_t is the average output gap. In this model, the output gap is the percentage deviation of the actual output from the potential output. Furthermore, r is the long-run equilibrium real interest rate and all expectations are computed with respect to the information set Ω_t. One can modify the model in Equation (1) into an estimable equation. If we rearrange the terms in Equation (1), we obtain:

$$r_t = r + \beta\left[\mathbb{E}\left(\pi_{t+k} \mid \Omega_t\right) - \pi^*_{t+k}\right] + \gamma x_t + \varepsilon_t \tag{2}$$

where $\varepsilon_t = -\gamma\left[x_t - \mathbb{E}\left(x_t \mid \Omega_t\right)\right] + i_t - i^*_t$. Note that this error term is not independent of the right-hand side variables, since the output gap and the deviation of the nominal interest rate from its target appears in the error term. Accordingly, the standard linear regression estimation is not applicable in this case. However, we can utilize an instrumental variable estimation procedure to get rid of the endogeneity problem. This method is a special case of the GMM estimation proposed by Clarida et al. (1998, 2000) for the estimation of the monetary policy rule. Moreover, we can strengthen the monetary policy equation by including information regarding the behavior of the central banks about smooth changes in the policy rate. This smoothing argument is generally represented with the following equation:

$$r_t = (1-\rho)r^*_t + \rho r_{t-1} + v_t \tag{3}$$

where ρ denotes the smoothing parameter and v_t is the disturbance term. Combining Equations (2) and (3) and rearranging the terms, we obtain:

$$r_t = (1-\rho)\left\{r + \beta\left[\tilde{\pi}_{t+k}\right] + \gamma x_t\right\} + \rho r_{t-1} + \xi_t \tag{4}$$

where $\tilde{\pi}_{t+k} = \mathbb{E}\left(\pi_{t+k} \mid \Omega_t\right) - \pi^*_{t+k}$. However, the new error term $\xi_t = -(1-\rho)\gamma\left[x_t - \mathbb{E}\left(x_t \mid \Omega_t\right)\right] + v_t$ also exhibits dependence with the regressors in the above equation. Consequently, we utilize an instrumental variable framework to estimate the monetary policy rule for Turkey.

In the instrumental variable estimation, we need instruments that are correlated with the regressors but not related to the error term ξ_t. Furthermore, it is clear that the only variable that possesses dependence with the error term is the output gap. Other right-hand side variables can be assumed to be orthogonal to the error term. Hence, we need to find a proper instrument for the output gap. Following Yazgan and Yılmazkuday (2007), we use the first two lags of the output gap as the instruments of the output gap.

Let Z_t be the vector that contains the first two lags of output gap, the first lag of the policy rate and the difference between inflation and inflation expectation between time t and $t+k$ such that $Z_t = \left[1, x_{t-1}, x_{t-2}, r_{t-1}, \tilde{\pi}_{t+k}\right]^{\mathrm{T}}$. Furthermore, define $X_t = \left[x_t, r_{t-1}, \tilde{\pi}_{t+k}\right]^{\mathrm{T}}$ as the vector of regressors in Equation (4). The following equation demonstrates the connection between the instruments and the regressors in Equation (4):

$$X_t = Z_t \Pi + u_t \tag{5}$$

In this model, we assume $cov(\xi_t \mid Z_t) = 0$ and $cov(\xi_t, u_t) \neq 0$. We can also write the main regression equation as

$$r_r = [1, X_t^{\mathrm{T}}]^{\mathrm{T}} \theta + e_t \tag{6}$$

where θ is the coefficient vector in Equation (4). Let θ_j denote the $j-th$ element of θ. Then, $\theta_1 = r(1-\rho)$, $\theta_2 = (1-\rho)\gamma$, $\theta_3 = \rho$ and $\theta_4 = (1-\rho)\beta$.

Using Equations (5) and (6), we can estimate the parameters in θ with a Two-Stage Least Squares (2SLS) method. According to this method, we first estimate the model in Equation (5) and obtain the fitted values $\hat{X}_t$. In the second stage, we estimate $r_t = [1, \hat{X}_t^{\mathrm{T}}]^{\mathrm{T}} \theta + e_t$ which is a modified version of Equation (6).

2.2 Structural Breaks in the 2SLS Model

The main purpose of this study is to reveal the changes in the monetary policy of Turkey. To examine this issue, we employ structural break tests on the 2SLS method proposed earlier. As we describe previously, we have two different equations in our analysis. Accordingly, it is essential to check for structural breaks in both equations. The main regression model in (6) has a single equation. In this case, we can employ Bai and Perron's (2003) structural break test on this equation. On the other hand, the second model in (5) consists of three equations. However, notice that the only endogenous variable is x_t. Thus, we have a single equation to estimate in this stage effectively. The fitted values for the exogenous regressors are equated to themselves. Consequently, in the first stage estimation we have a single equation to consider in the structural break analysis.

Let m_1 and m_2 denote the number of breaks in the first and second stage equations, respectively. Then, we can rewrite these equations as follows:

$$x_t = Z_t'\Pi_i + u_t \quad for \quad t \in \{T_{1,i-1}+1,\ldots,T_{1,i}\} \quad and \quad \forall i \in \{1,\ldots,m_1+1\} \tag{7}$$

$$r_t = \hat{X}_t'\theta_i + u_t \ for\, t \in \{T_{2,i-1}+1,\ldots,T_{2,i}\} and\, \forall i \in \{1,\ldots,m_2+1\} \tag{8}$$

where $\hat{X}_t = \left[\hat{x}_t, r_{t-1}, \tilde{\pi}_{t+k}\right]^{\mathrm{T}}$, $\hat{x}_t$ is the fitted value of x_t obtained from the model in (7) and $T_{j,i}$ is the ith break date in the jth equation. We also use the conventions $T_{1,0} = T_{2,0} = 0$ and $T_{1,m_1+1} = T_{2,m_2+1} = 0$. Since, we do not restrict the structural break dates in these two equations to be same, we can apply Bai and Perron's (2003) structural break-testing procedure separately. This procedure gives us the break dates, the value of coefficients and the significance of the coefficients in each regime. Moreover, Bai and Perron's (2003) method sequentially tests how many structural breaks there are in the model. This procedure can be summarized by the following steps:

1. We first fix the number of the regimes in each equation in (7) and (8) as m_1 and m_2.
2. Let $(T_1,\ldots,T_{m_1})$ and $(T_1,\ldots,T_{m_2})$ the partitions of the time horizon for each model. Then, we can define the sum of squared residuals for Equations (7) and (8) as follows:

$$S_{1,T}(T_1,\ldots,T_{m_1}) = \sum_{i=1}^{m_1+1} \sum_{t=T_{i-1}+1}^{T_i} \left(x_t - Z_t'\Pi_i\right)^2$$
$$S_{2,T}(T_1,\ldots,T_{m_2}) = \sum_{i=1}^{m_2+1} \sum_{t=T_{i-1}+1}^{T_i} \left(r_t - \breve{X}_t'\theta_i\right)^2$$

3. We can estimate the associated break partition from the following minimization problem:

$$\left(\hat{T}_1,\ldots,\hat{T}_{m_1}\right) = \text{argmin}_{T_1,\ldots,T_{m_1}} S_{1,T}(T_1,\ldots,T_{m_1})$$
$$\left(\hat{T}_1,\ldots,\hat{T}_{m_2}\right) = \text{argmin}_{T_1,\ldots,T_{m_2}} S_{2,T}(T_1,\ldots,T_{m_2})$$

One can employ a dynamic programming algorithm to efficiently estimate the break points.

4. After obtaining the break points, we can use the associated least squares estimates of the estimated partition (Bai and Perron, 2003).
5. Bai and Perron (2003) claim that one can sequentially test the hypothesis of having l breaks versus $l+1$ breaks. This test is labeled as $\sup F(l+1 \mid l)$ which is a special form of F test. For each segment, say $[T_{i-1}+1, T_i]$, we apply the F test that checks the absence of a structural break versus the presence of one structural break in every segment in the model with l structural breaks. We can compute the test statistic of interest by taking the maximum of the F statistic obtained from each segment. If we reject the null hypothesis (for the large values $\sup F(l+1 \mid l)$ statistic), then we can conclude there are $l+1$ structural breaks.
6. Step 5 is for testing $l+1$ breaks versus l. Starting from the case of no breaks, we can sequentially apply this step. If we reject the null of no break, we continue testing the null of 2 breaks versus 1 break. Iterating this procedure until we cannot reject the null, we can achieve the estimated number of breaks. However, note that we need a maximum number of breaks allowed for the model. In our study, we set this number as 5.

In our analysis, we allow all coefficients of the regressors to change simultaneously. However, we let each regression equation to have structural breaks at different periods as well as different number of structural breaks. On the other hand, we use heteroscedasticity and autocorrelation robust covariance matrix of Newey and West (1987) with Bartlett kernel and Newey-West Automatic bandwidth selection. Additionally, we apply a pre-whitening algorithm with automatic lag selection based on Akaike's Information Criterion for the variance-covariance estimation.

2.3 Data

As the money market short-term interest rate, we use the CBRT's effective policy rates that reflect the monetary policy stance of the CBRT. However, since 2002, the interest rate used for the policy rate changed a few times. Between 2002:02 and 2010:05, the market perceived the overnight interest rate on borrowing as the policy rate of the CBRT. However, the CBRT declared that one-week repo rate is the new policy rate on May 18, 2010. After 2011, the CBRT adopts a new policy mix and begin to conduct monetary policy using the weighted average funding rate. After 2011, the CBRT allowed the announced official policy rates and the effective rates to diverge from each other as a deliberate policy choice (Binici et al., 2016). Data for the overnight interest rate on borrowing, one-week policy rate, and the weighted average funding rate are obtained from the Turkish Data Manager. As inflation expectations, we use 12 months ahead inflation expectations retrieved from the CBRT's survey of expectations. Constructing monthly inflation target for Turkey is pretty tricky because the CBRT does not have a fixed inflation target throughout the period, so we follow the approach shown in Yazgan and Yilmazkuday (2007) to correct the discontinuity of year-end inflation targets. Inflation targets are also obtained from the CBRT.

3 Empirical Results

We first present estimation results of the Taylor rule without structural breaks in Tab. 1. Results show that the CBRT focuses on smoothing and the deviance of inflation expectations from the inflation target for setting monetary policy rate. According to this estimated monetary policy rule, the CBRT increases the real rate 0.53 points for each one percentage point deviation of inflation expectations from the actual inflation target. Interestingly, the output gap remains insignificant in this estimation result. It seems that the CBRT ignores the output gap while conducting monetary policy.

Tab. 1: The Taylor-rule estimation without structural breaks

Dependent Variable: r_t				
Variable	**Coefficient**	**Std. Error**	**t-Statistic**	**Prob.**
Constant	0.213444	0.417137	0.511689	0.6095
r_{t-1}	0.906575	0.024886	36.42959	0.0000
$\tilde{\pi}_{t+k}$	0.534366	0.149274	3.579757	0.0004
$\hat{x}_t$	−0.014530	0.114308	−0.127114	0.8990
Adjusted R^2	0.899735			

Tab. 2: The structural break test for the first stage regression

Breaks: 2005:02, 2008:10, 2011:09, 2015:03			
Breaking variables: Constant x_{t-1} x_{t-2} r_{t-1} $\tilde{\pi}_{t+k}$			
Break Test	**F-statistic**	**Scaled F-statistic**	**Critical Value**
0 vs. 1 *	4.808680	24.04340	18.23
1 vs. 2 *	8.679805	43.39903	19.91
2 vs. 3 *	6.716274	33.58137	20.99
3 vs. 4 *	12.14917	60.74586	21.71
4 vs. 5	0.000000	0.000000	22.37

* Significant at the 0.05 level.

Next, we begin estimating the forward-looking Taylor rule with structural breaks. To deal with the endogeneity problem, we utilize the 2SLS estimation. First, we determine the number of breaks in the first stage of the 2SLS by using Bai and Perron's (2003) procedure. As shown in Tab. 2, we detect the following structural break dates using the structural break testing procedure: 2005:02, 2008:10, 2011:09, and 2015:03. By using these structural breaks, we estimate the output gap equation in Tab. 3. As it can be seen from this equation, both sign and magnitude of coefficients change from one period to another. Therefore, using structural breaks in the first stage of the 2SLS estimations increases the robustness of the whole 2SLS procedure. From this point forward, we use the estimated output gap derived from this equation.

In the second stage of the 2SLS procedure, we first detect the structural breaks at the Taylor rule. As shown in Tab. 4, the Bai and Perron's (2003) structural

Tab. 3: The structural break estimation in the first stage regression

Dependent Variable: x_t				
Variable	**Coefficient**	**Std. Error**	**t-Statistic**	**Prob.**
2002:03 – 2005:01				
Constant	−0.080837	0.369405	−0.218829	0.8270
x_{t-1}	0.874106	0.319931	2.732169	0.0069
x_{t-2}	−0.635979	0.312985	−2.031978	0.0437
r_{t-1}	−0.014354	0.008110	−1.769821	0.0785
$\tilde{\pi}_{t+k}$	0.076968	0.073411	1.048455	0.2959
2005:02 – 2008:09				
Constant	0.510831	1.599386	0.319392	0.7498
x_{t-1}	0.681220	0.083210	8.186776	0.0000
x_{t-2}	0.168006	0.084348	1.991819	0.0480
r_{t-1}	−0.036668	0.120683	−0.303835	0.7616
$\tilde{\pi}_{t+k}$	0.180723	0.234650	0.770178	0.4422
2008:10 – 2011:08				
Constant	2.011614	1.006257	1.999105	0.0472
x_{t-1}	0.767092	0.143083	5.361170	0.0000
x_{t-2}	−0.088527	0.083037	−1.066117	0.2879
r_{t-1}	−0.351536	0.120035	−2.928621	0.0039
$\tilde{\pi}_{t+k}$	0.652705	0.414934	1.573032	0.1175
2011:09 – 2015:02				
Constant	0.585238	0.763994	0.766024	0.4447
x_{t-1}	0.109936	0.101495	1.083170	0.2802
x_{t-2}	0.341650	0.090183	3.788401	0.0002
r_{t-1}	−0.365375	0.202512	−1.804212	0.0729
$\tilde{\pi}_{t+k}$	1.131574	0.792104	1.428567	0.1549
2015:03 – 2018:08				
Constant	−3.296746	1.221296	−2.699384	0.0076
x_{t-1}	0.244622	0.170101	1.438101	0.1522

Tab. 3: (continued)

Dependent Variable: x_t				
Variable	**Coefficient**	**Std. Error**	**t-Statistic**	**Prob.**
x_{t-2}	0.148702	0.120588	1.233139	0.2192
r_{t-1}	0.945314	0.211776	4.463749	0.0000
$\tilde{\pi}_{t+k}$	−1.955362	0.396280	−4.934289	0.0000
Adjusted R^2	0.700446			

Tab. 4: The structural break test for the second stage regression

Breaks: 2004/09, 2008/12, 2011/11			
Breaking variables: Constant r_{t-1} $\tilde{\pi}_{t+k}$ $\hat{x}_t$			
Break Test	**F-statistic**	**Scaled F-statistic**	**Critical Value**[**]
0 vs. 1 [*]	4.416429	17.66572	16.19
1 vs. 2 [*]	10.68218	42.72870	18.11
2 vs. 3 [*]	8.263635	33.05454	18.93
3 vs. 4	3.502495	14.00998	19.64

[*] Significant at the 0.05 level.

break-testing procedure indicates that there are three structural breaks, which are 2004:09, 2008:12 and 2011:11. In the first period, extending in between 2002:03 and 2004:09, Turkey experienced a rapid decline in inflation, and the CBRT reduced the policy rate slowly while inflation was declining quickly. According to Tab. 5, only the smoothing coefficient is significant at the 5 percent significance level in this period. In the second period between 2004:10 and 2008:11, Turkey had a stable inflation fluctuating between 7 percent and 11 percent. Still, the CBRT were over cautious and pursued a monetary policy with a high real interest rate. As expected, the output gap is insignificant in this period, and the CBRT mainly focused on the inflation gap. According to the estimated Taylor rule, the CBRT raises the real rate by 0.37 points for each one-percentage point deviation of inflation expectations from the inflation target. The third period between 2018:12 and 2011:10 includes both the 2009 crisis when Turkey's GDP fell by 4.7 percent and the high recovery period of 2010 and 2011. All coefficients are significant in this period. Compared to the previous period, the coefficient on

Tab. 5: The Taylor-rule estimation with structural breaks

Dependent Variable: r_t				
Variable	**Coefficient**	**Std. Error**	**t-Statistic**	**Prob.**
2002:03 – 2004:08				
Constant	5.133354	2.778448	1.847562	0.0663
r_{t-1}	0.726666	0.150274	4.835592	0.0000
$\tilde{\pi}_{t+k}$	0.965103	0.674869	1.430058	0.1544
$\hat{x}_t$	−0.717790	0.714262	−1.004939	0.3163
2004:09 – 2008:11				
Constant	2.358198	0.595869	3.957578	0.0001
r_{t-1}	0.816848	0.038588	21.16846	0.0000
$\tilde{\pi}_{t+k}$	0.370894	0.083388	4.447818	0.0000
$\hat{x}_t$	−0.070971	0.051037	−1.390574	0.1661
2008:12 – 2011:10				
Constant	0.795291	0.064733	12.28570	0.0000
r_{t-1}	0.830998	0.010034	82.81651	0.0000
$\tilde{\pi}_{t+k}$	0.253541	0.056240	4.508212	0.0000
$\hat{x}_t$	−0.047028	0.019376	−2.427112	0.0162
2011:11 – 2018:08				
Constant	0.784808	0.205787	3.813690	0.0002
r_{t-1}	0.692460	0.035816	19.33403	0.0000
$\tilde{\pi}_{t+k}$	0.818956	0.088156	9.289878	0.0000
$\hat{x}_t$	0.161435	0.067465	2.392859	0.0177
Adjusted R^2	0.907771			

the inflation gap is smaller in this period. It seems that the CBRT is less hawkish about inflation between 2009 and 2011.

Interestingly, the sign of the output gap is negative which means that the monetary policy is pro-cyclical. The CBRT's dovish approach on inflation and the pro-cyclical monetary policy may explain the very high growth rates that occurred in 2010 and 2011; Turkey grew by 8.5 and 11.1 percent in 2010 and

2011, respectively. The last period is between 2011:11 and 2018:08. In this period, the CBRT conducts a non-orthodox monetary policy. All coefficients are significant. The coefficient of the inflation gap is higher than it is in the two previous periods. The sign of output gap is also positive and significant. This, in turn, implies that during the last period, the CBRT followed a very cautious monetary policy that aimed to combat inflation and smooth the business cycle.

4 Conclusion

Quite a few studies estimate the Taylor rule for the CBRT. Even though the Turkish economy experienced many structural changes since 2002, the previous studies that estimate the monetary policy rule for Turkey disregard structural breaks while fitting a policy reaction function. In this study, we adopt the Bai and Perron's (2003) structural break-testing procedure that allows us to find the structural breaks with unknown dates while using a Two-Stage Least Squares (2SLS) method to deal with the endogeneity problem of the Taylor-rule estimation.

Our results show that there are four different monetary policy periods which are 2002:03 - 2004:08, 2004:09 - 2008:11, 2008:12 - 2011:10, and 2011:11 - 2018:08. In the first period, only the smoothing parameter is significant in our estimated Taylor rule. In the second period, the deviance of inflation expectations from the inflation target also becomes significant, and the output gap remains insignificant. This result indicates that the CBRT's main focus was on inflation and disregarded the growth. In the third period, the coefficient of the inflation gap gets smaller, and the sign of the output gap becomes negative and significant. According to these results, the CBRT seems to pursue pro-cycle monetary policy with less focus on inflation between 2008:12 and 2011:10. In the final period, the sign of the output gap is positive and significant, and the coefficient of the inflation gap is higher than both the second and the third period. Our estimated Taylor rule indicates that the CBRT is hawkish and try to smooth the business cycle during the final period. Our estimated Taylor with multiple structural breaks clearly shows that the results of estimated Taylor rules that do not take into account the parameter instability would yield incorrect results. Therefore, future studies should pay attention to structural breaks while estimating Taylor rules.

References

Aklan, N., & Nargeleçekenler, M. (2008). Taylor Kuralı: Türkiye Üzerine Bir Değerlendirme. *Ankara Üniversitesi SBF Dergisi*, 63(2), 21–41.

Bai, J., & Perron, P. (2003). Computation and analysis of multiple structural change models. *Journal of Applied Econometrics*, 18(1), 1–22.

Binici, M., Kara, H., & Özlü, P. (2016). Unconventional interest rate corridor and the monetary transmission: Evidence from Turkey. Working Paper No. 16/08, The Central Bank of the Republic of Turkey retrieved from http://www.tcmb.gov.tr/wps/wcm/connect/91e501be-4fc1-483a-b84d-121577f0d96e/wp1608e.pdf?MOD=AJPERES&CACHEID=ROOTWORKSPACE-91e501be-4fc1-483a-b84d-121577f0d96e-m3fw6gE.

Clarida, R., Gali, J., & Gertler, M. (1998). Monetary policy rules in practice: Some international evidence. *European Economic Review*, 42(6), 1033–1067.

Clarida, R., Gali, J., & Gertler, M. (1999). The science of monetary policy: A new Keynesian perspective. *Journal of Economic Literature*, 37(4), 1661–1707.

Clarida, R., Gali, J., & Gertler, M. (2000). Monetary policy rules and macroeconomic stability: Evidence and some theory. *Quarterly Journal of Economics*, 115(1), 147–180.

Demirbaş, E., & Kaya, M. (2012). Testing the validity of Taylor principle for Turkey from a different perspective. *AİBÜ Sosyal Bilimler Enstitüsü Dergisi*, 12, 81–110.

Kara, H., 2008. Turkish experience with implicit inflation targeting. *Central Banking Review*, 8 (1), 1–16.

Kayhan, S., Bayat, T., & Koçyiğit, A. (2013). Enflasyon Hedeflemesi Rejiminde Öğrenme Süreci ve Asimetri: Markov Switching Yaklaşımı. *Eskişehir Osman Gazi Üniveristesi İİBF Dergisi*, 8(1), 191–212.

King, M. (1996). How should central banks reduce inflation? Conceptual issues. *Economic Review-Federal Reserve Bank of Kansas City*, 81, 25–52.

Newey, W. K., & West, K. D. (1987). A simple, positive semi-definite, heteroskedasticity and autocorrelation consistent covariance matrix. *Econometrica*, 55(3), 703–708.

Pesaran, M. H., Shin, Y., & Smith, R. J. (2001). Bounds testing approaches to the analysis of level relationships. *Journal of applied econometrics*, 16(3), 289–326.

Taylor, J. B. (1993). Discretion versus policy rules in practice. In *Carnegie-Rochester conference series on public policy*, 39, 195–214.

Yapraklı, S. (2011). Türkiye'de Açık Ekonomi Para Politikası Kuralının Geçerliliği: Sınır Testi Yaklaşımı İş Güç. *Endüstri İlişkileri ve İnsan Kaynakları Dergisi*, 13(1), 127–142.

Yazgan, M., & Yılmazkuday, H. (2007). Monetary policy rules in practice: Evidence from Turkey and Israel. *Applied Financial Economics*, 17(1), 1–14.

Zortuk, M. (2007). Koşulluluk Aracı Olma Bağlamında Kısa Vadeli Faiz Oranlarının Hedeflenen Enflasyondan Sapmada Kullanımı: Bounds Test Yaklaşımı (Türkiye Örneği). *Ekonometri ve İstatistik Sayı*, 6, 41–68.

Bilge Eriş Dereli

Returns to Overeducation

Returns to Overeducation by College Major: Evidence from Turkey

Abstract: This study uses the latest available 2017 Turkish Household Labor Force Surveys and analyzes the incidence of and returns to overeducation by college major, where overeducation indicates a position in which a worker's education level is one standard deviation above the average education level in her occupation. This chapter seeks to answer two questions: Which college majors yield to greater incidence of overeducation? Do earnings effects of being overeducated vary by college major? Two different specifications are estimated to answer these questions. First, separate logit models for male and female are estimated to see whether there are differences in the incidence of overeducation across majors. The findings indicate that there are substantial differences. Most of the fields that teach occupation-specific skills are observed not to yield high incidence of overeducation. In addition, it is found that likelihood of overeducation decreases by age both for male and female. Second, conditional earnings functions are estimated using quantile regressions to see whether earnings differences of being overeducated exist and vary by college major. The results reveal that there are earnings penalties of being overeducated and different college majors lead to strikingly different earnings losses of being overeducated.

Keywords: overducation, college major, Turkish labor market

JEL: C21, J31, I26

1 Introduction

Over the last decades, there has been a substantial expansion in the share of workers with tertiary degree in Turkish labor market as well as in most of the developed and developing economies. Along with this expansion in higher education, the incidence of overeducation has started to rise as well, where overeducation indicates a position in which a worker's acquired level of schooling is higher than the worker's job's required level of schooling. The main reason of the rise in the incidence of overeducation can be thought as demand to workers with tertiary degree being lower than the supply of the workers with tertiary degree. In addition to this aspect of the labor market, college major[1] has been an important

1 Field of study, field of education, field of graduation are the terms used interchangeably by college major.

dimension in empirical studies to evaluate basic labor market outcomes. This study investigates the incidence of and returns to overeducation by college major in Turkish Labor Market using the latest 2017 Household Labor Force Surveys. There are two basic questions this chapter seeks for answer: Which college majors yield to greater incidence of overeducation? Do earnings effects of being overeducated vary by college major?

This study explores returns to overeducation by college major which can be considered as an intersection of two research fields: Overeducation and returns to tertiary education by college major. Initial studies of the growing literature overeducation concentrate on the incidence of and returns to overeducation. Among those studies are Duncan and Hoffman (1981), Tsang and Levin (1985), Hartog and Oosterbeek (1988), Verdugo and Verdugo (1989), Sicherman (1991), Alba-Amirez (1993), Cohn and Kahn (1995), Sloane and Barru (1999). More recent studies in the overeducation literature are Linsley Hartog (2000), (2005), McGuiness (2006), Galasi (2008), Hung (2008), Korpi and Tahlin (2009), Mehta et al. (2011), Gervasi and McGuiness (2018). Main findings of the studies on returns to overeducation indicate that the returns to schooling is lower than the returns to required schooling, regardless of how required schooling is determined.

The literature on returns to tertiary education by college major concentrates on earnings heterogeneities across majors. Loury and Garman (1995), Finnie and Frenette (2003) Arcidiacono (2004), Kelly et al. (2008), Chevalier (2011), Grave and Goerlitz (2012), Altonji et al. (2014). These studies mainly indicate that college major is an important variable that should be taken into account to control for returns to education and there are statistically significant differences across returns by major.

However, there are few studies on the relationship between overeducation, college major and returns to schooling. Frenette (2004), Ortiz and Kucel (2008) and Baron and Ortiz (2011) are among those studies and their findings imply substantial differences across incidence of and returns to overeducation by college major. This study advances the literature on educational mismatch by linking returns to overeducation by college major and to the best of my knowledge, there is no prior study analyzing the returns to overeducation by college major in Turkish labor market.[2]

2 The number of studies related with overeducation and returns to tertiary education by college major in Turkey are limited. Filiztekin (2011) and Orbay and Aydede (2015) are the only studies that analyze the wage differences and economic returns of educational mismatch. Di Paolo and Tansel (2017) is the only study that analyzes wage differentials by field of study.

There are important policy-relevant issues that are linked with the findings of this paper. First, existence of overeducation signals underutilization and a productivity loss in the economy. Evaluation of the incidence of overeducation by college majors guides policy makers for designing education policies that efficiently designs and allocates the college majors across universities. Second, it is related with college major choice and Berger (1988) documented that expected earnings are one of the important factors that affect major choice. Choice of a college major with greater likelihood of being overeducated with lower earnings should be considered by potential university entrants.

Section 2 and Section 3 describe the data and methodology used in the analysis, respectively. The estimation results are presented in Section 4. Section 5 concludes.

2 Data Description

The data are derived from the 2017 Turkish Household Labor Force Surveys from the Turkish Statistical Institution (TURKSTAT) taking into account the availability of college major variable. In fact, college major variable is available since 2009 wave of the survey; however, the college major classification changes from Fields of Education and Training 1999 (FOET-99) to International Standard Classification of Education 2013 (ISCED–13) in 2016.[3] This change in the college major classification makes it impossible to conduct and compare results between 2009 and 2017. The year 2016 is not included in the analysis, because all empirical and intuitive results are the same as they are for 2017.[4] There are 22 narrowly defined college major categories. The sample of the study consists of tertiary-educated workers aged between 15 and 64, working in non-agriculture sector at the time of the survey. To get nationwide representative results, all observations are weighted.

Educational mismatch is calculated as the difference between worker's acquired years of schooling and job's required years of schooling. The critical point in calculating educational mismatch is defining the required years of schooling to perform a job. This study employs the realized measure of Verdugo

3 A mapping from FOET-99 to ISCED-13 cannot be carried since the college majors are not reported at a sufficiently disaggregated level.

4 Simple hypothesis tests are conducted to test the equality of incidence of overeducation across 2016 and 2017. Results indicate that the differences in the incidence of overeducation between 2016 and 2017 are statistically insignificant. Moreover, all of the descriptive analysis yields the same results for 2016 and 2017.

and Verdugo (1989) where required education level is calculated as the average education level of all workers employed in a specific occupation.[5] Then a worker is classified as overeducated (undereducated) if his acquired education level is one standard deviation above (below) that average education level.

3 Methodology

The goal of this chapter is to answer two basic questions whose answers are expected to be policy relevant: Which college majors yield to greater incidence of overeducation? Do earnings effects of being overeducated vary by college major?

To answer the first question, a logit regression with a dichotomous-dependent mismatch variable is estimated as in Equation 1. The mismatch variable takes the value 0 indicating a worker is adequately educated and 1 indicating a worker is overeducated.

$$P(mismatch) = \beta X_{ij} + \alpha C_{ij} + \gamma M_j + u_{ij} \quad (1)$$

X_{ij} is a vector of demographic variables of age, squared age, marital status, place of birth for ith individual in major j, C_{ij} is a vector of control variables of regions and occupations for ith individual in major j and M_j denotes the college major. Separate regressions are run for male and female assuming labor market characteristics differences across gender.

To answer the second question, conditional earnings functions are estimated using quantile regressions similar to see Hamermesh and Donald (2008) and Chevalier (2011). The rationale behind using the quantile regression is the assumption that the effects of the covariates on earnings will be different at different quantiles of the earnings distribution.[6]

The specification includes the interaction of being overeducated and college major as shown in Equation 2.[7] The logarithm of monthly earnings inserts as the dependent variable.

5 Other methodologies used to calculate required years of schooling are objective methodology employed by Rumberger (1987) and Tsang and Levin (1985) and subjective methodology employed by Duncan and Hoffman (1981) and Sicherman (1991).

6 Empirical cumulative distribution of logarithm of monthly earnings of tertiary degree workers is given in appendix (Fig. A6).

7 Before this estimation, quantile earnings functions incorporating *overeducation* as a dummy variable are estimated to see whether overeducated workers earn more or less. Results are reported in appendix (Tab. A1 and Tab. A2) and indicate that

$$Q_g\left(logearnings / X\right) = \beta X_{ij} + \alpha C_{ij} + \delta(Overeducated * M)_j + \gamma M_j + u_{ij} \quad (2)$$

X_{ij} is a vector of demographic variables of age, squared age, marital status, place of birth, tenure and squared tenure for i^{th} individual in major j, C_{ij} is a vector of control variables of regions and occupations for i^{th} individual in major j, *overeductaed* is a dummy variable taking the value 1 if the worker is overeducated and M_j denotes the college major. Once again, separate regressions are run for male and female.

4 Results

Before presenting basic descriptive statistics and estimation results relating overeducation and college major, Tab. 1 presents the distribution of labor force status over college major to see how college major matters even for this basic labor market indicator. It is observed that there are substantial differences between employment and unemployment rates by college major. The majors with highest employment level are veterinary, engineering and engineering trades and health, whereas majors with highest unemployment level are welfare, information and communication technologies and arts.

Tab. 2 presents the distribution of mismatch over basic demographics.[8] Fifty-nine percent of the workers are classified as adequately educated, whereas 41 % of the workers are classified as overeducated. The incidence of overedcuation is higher for female. Young and older workers have a similar distribution of mismatch and more than half of them are categorized as overeducated. On the other hand, the incidence of overeducation is much lower (28 %) for middle-aged workers. Distribution of mismatch varies by marital status and married workers have the least incidence of overeducation. Like labor force status, incidence of overeducation varies substantially by college major. Welfare, occupational health and transformation and manufacturing and processing are among the college majors with highest incidence of overeducation (63 %, 60 % and 60 %, respectively).

---

both overeducated male and female suffer from earnings losses, while compared with adequately educated workers. Being overeducated lowers the rate of return to schooling. This finding is in accordance with the findings of the extensive literature on returns to overeducation.

8 Additional graphs for the distribution of overeducated tertiary degree workers over basic demographics are presented in appendix.

Tab. 1: Labor force statistics by college major

	employed	**unemployed**	**nilf**
Education sciences	70.90	7.590	21.51
Arts	62.12	15.38	22.50
Humanities	68.73	8.310	22.96
Languages	63.71	11.69	24.60
Social and behavirol	66.68	10.77	22.55
Journalism and inform	59.15	14.02	26.83
Business Administrati	69.28	10.48	20.24
Law	75.25	9.370	15.38
Biology and environme	68.53	13.66	17.81
Physical science	73.89	12.54	13.57
Mathematics and stati	70.75	9.980	19.26
ICT	66.85	15.80	17.34
Engineering and engin	79.67	7.980	12.35
Manufacturing and pro	62.97	10.41	26.63
Architecture and cons	73.72	10.78	15.50
Agriculture, forestry	71.63	9.830	18.54
Veterinary	80.25	8	11.75
Health	78.09	7.420	14.49
Welfare	51.79	18.57	29.64
Personel services	64.31	10.65	25.04
Occ. health and trans	65.57	13.93	20.49
Security services	77.14	3.740	19.12
Total	70.71	9.750	19.54

Tab. 3 presents the results from the logit regression of Equation 1. The effects of basic demographics can be summarized as follows: Likelihood of overeducation decreases by age both for male and female. The effect of being married varies for male and female. Relative to being single, being married decreases the likelihood of overeducation for male whereas it increases the likelihood for female. Workers born abroad are found to have higher probability of being educated in comparison with workers born in Turkey.

It is observed that the extent of overeducation varies across college major both for male and female. The base category for the college major is law. Results indicate that graduates of all college majors—with statistically significant effect—have a greater likelihood of being overeducated compared to the base category of law. The majors with statistically insignificant effects are education sciences, mathematics

Tab. 2: Distribution of adequately educated and overeducated tertiary degree workers over basic demographics

	Adequately Educated (%)	**Overeducated (%)**
Total	59.26	40.74
Male	65.68	34.32
Female	51.87	48.13
Young	44.86	55.14
Middle	71.69	28.31
Older	47.76	52.24
Single	47.31	52.69
Married	65.65	34.35
Divorced	59.92	40.08
Widowed	36.15	63.85
Education sciences	66.74	33.26
Arts	47.81	52.19
Humanities	61.94	38.06
Languages	56.93	43.07
Social and behavirol sciences	57.25	42.75
Journalism and information	46.34	53.66
Business Administration	55.65	44.35
Law	70.88	29.12
Biology and environmental sciences	63.77	36.23
Physical sciences	65.88	34.12
Mathematics and statistics	66.2	33.8
ICT	41.4	58.6
Engineering and engineering trades	57.25	42.75
Manufacturing and processing	40.24	59.76
Architecture and construction	61.73	38.27
Agriculture, forestry and fishery	53.7	46.3
Veterinary	76	24
Health	74.77	25.23
Welfare	36.96	63.04
Personel services	43.51	56.49
Occ. health and transportation services	40.16	59.84
Security services	71.58	28.42

Tab. 3: Logit Results—Which fields lead to greater overeducation?

Dependent variable: Mismatch	Male	Female
Demographics		
Age	−0.42***	−0.49***
	(0.025)	(0.028)
Age*Age	0.0053***	0.0062***
	(0.00030)	(0.00036)
Married	−0.73***	0.36***
	(0.091)	(0.085)
Place of birth	0.60***	0.89***
	(0.20)	(0.17)
College major		
Education sciences	0.41	−0.22
	(0.27)	(0.25)
Arts	0.80**	1.12***
	(0.34)	(0.28)
Humanities	0.58*	0.86***
	(0.32)	(0.28)
Languages	0.90**	0.48
	(0.36)	(0.30)
Social and behavioral sciences	0.94***	0.71***
	(0.27)	(0.26)
Journalism and information	1.75***	0.58
	(0.61)	(0.60)
Business administration	0.94***	0.86***
	(0.26)	(0.24)
Biology and environment	0.78*	0.30
	(0.46)	(0.37)
Physical science	0.78**	0.34
	(0.33)	(0.32)
Mathematics and statistics	0.19	0.27
	(0.44)	(0.37)
ICT	1.28***	0.87**
	(0.35)	(0.36)
Engineering and engineering trades	1.09***	0.20
	(0.26)	(0.29)
Manufacturing and processing	1.57***	1.35***
	(0.34)	(0.31)

Tab. 3: (continued)

Dependent variable: Mismatch	Male	Female
Architecture and construction	0.63**	0.59*
	(0.29)	(0.32)
Agriculture, forestry and fishery	1.22***	0.85**
	(0.33)	(0.36)
Veterinary	0.24	0.045
	(0.55)	(0.48)
Health	−0.067	−0.51**
	(0.32)	(0.26)
Welfare	1.10	0.96***
	(0.72)	(0.33)
Personel services	1.50***	1.21***
	(0.32)	(0.31)
Occ. health and transport services	1.69***	0.83
	(0.59)	(0.84)
Security services	0.29	0.18
	(0.33)	(0.57)
Constant	5.61***	6.86***
	(0.55)	(0.56)
Observations	25,790	22,076
Pseudo R2	0.13	0.11

Standard errors in parentheses. ***, ** and * denotes statistical significance at 10 %, 5 % and 1 % level, respectively. Regressions include regional dummies at NUTS1 regional classification. Base category for the mismatch variable is "being adequately educated" and base category for the college major variable is "Law".

and statistics, veterinary, health, welfare and security services for male and education sciences, languages, journalism and information, biology and environment, physical sciences, mathematics and statistics, engineering and engineering trades, veterinary, occupational health and transportation services and security services for female. Most of the majors that teach occupation-specific skills are observed not to yield overeducation. Majors with the highest prevalence rates are journalism and information, occupational health and transportation services and manufacturing and processing for male and manufacturing and processing, personel services and arts for female. The majors with lowest prevalence rates are humanities and social and behavioral sciences for male and female, respectively.

The results of the quantile regressions of Equation 2 are presented in Tab. 4 and Tab. 5 for male and female, respectively. It is observed that earnings penalties

Tab. 4: Conditional earnings function—Male

Dependent variable: Log(earnings)	**q10**	**q50**	**q90**
*Overeducation*college major interactions*			
Education sciences	−0.67***	−−0.92***	−1.11***
	(0.097)	(0.060)	(0.12)
Arts	−0.53***	−0.87***	−1.47***
	(0.13)	(0.080)	(0.16)
Humanities	−0.71***	−0.92***	−1.35***
	(0.11)	(0.071)	(0.14)
Languages	−0.60***	−1.03***	−1.31***
	(0.15)	(0.096)	(0.19)
Social and behavirol sciences	−0.68***	−0.90***	−1.32***
	(0.095)	(0.059)	(0.12)
Journalism and information	−0.77***	−0.93***	−1.46***
	(0.27)	(0.17)	(0.33)
Business Administration	−0.64***	−0.89***	−1.31***
	(0.082)	(0.051)	(0.100)
Law	−0.90***	−1.15***	−2.26***
	(0.22)	(0.13)	(0.26)
Biology and environment	−0.45*	−0.97***	−1.81***
	(0.25)	(0.16)	(0.31)
Physical science	−0.45***	−0.69***	−1.32***
	(0.13)	(0.082)	(0.16)
Mathematics and statistics	−0.99***	−1.12***	−1.54***
	(0.22)	(0.13)	(0.26)
ICT	−0.40***	−0.74***	−1.61***
	(0.11)	(0.068)	(0.13)
Engineering and engineering trades	−0.66***	−0.90***	−1.45***
	(0.084)	(0.052)	(0.10)
Manufacturing and processing	−0.52***	−0.91***	−1.38***
	(0.10)	(0.065)	(0.13)
Architecture and construction	−0.57***	−0.95***	−1.44***
	(0.10)	(0.064)	(0.12)
Agriculture, forestry and fishery	−0.49***	−0.95***	−1.34***
	(0.11)	(0.070)	(0.14)
Veterinary	−0.42*	−1.25***	−1.99***
	(0.22)	(0.14)	(0.27)
Health	−0.71***	−1.20***	−2.07***
	(0.14)	(0.086)	(0.17)

Tab. 4: (continued)

Dependent variable: Log(earnings)	**q10**	**q50**	**q90**
Welfare	−0.81***	−0.99***	−1.58***
	(0.20)	(0.12)	(0.24)
Personel services	−0.46***	−0.79***	−1.17***
	(0.10)	(0.063)	(0.12)
Occ. health and transport services	−0.44**	−0.79***	−1.70***
	(0.19)	(0.12)	(0.23)
Security services	−0.89***	−0.90***	−1.40***
	(0.13)	(0.082)	(0.16)
Constant	7.37***	7.85***	8.29***
	(0.095)	(0.059)	(0.11)
Observations	17,726	17,726	17,726
Pseudo R2	0.27	0.31	0.25

Standard errors in parentheses. ***, ** and * denotes statistical significance at 10 %, 5 % and 1 % level, respectively. Regressions include age, squared age, marital status, place of birth, tenure, squared tenure, occupation dummies, college major dummies and regional dummies at NUTS1 regional classification.

of being overeducated vary by major and are different at different quantiles of earnings both for male and female. Moreover, earnings effects for male are significant at all quantiles for all majors. At the 10th quantile, male workers majored in law, mathematics and statistics face more than 90 % earnings penalties for being overeducated. This percentage increases as moved to higher quantiles of the earnings distribution. The majors with greatest earnings penalty at the 90th quantile are law, veterinary and biology and environment for males.

Earnings effects for female are significant at 50th and 90th quantiles for all majors.[9] At the 50th quantile, biology and environment, mathematics and statistics and journalism and information are the majors with greatest earnings penalties. Similar to the results for male, this percentage increases as moved to the 90th quantile of the earnings distribution. The majors with greatest earnings penalty at the 90th quantile are law, occupational health and transportation services, journalism and information and health for female.

9 The majors with insignificant earnings effects at 10th percentile are journalism and information, law, physical science, manufacturing and processing, veterinary, welfare, personnel services, occupational health and transportation services and security services.

Tab. 5: Conditional earnings function—Female

Dependent variable: Log(earnings)	**q10**	**q50**	**q90**
*Overeducation*college major interactions*			
Education sciences	−0.70***	−0.98***	−0.99***
	(0.24)	(0.17)	(0.27)
Arts	−0.48**	−0.83***	−1.06***
	(0.24)	(0.17)	(0.27)
Humanities	−0.44*	−0.97***	−0.97***
	(0.26)	(0.18)	(0.29)
Languages	−0.53**	−0.90***	−0.99***
	(0.26)	(0.18)	(0.29)
Social and behavirol sciences	−0.45*	−1.00***	−1.13***
	(0.24)	(0.17)	(0.27)
Journalism and information	−0.36	−1.10***	−1.50***
	(0.38)	(0.27)	(0.43)
Business Administration	−0.40*	−0.91***	−1.08***
	(0.23)	(0.16)	(0.26)
Law	−0.35	−1.08***	−1.63***
	(0.27)	(0.19)	(0.31)
Biology and environment	−0.63*	−1.23***	−1.48***
	(0.35)	(0.24)	(0.39)
Physical science	−0.39	−0.81***	−0.92***
	(0.27)	(0.19)	(0.31)
Mathematics and statistics	−0.87***	−1.16***	−0.45
	(0.33)	(0.23)	(0.37)
ICT	−0.44*	−0.85***	−1.06***
	(0.24)	(0.17)	(0.27)
Engineering and engineering trades	−1.12***	−1.07***	−1.37***
	(0.25)	(0.18)	(0.29)
Manufacturing and processing	−0.36	−0.84***	−0.98***
	(0.24)	(0.17)	(0.27)
Architecture and construction	−0.44*	−1.06***	−1.32***
	(0.25)	(0.18)	(0.28)
Agriculture, forestry and fishery	−0.53**	−0.93***	−1.10***
	(0.25)	(0.18)	(0.29)
Veterinary	−0.14	−0.88***	−1.11***
	(0.37)	(0.26)	(0.41)
Health	−0.67***	−1.03***	−1.50***
	(0.25)	(0.17)	(0.28)

Tab. 5: (continued)

Dependent variable: Log(earnings)	q10	q50	q90
Welfare	−0.29	−0.79***	−1.15***
	(0.24)	(0.17)	(0.27)
Personel services	−0.36	−0.95***	−1.18***
	(0.24)	(0.17)	(0.27)
Occ. health and transport services	0.19	−0.90***	−1.62***
	(0.49)	(0.34)	(0.55)
Security services	−0.18	−1.03***	−1.04**
	(0.38)	(0.26)	(0.42)
Constant	7.26***	7.90***	8.06***
	(0.12)	(0.086)	(0.14)
Observations	11,814	11,814	11,814
Pseudo R2	0.27	0.31	0.26

Standard errors in parentheses. ***, ** and * denotes statistical significance at 10 %, 5 % and 1 % level, respectively. Regressions include age, squared age, marital status, place of birth, tenure, squared tenure, occupation dummies, college major dummies and regional dummies at NUTS1 regional classification.

5 Conclusion

This chapter provides an empirical evaluation of the earnings effects of overeducation by college major using the latest available 2017 Turkish Household Labor Force Surveys. The basic descriptives indicate that the incidence of overedcuation is higher for female, lower for middle-aged workers and married workers have the least incidence of overeducation across workers with other marital status. Results of the logit estimations show that the extent of overeducation varies across college majors both for male and female. As there are differences in choice of major and career between male and female in general, majors with high prevalence rates differ by gender, too. Estimation of quantile earnings functions point out that earnings penalties of being overeducated exist, vary by major and are different at different quantiles of earnings both for male and female.

The estimation findings reveal that most of the results differ by gender. This finding should be considered both by university entrants and policy makers. Entrants should carefully evaluate the future labor market prospects of a major taking into account gender differentials. Policy makers should consider allocating vacancies in majors considering this differential. As an example, more vacancies can be devoted to female than male in information and communication technologies major.

Law is found to be the major whose graduates have the lowest probability of being overeducated. However, once they are overeducated, earnings penalties are high for graduates of law. Still, as a major teaching occupation-specific skills, law is among the majors that potential university entrants would like to choose. Compared to law, the extent of overeducation is insignificant for education sciences, veterinary, health, welfare, security services and languages. The allocation of majors to recently founded universities might be designed taking into account this prominent result of the study.

There are earnings penalties of being overeducated for all majors. Nevertheless, a documentation of the majors with greatest and lowest penalties is important to be able to prevent workers from those losses. For the median regression, physical science is the major with lowest earnings penalties both for male and female. Then, information and communication technologies comes for male and art comes for female. It can be claimed that these majors compensate earnings losses better than other majors.

Appendix

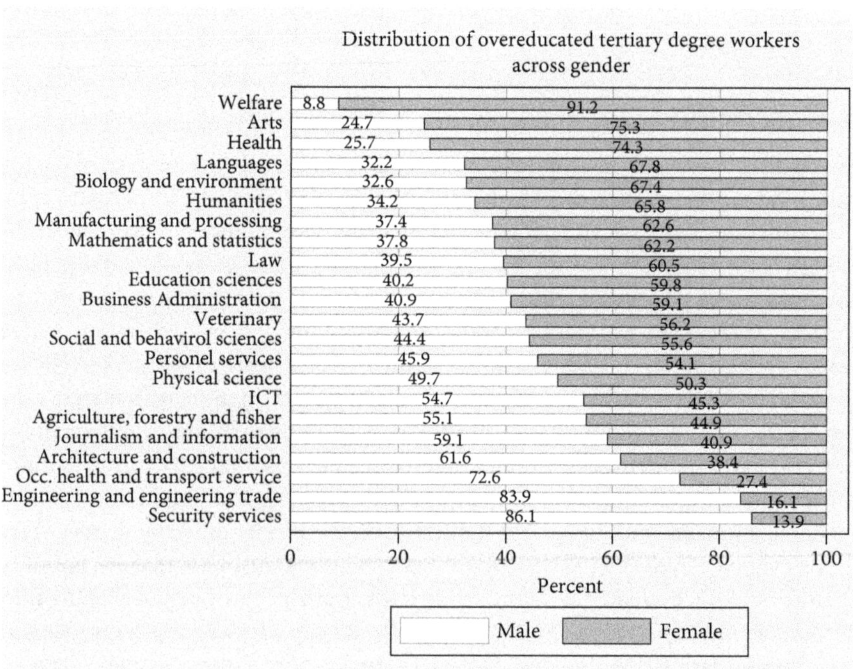

Fig. A1: Distribution of overeducated tertiary degree workers across gender

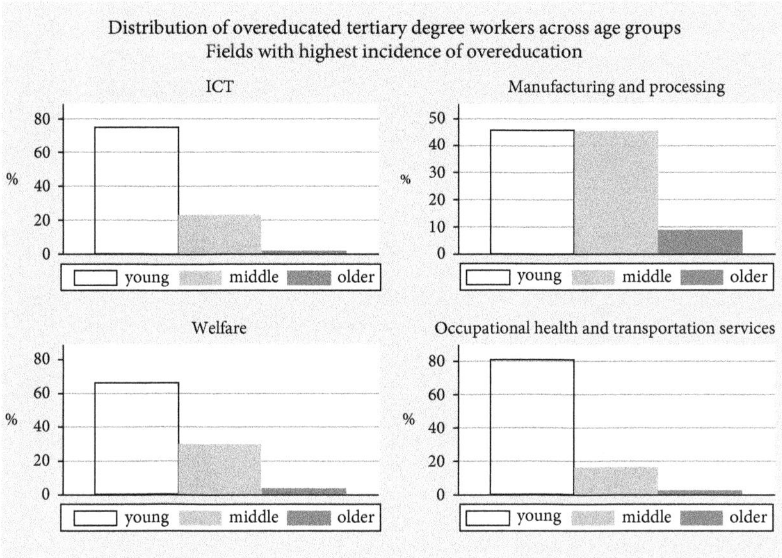

Fig. A2: Distribution of overeducated tertiary degree workers across age groups

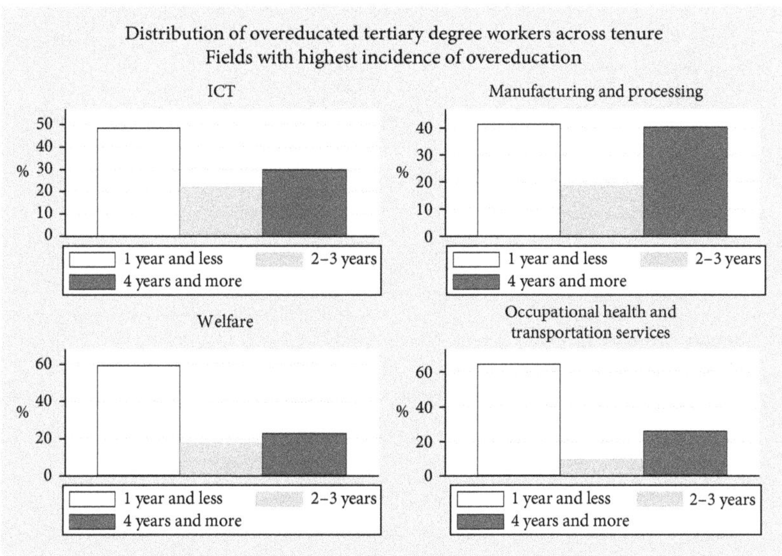

Fig. A3: Distribution of overeducated tertiary degree workers across tenure

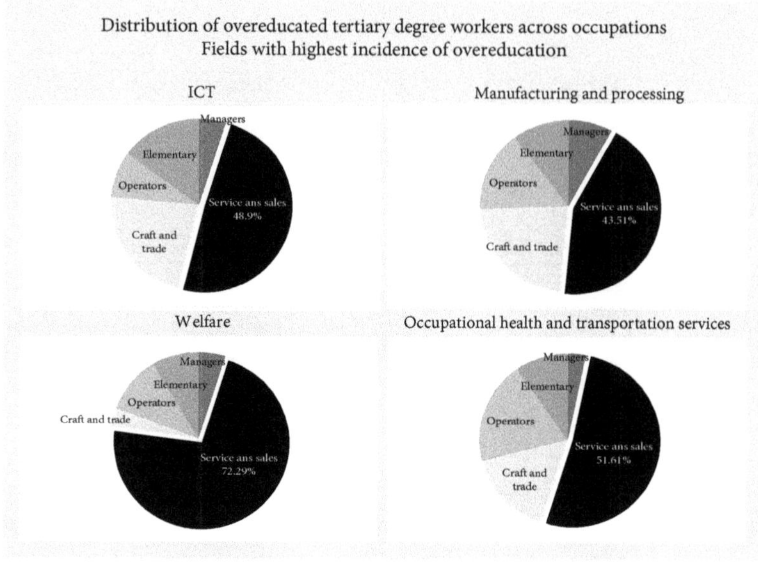

Fig. A4: Distribution of overeducated tertiary degree workers across occupations

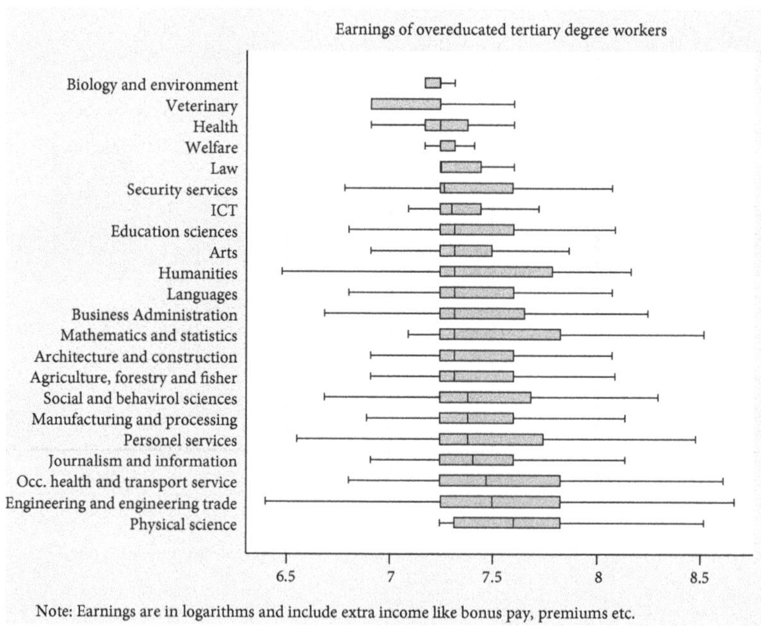

Fig. A5: Monthly earnings of overeducated tertiary degree workers

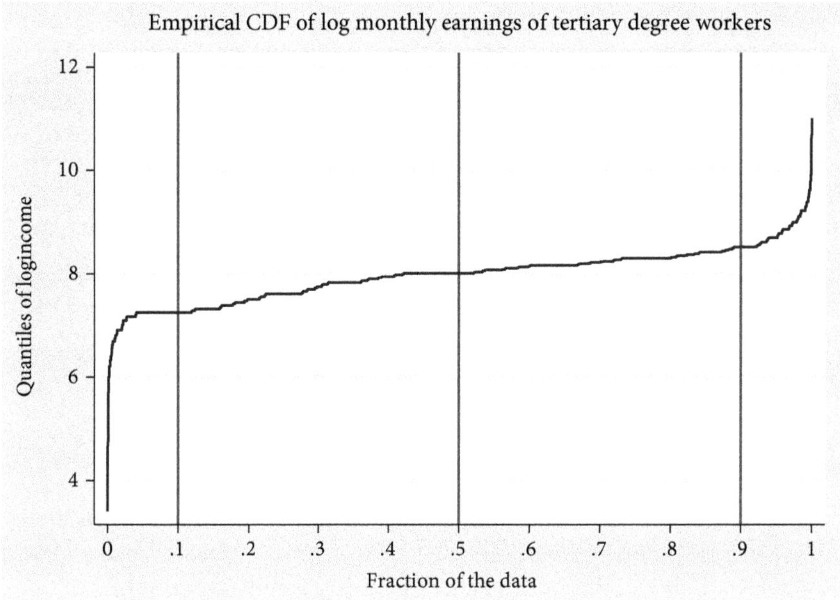

Fig. A6: Cumulative distribution function of monthly earnings of tertiary degree workers

Tab. A1: Quantile regressions—Male

Dependent variable: Log(earnings)	**q10**	**q50**	**q90**
Overeducation	−0.59***	−0.91***	−1.36***
	(0.083)	(0.050)	(0.098)
Constant	7.33***	7.85***	8.30***
	(0.099)	(0.059)	(0.12)
Observations	17,726	17,726	17,726
Pseudo R2	0.31	0.34	0.29

Standard errors in parentheses. ***, ** and * denotes statistical significance at 10 %, 5 % and 1 % level, respectively. Regressions include age, squared age, marital status, place of birth, tenure, squared tenure, occupation dummies, college major dummies and regional dummies at NUTS1 regional classification.

Tab. A2: Quantile regressions—Female

Dependent variable: Log(earnings)	**q10**	**q50**	**q90**
Overeducation	−0.45**	−0.91***	−1.20***
	(0.22)	(0.16)	(0.26)
Constant	7.26***	7.94***	8.07***
	(0.12)	(0.085)	(0.14)
Observations	11,814	11,814	11,814
Pseudo R2	0.27	0.32	0.26

Standard errors in parentheses. ***, ** and * denotes statistical significance at 10 %, 5 % and 1 % level, respectively. Regressions include age, squared age, marital status, place of birth, tenure, squared tenure, occupation dummies, college major dummies and regional dummies at NUTS1 regional classification.

References

Alba-Amirez, A. (1993). "Mismatch in the Spanish labor market: Overeducation?", *Journal of Human Resources*, 27(2): 259–278.

Altonji, J. G., Kahn, L. B., and Speer, J. D. (2014). "Trends in earnings differentials across college majors and the changing task composition of jobs", *The American Economic Review*, 104(5): 387–393.

Arcidiacono, P. (2004). "Ability sorting and the returns to college major", *Journal of Econometrics*, 121(1): 343–375.

Barone, C., and Ortiz, L. (2011). "Overeducation among European University Graduates: A comparative analysis of its incidence and the importance of higher education differentiation", *Higher Education*, 61(3): 325–337.

Bauer, T. K. (2002). "Educational mismatch and wages: A panel analysis", *Economics of Education Review*, 21: 221–229.

Berger, M. C. (1988). "Predicted future earnings and choice of college major", *Industrial and Labor Relations Review*, 41(3): 418–429.

Chevalier, A. (2011). "Subject choice and earnings of UK graduates", *Economics of Education Review*, 30(6): 1187–1201.

Cohn, E., and Chu Ng, Y. (2000). "Incidence and wage effects of overschooling and underschooling in Hong Kong", *Economics of Education Review*, 19(2): 159–168.

Cohn, E., and Kahn, S. (1995). "The wage effects of overschooling revisited", *Labour Economics*, 2(1): 67–76.

Di Paolo, A., and Tansel, A. (2017). "Analyzing wage differentials by field of study: Evidence from Turkey", Turkish Economic Association Discussion Paper 2017/4.

Duncan, G. J., and Hoffman, S. D. (1981). "The incidence and wage effects of eovereducation", *Economics of Education Review*, 1(1): 75–86.

Filiztekin, A. (2011). Education-occupation mismatch in Turkish labor market. MPRA Paper 35123.

Finnie, R., and Frenette, M. (2003). "Earning differences by major field of study: Evidence from three cohorts of recent Canadian graduates", *Economics of Education Review*, 22(2): 179–192.

Frenette, M. (2004). "The overqualified Canadian graduate: The role of the academic program in the incidence, persistence, and economic returns to overqualification", *Economics of Education Review*, 23(1): 29–45.

Galasi, P. (2008). "The effect of educational mismatch on wages for 25 countries", Budapest Working Papers on the Labour Market: 8.

Gervasi, L. O., and McGuiness, S. (2018). "Overeducation among European university graduates: A constraint or a choice?", European Youth Labor Markets. Switzerland, Springer, 154–174.

Grave, B. S., and Goerlitz, K. (2012). "Wage differentials by field of study–the case of German university graduates", *Education Economics*, 20(3): 284–302.

Hamermesh, D. S., and Donald, S. G. (2008). "The effect of college curriculum on earnings: An affinity identifier for non-ignorable non-response bias", *Journal of Econometrics*, 144(2): 479–491.

Hartog, J. (2000). "Over-education and earnings: Where are we, where should we go?", *Economics of Education Review*, 19(2): 131–147.

Hartog, J., and Oosterbeek, H. (1988). "Education, allocation and earnings in the Netherlands; Overschooling?", *Economics of Education Review*, 7(2): 185–194.

Hung, C.-Y. (2008). "Overeducation and undereducation in Taiwan", *Journal of Asian Economics*, 19(2): 125–137.

Kelly, E., O'Connell, P., and Smyth, E. (2008). "The economic returns to field of study and competencies among higher education graduates in Ireland", ESRI Working Paper No: 42.

Korpi, T., and Tahlin, M. (2009). "Educational mismatch, wages, and wage growth: Overeducation in Sweden, 1974–2000", *Labor Economics*, 16: 183–193.

Linsley, I. (2005). "Causes of Overeducation in the Australian Labour Market", *Australian Journal of Labor Economics*, 5: 121–143.

Loury, L. D., and Garman, D. (1995). "College Selectivity and Earnings", *Journal of Labor Economics*, 13(2): 289–308.

McGuiness, S. (2006). "Overeducation in the Labor Market", *Journal of Economic Surveys*, 20 (3): 387–418.

Mehta, A., Felipe, J., Quising, P., and Camingue, S. (2011). "Overeducation in developing economies: How can we test for it, and what does it mean?", *Economics of Education Review*, 30: 1334–1347.

Orbay, B., and Aydede, Y. (2015). Educational mismatch and the cost of underutilization in Turkish labour markets, MPRA Paper 65713.

Ortiz, L., and Kucel, A. (2008). "Do fields of study matter for over-education?: The cases of Spain and Germany", *International Journal of Comparative Sociology*, 49(4–5): 305–327.

Robst, J. (2007). "Education and job match: The relatedness of college major and work", *Economics of Education Review*, 26: 397–407.

Rumberger, R.W. (1987). "The Impact of Surplus Schooling on Producitivity and Earnings", *The Journal of Human Resources*, 22(1): 24–50.

Sicherman, N. (1991). "Overeducation in the Labor Market", *Journal of Labor Economics*, 9(2): 101–122.

Sloane, P., Battu, H., & Seaman, P. (1999). "Overeducation, undereducation and the British labour market", *Applied Economics*, 31: 1437–1453.

Tsang, M. C., & Levin, H. M. (1985). "The economics of overeducation", *Economics of Education Review*, 4(2): 93–104.

Verdugo, R. R., & Verdugo, N. T. (1989). "The impact of surplus schooling on earnings", *The Journal of Human Resources*, 24(4): 629–643.

Burcu Düzgün-Öncel and Deniz Karaoğlan

Adult Obesity: Decomposition Analysis

Socio-Economic Determinants of Adult Obesity: Decomposition Analysis on Turkey

Abstract: Obesity is an essential and growing public health problem worldwide, and obesity growth rates are high in both developed and developing countries. Individuals with lower socio-economic status are more likely to be exposed to risk of obesity than their counterparts. We believe that socio-economic status-related inequalities in obesity have various factors and addressing these inequalities requires coordinated public policies. In this respect, the aim of this chapter is to disentangle and decompose the socio-economic determinants of adult obesity in Turkey. We perform the empirical analysis using Turkish Health Survey data set prepared by Turkish Statistical Institute (TURKSTAT) for the years 2014 and 2016. We conduct the analysis separately for males and females. We estimate the concentration indices to find the extent of socio-economic inequalities in obesity. Negative concentration indices show prevalence of obesity is higher among those with relatively low socio-economic status. Furthermore, we apply Fairlie decomposition analysis to determine the determinants of inequality in obesity. Fairlie decomposition results suggest that the probability of obesity is approximately 30 % for low-educated individuals and 15 % for the others. The difference between two groups indicates the degree of contribution of other factors to inequality in obesity. Decomposition results show that age, gender and certain chronic illnesses make the highest contribution to inequality in obesity.

Keywords: obesity, concentration index, socio-economic status, decomposition

JEL: C31, C34, I12, J21, J24

1 Introduction

Obesity is an essential and increasing public health problem in both developed and less developed countries. Obesity reduces quality of life (Jia and Lubetkin, 2005; Forste and Moore; 2012; Walsh and Cullinan, 2015), increases morbidity such as cancer, heart disease, stroke, diabetes and musculoskeletal problems (Renehan et al., 2008; Walsh and Cullinan, 2015; Aizawa and Helble, 2017; Emamian et al., 2017) and leads to an increase in health-care expenditures (Wang et al., 2011; Cawley and Meyerhoefer, 2011). Obesity is strongly associated with age, gender, household income, and urbanization. Furthermore, it is considered to be one of the most striking diseases that have recently been targeted for a global response. Despite the existence of diversified conclusions, several studies have shown that socio-economic gradient of obesity exists in different countries.

The chapter has focused on the determinants of inequality in obesity recently. For instance, Hajizadeh et al. (2014) investigate trends in socio-economic-related inequalities in obesity among Canadian adults between 2000 and 2010. The estimated concentration index suggests that obesity is more concentrated among rich men and more prevalent among economically disadvantaged women. The decomposition analysis shows that factors such as demographics, income, immigration, education, drinking habits and physical activity are key factors explaining inequality in obesity. Ventosa and Urbanos-Garrido (2016) use micro data from the Spanish National Health Survey for the years 2011 and 2012 to estimate socio-economic inequalities in obesity. Their results present significant pro-rich inequality in the distribution of obesity and this inequality is higher for women. Walsh and Cullinan (2015) try to quantify and decompose the socio-economic gradient in childhood obesity in the Republic of Ireland by using concentration indices and decomposition analysis. Their results show that gradient is more pronounced in obese children and inequality in childhood obesity is mostly explained by parents' characteristics. Devaux and Sassi (2011) present an international comparison of inequalities by education level and socio-economic status (SES) for men and women for 11 OECD countries. They observe persistent social inequalities in obesity by education and SES in all countries. According to their calculations, USA and England have the greatest rates of obesity and overweight. Their results also suggest that large social inequalities for women are consistently detected in all countries. The authors also point out the fact that Hungary and Spain have the largest absolute inequalities, whereas France and Sweden have the largest relative inequalities. Alaba and Chola (2014) examine the socio-economic inequality in obesity among South African adults by using an asset index that proxy SES. They estimate concentration indices and perform decomposition analysis to determine the factors that contribute to socio-economic–related inequalities. The results indicate that women are more likely to be obese than men and individuals with higher SES are more likely to be more obese than their poorer counterparts. Decomposition results show that education and asset index contribute to inequality more for men.

Remarkable literature also exists for less developed countries. Fernald (2007) explores the association between SES and BMI for Mexican adults in 2003. The author concludes that greater education level is significantly related with higher body mass index (BMI) both for men and women. Aekplakorn et al. (2014) study the trends in BMI and obesity for the years 1991 and 2009 for Thai adults. Their results suggest that individuals living in urban areas and belong to high SESs were more likely to be obese previously. However, as economic growth increases, obesity becomes more prevalent among the individuals belonging to lower SES. Aizawa and Helble (2017) examine the transition of socio-economic–related excessive body weight from 1993 to 2014 in Indonesia by calculating concentration indexes and implementing decomposition analysis. Their results confirm that the prevalence of obesity has a larger impact on poorer segments, but concentration has decreased throughout the analyzed period. The change in inequality can be explained by the reduction in the elasticity of wealth and improved sanitary conditions in poorer households. Emamian et al. (2017) study socio-economic inequality in obesity and its determinants in Iran by applying Oaxaca-Blinder decomposition analysis. Their results indicate that obesity persists more in lower socio-economic groups and varies remarkably between different provinces and is more widespread in women and in urban population. Dinsa et al. (2012) study the relationship between SES and obesity in low- and middle-income countries among adults and children. Their results point out the positive relationship between SES and obesity in low-income countries. However, the relationship is mixed for men and negative for women in middle-income countries. Nevertheless, the authors conclude that child obesity appears to be predominantly a problem of the rich in low- and middle-income countries.

There are a few studies that examine the determining factors of obesity in Turkey. Earlier studies are generally conducted for specific regions [see, Erem et al. (2004), Hatemi et al. (2003) and Yumuk (2005)]. More recent studies examine the determinants of individual's BMI as well as the causal effect of education on individual's BMI levels by using earlier waves of Turkish Health Survey (THS) data set, which is a cross-sectional data set at country-based level [see, Tansel and Karaoglan (2014), Tansel and Karaoglan (2016)]. Later, Karaoglan and Tansel (2017) reinvestigate the determinants of BMI by using quantile regression (QR) technique in order to see how education and other demographic factors affect the individual's BMI at various quantiles of BMI quantiles. Although those studies are the first to examine the determinants of individual's BMI by using a rich micro data set, they are insufficient in explaining the inequality in obesity. To our knowledge, Ergin et al. (2011) conduct the first regional study to describe educational and wealth-related inequalities in Turkey by using World Health Survey 2002. Their findings suggest that for men, the prevalence of overweight is the highest for highest-wealth groups whereas for women, the prevalence of overweight is the highest among low-educated and middle-wealth groups. Ankara (2016) analyzes socio-economic determinants of obesity in different regions in Turkey for women aged 15–49 by using 2008 wave of Turkish Demographic Health Survey (TDHS) data set. The results show that obesity is more concentrated among wealthier women in eastern Turkey while it is more concentrated among poorer women in western Turkey. The author concludes that inequality in obesity is more associated with wealth and ethnicity.

Literature above reveals that socio-economic status (SES)–related inequality in health has diversified factors and understanding the nature of this inequality is important for policy makers who are trying to determine the effective intervention policies. In this respect, the aim of this study is to disentangle the socio-economic status inequality in obesity and reveal the contributors by decomposing inequality in obesity for Turkish adults. This study differs from the previous studies in various manners: First, in this chapter, we use the latest waves (2014 and 2016) of THS data set. Second, we use concentration indices and concentration curves to show SES inequality, which are not targeted by the previous studies by using the previous waves of THS data set. Last, this is the first study that uses Fairlie decomposition method to find the contributors of the inequality in obesity in Turkey. Hence, we believe that this chapter will inspire the future research on obesity and will be a good tool to implement policies targeted to combatting obesity.

Our results confirm the existence of a significant socio-economic gradient in the prevalence of obesity in Turkey, in line with previous literature. Our results show that educational attainment inequality in the distribution of obesity is higher for women than for men. Normalized concentration index are found to be negative for both genders. These negative indices suggest that obesity is higher among those with relatively low socio-economic status which is represented by low-education levels in this study. Decomposition results show that several demographic factors, especially age, has essential contributions to inequality in obesity. The results do not indicate a significant contribution of household income in explaining the inequality in obesity for different levels of education. Our results also suggest that having hypertension and lumbar region problems also significantly contribute to inequality in obesity for all education levels.

The rest of the chapter is organized as follows: Section 2 gives information about the data used. Section 3 presents the methods that are used. Results are shown in Section 4. Section 5 presents concluding remarks and suggest policy implications.

2 Data

Data used in this study is Turkish Health Survey (THS) for the years 2014 and 2016 conducted by Turkish Statistical Institute (TURKSTAT). This is a cross-sectional survey representative at country level. Our focus group is individuals between 25 and 64 of whom 11,261 are men and 13,820 are women. By considering the individuals over 25, our objective is to circumvent the problem related to individual's incomplete years of schooling, since individuals complete their education approximately at the age of 25 in Turkey. Institutional population (soldiers, individuals living in dormitories, prisons, hospitals at the long-terms homes for elderly, etc.) and not to exceed 1 % of the population of the total population (small villages, etc.) are thought to be reached settlements with adequate number of households in the sample are excluded. The survey includes information about personal and demographic characteristics, labor market characteristics, lifestyles and health determinants, use of health services and health indicators both for men and women.

Body mass index (BMI), which is used to determine obesity, is at interest in this study. We calculate BMI by dividing weight in kilograms by height in squared meters. BMI greater than 30 implies obesity in adults. Individuals with BMI between 30 and 25 are considered as overweight, individuals with BMI between 18.5 and 25 are classified as normal and individuals with BMI lower than 18.5 shows underweighted individuals. These cutoffs are chosen according to related literature.

In the related literature, socioeconomic status (SES) is generally defined according to the individual's education level and income. In THS data set, education attainment is a categorical variable with categories of illiterate, primary school, secondary school, high school and university or higher degree. We also group educational level as low, medium and high in Fairlie decomposition analysis. Low education includes illiterate and primary school, medium education has medium and high school, whereas high education incorporates individuals with university or higher education. Income is the household income and a categorical variable in the survey. However, equalized per capita household income is not available due to data set constraints. In this respect, we use only educational attainment as the indicator of socio-economic status.

Regarding labor force status, we classify the individuals into two groups: "out of labor force" and "in labor force". Individuals who state that they are seasonal workers, students, pensioners, the individuals who have other income resources and the individuals who are unable to work are considered as out of labor force. The respondents who are working in a regular job is referred as "employed", while the individuals who are not working but seeking for job is considered as "unemployed".

Last, health status variable is also a categorical variable with very poor, poor, fair, good and very good categories. We also include certain chronic illnesses in the decomposition analysis such as asthma, bronchitis, coronary heart diseases, hypertension, lumbar region and neck problems, diabetes, liver disease, allergies, and depression. We also compromise use of prescribed drugs and walking, biking, doing sports, smoking and alcohol consumption as other indicators of health.

3 Methods

3.1 Concentration Index and Concentration Curve

We use concentration index (CI) and concentration curve as the measurement of socio-economic inequality in obesity in this study and calculate country-wide concentration indices for both genders. Concentration indices are commonly utilized as a means of quantifying socio-economic inequalities and are derived from the well-known Gini coefficient (Walsh and Cullinan, 2015). While the Gini coefficient measures income inequality across income distribution, concentration index measures inequality in a health variable across socio-economic status. Concentration indices capture the socio-economic dimension of inequalities, take into account the whole population, are sensitive to changes in population distribution along the socio-economic scale, offer the possibility of visual representation through concentration curve and allow testing dominance relationships (Wagstaff et al.,1991). Concentration index is calculated as twice the area between the concentration curve and the 45-degree line. A negative index shows that poor health is higher among those with relatively low socio-economic status and is represented by a concentration curve above the 45-degree line (Ventosa and Garrido, 2016).

Concentration index is calculated as the following (Kakwani et al., 1997; Van Doorslaeer et al., 1997; Aizawa and Helble, 2017):

$$CI = \frac{2}{\mathrm{N}\mu}\sum_{1}^{n} H_i R_i - 1 - \frac{1}{\mathrm{N}} \tag{1}$$

where N is the sample size, H_i is the health outcome for individual *i*, and μ is the mean of health variable. Our health outcome variable is the binary variable for obesity in this study (it takes value of 1 if the individual's BMI level is equal to or greater than 30, 0 otherwise) R_i is the fractional rank of individual *i* in the socio-economic status (Aizawa and Helble, 2017). When health outcome is a binary variable, the minimum and maximum possible values of the concentration index become $\mu-1$ and $1-\mu$ (Wagstaff, 2005). Thus, we need to apply a normalization to keep the concentration index in the range between −1 and 1. By following Aizawa and Helble (2017) and Walsh and Cullinan (2015), we implement Wagstaff (2005) normalization method and provide both the original concentration index (CI) and Wagstaff Index (WI) for the binary obesity variable. The normalized index is calculated as the following:

$$WI = \frac{1}{1-\mu} CI \tag{2}$$

where CI is the original concentration index given by the Equation (1).

3.2 Fairlie Decomposition

Socio-economic status-related inequality in health has diversified factors and understanding the nature of this inequality is important for policy makers who are trying to determine the effective intervention policies. The concentration index and the concentration curve use one socio-economic variable to compute inequality in health variable and this inequality can be decomposed to estimate the effect of other explanatory variables. Hence, the decomposition allows us to examine other variables that contribute to inequality to be included within the analysis and permits a clearer quantification of the impact of the variables underpinning any inequality in health (Van Doorslaer and Koolman, 2004). In order to disentangle direct and indirect effects of SES on obesity, we use Fairlie decomposition technique which is an extension of the classical Oaxaca-Blinder decomposition method. Basically, the technique estimates the contributions of the explanatory variables among different education levels (low, medium and high).

For a linear regression, the standard Blinder-Oaxaca decomposition of education gap in the average value of dependent variable, which is obesity in this study, can be expressed as (Fairlie, 1999; Fairlie, 2006):

$$\bar{H}_i - \bar{H}_0 = [(\bar{X}_i - \bar{X}_0)\hat{\beta}_i] + [\bar{X}_0(\hat{\beta}_i - \hat{\beta}_0)] \tag{3}$$

where the difference $\bar{H}_i - \bar{H}_0$ shows the change in obesity level among education, $\bar{X}_i$ is a row vector of average values of the independent variables and $\hat{\beta}_i$ is a vector of coefficient estimates for education i. With X representing the control variables and $\hat{\beta}$ the coefficient estimates, the logit equation can be written as:

$$H = F\left(X\hat{\beta}\right) \tag{4}$$

Following Fairlie (1999) and Fairlie (2006), the decomposition for a nonlinear function such as logit or probit, is as the following:

$$\bar{H}_i - \bar{H}_0 = \left[\sum_{i=1}^{N_{t1}} \frac{F\left(X_{i,t1}\hat{\beta}_{t0}\right)}{N_{t1}} - \sum_{i=1}^{N_{t0}} \frac{F\left(X_{i,t0}\hat{\beta}_{t0}\right)}{N_{t0}}\right] + \left[\sum_{i=1}^{N_{t1}} \frac{F\left(X_{i,t1}\hat{\beta}_{t1}\right)}{N_{t1}} - \sum_{i=1}^{N_{t1}} \frac{F\left(X_{i,t1}\hat{\beta}_{t0}\right)}{N_{t1}}\right] \tag{5}$$

where N denotes the sample size. In Equation (5), the first square brackets is related to changes in the distributions of control variables and the second square brackets is related to changes in the process that determines H (Caner et al., 2018). In order to calculate decomposition, we substitute the average probability of a transition into obesity for $\bar{H}$ and the logistic function for F.

4 Results

4.1 Descriptive Statistics

Tab. 1 shows the descriptive statistics, distinguishing between adults who are grouped as obese, overweight, recommended weight and underweight. We use education as the ranking variable in the construction of concentration index and concentration curves. The descriptive statistics suggest that prevalence of obesity decreases with the increase in education level. Only 13.65 % of individuals with university or higher degree are obese, whereas this ratio rises to 36.06 % and 30.92 % for illiterate individuals and individuals with primary school degree, respectively. On the other hand, we observe higher share of individuals have recommended body mass index (BMI) among high-educated individuals. Increase in the prevalence of obesity with the decrease in education level can also be observed from Fig. 1 which exhibits distribution of mean obesity over educational attainment.

Tab. 1 also presents distribution of BMI according to income quintiles. However, income variable in the survey is household income and is a categorical variable. Since household identification variables are not available in the data set, it is not possible to calculate per capita household income. In this respect, we cannot use income as a socio-economic status indicator. Additionally, according to descriptive statistics, we do not observe any pattern in obesity prevalence according to income quintiles.

When we examine labor market indicators, weighted statistics suggest prevalence of obesity and being overweight are lower for the individuals in the labor force. For instance, obesity rate is 19.52 % and overweight ratio is 41.51 % for individuals who are employed. Descriptive statistics show that the share of obese individuals rises with poor health. Tab. 1 indicates that 42.44 % of people among the individuals with poor health are obese and this ratio is only 14.99 % for the individuals who report very good health. We also observe increase in the obesity prevalence with respect to age. In other words, older individuals have more probability of being obese or overweight. Finally, we monitor that 25 % of whole adult population is obese, whereas this share is 20.08 % for males and 29.08 % for females implying that prevalence of higher BMI is more common among females.

Tab. 1: Sample Statistics by BMI Category (%)

	obese	overweight	recommended	underweight
Socio-economic variables				
Educational attainment				
illiterate	36.06	35.01	27.00	1.93
primary	30.92	39.77	28.20	1.11
secondary	19.55	39.27	39.27	1.91
high school	17.80	40.66	39.61	1.92
university or higher	13.65	37.28	46.67	2.40
Education level				
low education	31.99	38.78	27.95	1.28
medium education	18.49	40.12	39.48	1.92
high education	13.65	37.28	46.67	2.40
Income				
1st quintile	26.50	37.11	34.71	1.68
2nd quintile	26.62	38.72	33.12	1.54
3rd quintile	26.46	39.60	32.46	1.47
4th quintile	23.89	40.73	33.35	2.04
5th quintile	20.80	40.16	37.60	1.44
Labor force status				
out of labor force	30.19	36.53	31.56	1.72
Employed	19.52	41.51	37.39	1.57
Unemployed	18.89	38.71	41.01	1.38
Health status				
very poor	42.44	30.26	22.51	4.80
poor	38.89	35.39	24.21	1.51
fair	31.22	38.72	28.45	1.61
good	20.03	39.99	38.36	1.62
very good	14.99	37.98	45.30	1.73
Age				
25–34	11.60	32.71	52.19	3.50
35–44	23.27	40.79	34.49	1.45
45–54	32.80	42.34	24.14	0.73
55–64	35.84	40.15	23.38	0.63
Gender				
Male	20.08	44.88	34.22	0.82
female	29.08	34.04	34.54	2.33
Sample size (n)	6280	9759	8628	414
Sample size (%)	25.04	38.91	34.40	1.65

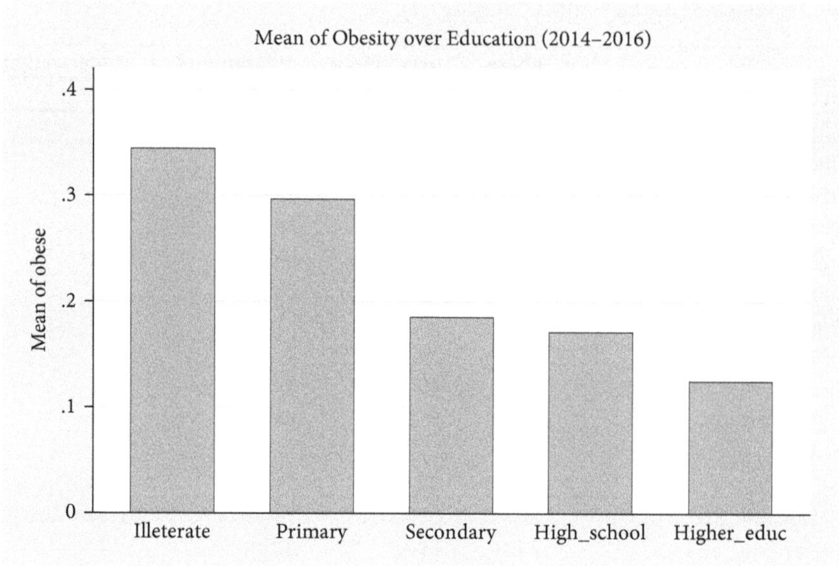

Fig. 1: Prevalence of Mean Obesity over Educational Attainment

4.2 Concentration Index Estimation

In order to quantify SES inequality in obesity, we calculate both standard and normalized concentration indices (CI) based on Wagstaff normalization (WI). Tab. 2 presents concentration indices for individuals who are obese. Since our health outcome is a binary variable, we need to adjust the boundaries of the index and thus focus more on WI. The results confirm the existence of significant inequalities. We observe negative indices in both CI and WI and for both genders showing that obesity is higher among individuals with lower levels of education. Standard concentration index is −0.180 for all sample and changes to −0.235 when we use Wagstaff normalization. WI measure is −0.108 for males and −0.272 for females indicating the fact that SES inequality in obesity is higher for women.

Fig. 2 presents concentration curves with respect to gender. Concentration curves also show the presence of a marked socio-economic gradient in the prevalence of obesity, which is greater for females. We observe concentration curves above the 45-degree line again implying prevalence of obesity is higher among lower socio-economic groups.

Tab. 2: Standard and Wagstaff Concentration Indices (2014, 2016)

	All sample	Males	Females
Sample size	25081	11261	13820
Standard concentration index (CI)	−0.180	−0.088	−0.196
standard error	(0.0061)	(0.0107)	(0.0073)
Wagstaff concentration index (WI)	−0.235	−0.108	−0.272
standard error	(0.0080)	(0.0130)	(0.0101)

Notes: Data is from TURKSTAT Health Survey 2014 and 2016. Sample weight applied.

4.3 Fairlie Decomposition Results

Fairlie decomposition results show us the predicted probabilities of obesity for different levels of education. The contribution of the change in the control variables is estimated as in Equation (5) relying on the pooled coefficients. For instance, column (1) of Tab. 3 shows the results for the dependent variable "being obese" for low-educated individuals, and column (3) shows the results for highly educated individuals. In other words, individuals with low education are our treatment group where individuals with other levels of education are our control group in column (1). The results in columns (2) and (3) can be interpreted in the same manner. Our demographic controls are gender dummy (equals to 1 for females) and age categories, where age group 25–34 is the reference group. We use household income variable to check whether household income contributes to inequality, even though per capita household income is not available. First income quintile is the reference group. The variable "in the labor force" is also a binary variable which is equal to 1 for the individuals who are employed or unemployed. We use the individual's self-assessed health status of and certain chronic illnesses as the other health indicators. Finally, we include physical activity indicators along with smoking and alcohol consumption as additional control variables.

Results in column (1) shows that probability of obesity is about 30 % for low-educated individuals and about 15 % for the others. The difference of −14.93 % shows the contribution of control variables to inequality in obesity other than education. Female dummy, age, being in 4th or 5th income quintiles, having chronic illnesses of asthma, hypertension, lumbar region problems, diabetes, walking and smoking have significant contributions to SES inequality in obesity for low-educated individuals. According to estimates in column (3), probability of obesity is about 12 % for high-educated individuals and about 25.98 %

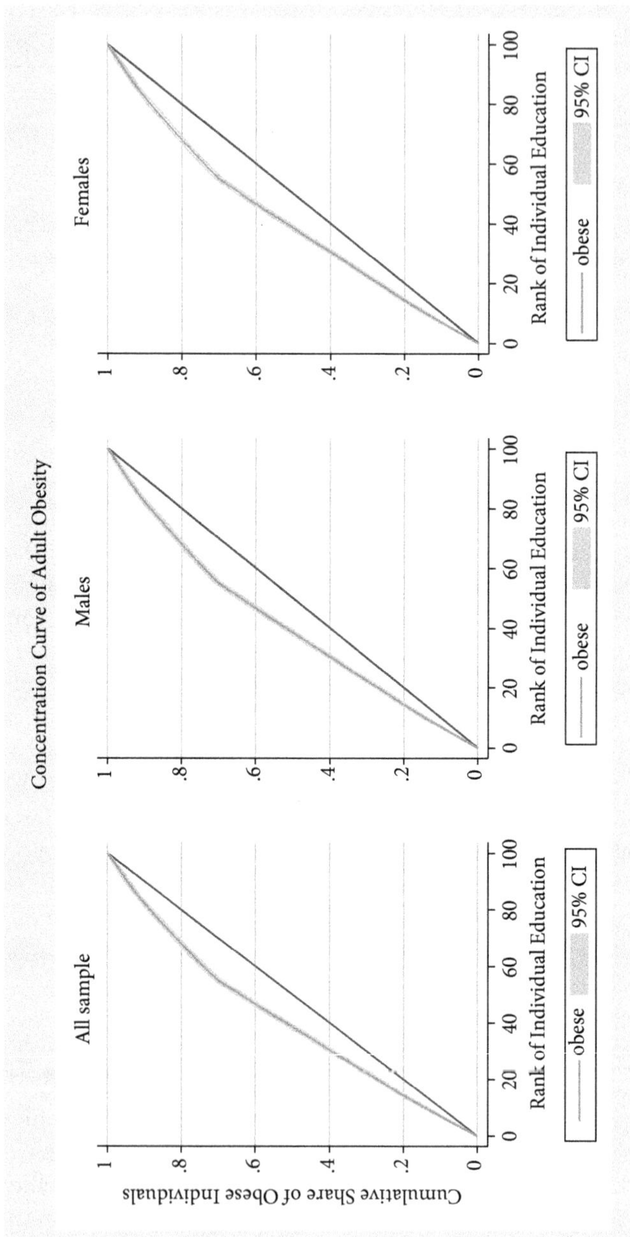

Fig. 2: Concentration Curves of Adult Obesity According to Gender

Tab. 3: Fairlie Decomposition Estimation Results

	Low education dep var: obesity	Medium education dep var: obesity	High education dep var: obesity
Predicted H_i (for treatment)	0.3066	0.1766	0.1251
Predicted H_i (for control)	0.1572	0.2606	0.2598
Difference	−0.1493	0.0839	0.1346
Percent explained	-9.63	4.5	5.27
Control variables			
female	−0.0158***	−0.0038	−0.0048**
	(0.0023)	(0.0024)	(0.0022)
age 35–44	0.0035***	−0.0017*	−0.0016
	(0.0010)	(0.0009)	(0.0012)
age 45–54	−0.0246***	0. 0077***	0.0125***
	(0.0020)	(0.0014)	(0.0032)
age 55–64	−0.0221***	0.0088***	0.0132***
	(0.0022)	(0.0022)	(0037)
2nd income quintile	−0.0004	−0.0001	0.0036
	(0.0005)	(0.0001)	(0.0036)
3rd income quintile	−0.0001	−0.0007	0.0011
	(0001)	(0.0007)	(0.0017)
4th income quintile	0.0017**	−0.0004	0.0009
	(0.0008)	(0.0008)	(0020)
5th income quintile	0.0107***	−0.0001	0.0084
	(0.0034)	(0.0002)	(0.0095)
in the labor force	−0.0023	−0.0004	−0.0066
	(0.0026)	(0.0016)	(0.0050)
fair health	−0.0024	0.0010	0.0231*
	(0.0018)	(0.0015)	(0.0136)
good health	0.0006	−0.0027	−0.0316*
	(0.0037)	(0.0036)	(0.0167)
asthma	−0.0044***	0.0015	−0.0017
	(0.0011)	(0.0015)	(0.0021)
bronchitis	−0.0014	0.0012	0.0008
	(0.0009)	(0.0010)	(0.0018)
coronary heart disease	0.0001	−0.0010	0.0004
	(0.0008)	(0.0007)	(0.0021)
hypertension	−0.0139***	0.0105***	0.0153***
	(0.0016)	(0.0017)	(0.0040)

(continued on next page)

Tab. 3: (continued)

	Low education dep var: obesity	**Medium education dep var: obesity**	**High education dep var: obesity**
lumbar region problems	−0.0041***	0.0036***	0.0075***
	(0.0015)	(0.0012)	(0.0026)
neck region problems	0.0017*	−0.0006	−0.0036
	(0.0010)	(0.0009)	(0.0019)
diabetes	−0.0097***	0.0063***	0.0083
	(0.0011)	(0.0013)	(0.0024)
liver disease	0.0002	0.0002	−0.0003
	(0.0004)	(0.0005)	(0.0008)
depression	0.0001	−0.0001	−0.0004
	(0.0005)	(0.0004)	(0.0012)
prescribed drug use	−0.0025**	0.0016	0.0001
	(0.0012)	(0.0010)	(0.0018)
daily activity	0.0002	0.0027***	−0.0026**
	(0.0001)	(0.0007)	(0.0013)
walking	−0.0036***	0.0015**	0.0029**
	(0.0008)	(0.0007)	(0.0015)
biking	−0.0001	0.0008**	0.0004
	(0.0007)	(0.0004)	(0.0005)
doing sports	−0.0018	−0.0001	0.0039**
	(0.0020)	(0.0003)	(0.0018)
smoking	−0.0066***	0.0069***	−0.0002
	(0.0010)	(0.0015)	(0.0004)
alcohol use	0.0018	0.0001	0.0035
	(0.0025)	(0.0015)	(0.0022)
Sample size (n)	13671	7204	4206

Notes:***p < 0.01, **p < 0.05, *p < 0.1. Data is from TURKSTAT Health Survey 2014 and 2016. Sample weight applied.

for the other education levels and the difference of 13 % suggests the contribution of control variables to the probability of obesity. Positive estimates indicate that variation in the control variable by different education levels leads to an increase in inequality in obesity and accordingly a negative estimate leads to a reduction in inequality in obesity. For instance, being a female negatively contributes to inequality for all education levels, while having hypertension negatively contributes to inequality for low-educated individuals and positively for high-educated individuals. The largest factor explaining the difference in all specifications is the age. Individuals are more likely to be obese at older ages regardless of their education levels.

5 Conclusion

This study confirms the existence of a significant socio-economic gradient in the prevalence of obesity in Turkey, in line with previous literature. Our results show that educational attainment inequality in the distribution of obesity is higher for women than for men. Normalized concentration index is calculated as −0.235 for whole sample, −0.108 for males and −0.272 for females. These negative indices suggest that obesity is higher among those with relatively low socio-economic status which is represented by education level in this study. The concentration index and the concentration curve use one socio-economic variable, namely individual's education level to compute inequality in health variable and this inequality can be decomposed to estimate the effect of other explanatory variables. In this respect, we apply Fairlie decomposition method which is nonlinear extension of the classical Oaxaca-Blinder decomposition technique. Decomposition results show that control variables, especially age, has essential contributions to inequality in obesity for different education levels. Revealing socio-economic status-related inequality in obesity has several factors and comprehending the nature of this inequality is important for policy makers who are trying to determine the effective intervention policies that aim to improve health of population.

5.1 Policy Implications

Concentration Index estimation results suggest that inequality in obesity is high for lower-educated individuals. This finding points out the importance of education to reduce obesity rates. The government should spend more on education and increase both literacy and compulsory schooling completion rates.

To increase the awareness of society regarding the dangers of obesity, quality of schooling is as important as years of schooling completed. For instance, both families and children should be informed about healthy nutrition processes and the importance of exercising. In addition to formal education, media and Non-Governmental Organizations (NGOs) can be important actors to increase the society's knowledge about the dangers of obesity.

The inequality in obesity is significantly higher among women compared to men. First, this phenomenon can be linked to physical factors. For instance, in post-menopause period women tend to gain more weight. Again, awareness of healthy nutrition and importance of exercising are important to reduce the obesity rates among women. Second, inequality in obesity rates can be also explained by more sedentary life style of women compared to men, as approximately 61 % of the women in reproductive age are inactive (neither employed nor searching for job), according to latest Turkish Demographic and Health Survey (TDHS) data set. Therefore, implementing policies to encourage women to participate in the labor force will help to decrease inequality in obesity.

Last, according to Fairlie decomposition results, being at older age and having specific chronic illnesses, such as hypertension and lumber region problems, significantly contribute to the inequality in obesity for each education level. Necessary medical interventions should be taken into consideration by hospitals and family health centers.

References

Aekplakorn, Wichai, Rungkarn Inthawong, Pattapong Kessemboon, Rassamee Sangthong, Suwat Chariyalertsak, Panwadee Putwatana, and Surasak Taneepanichskul. 2014. "Prevalence and Trends of Obesity and Association with Socioeconomic Status in Thai Adults: National Health Examination Surveys, 1991–2009." *Journal of Obesity*, 14: 1–8.

Aizawa, Toshiaki, and Matthias Helble. 2017. "Socioeconomic Inequality in Excessive Body Weight in Indonesia." *Economics and Human Biology*, 27: 315–327.

Alaba, Olufunke, and Lumbwe Chola. 2014. "Socioeconomic Inequalities in Adult Obesity Prevalence in South Africa: A Decomposition Analysis." *International Journal of Environmental Research and Public Health*, 11: 3387–3406.

Ankara, Hasan Giray. 2016. "Inequality Analyses of Obesity in Turkey." *International Journal of Social Science and Humanity*, 6: 742–755.

Caner, Asena, Deniz Karaoğlan, and Gülbiye Yaşar. 2018. "Utilization of Healthcare Services by Young Children: The Aftermath of the Turkish Health Transformation Program." *International Journal of Health Planning and Management*, 33(3): 596–613.

Cowley, J., and C. Meyerhoefer. 2011. "The Medical Care Cost of Obesity: An Instrumental Variables Approach." *Journal of Health Economics*, 31: 219–230.

Devaux, Marion, and Franco Sassi. 2011. "Social Inequalities in Obesity and Overweight in 11 OECD Countries." *European Journal of Public Health*, 23: 464–469.

Dinsa, G. D., Y. Goryakin, E. Fumagalli, and M. Suhrckle. 2012. "Obesity and Socioeconomic Status in Developing Countries: A Sytematic Review." *Obesity Reviews*, 13: 1067–1079.

Emamian, Mohammad Hassan, Mansooreh Fateh, Ahmad Reza Hosseinpoor, Ali Alami, and Akbar Fotouhi. 2017. "Obesity and Its Socioeconomic Determinants in Iran." *Economics and Human Biology*, 26: 144–150.

Erem, C., et al. 2004. "Prevalence of Obesity and Associated Risk Factors in a Turkish Population (Trabzon City, Turkey)." *Obesity Research*, 12(7): 1117–1127.

Ergin, Isil, Hur Hassoy, and Anton Kunst. 2011. "Socioeconomic Inequalities in Overweight among Adults in Turkey: A Regional Evaluation." *Public Health Nutrition*, 15: 58–66.

Fairlie, W. Robert. 1999. "The Absence of the African-American Owned Business: An Analysis of the Dynamics of Self Employment." *Journal of Labor Economics*, 17: 80–108.

Fairlie, W. Robert. 2006. "An Extension of the Blinder-Oaxaca Decomposition Technique to Logit and Probit Models." *IZA Discussion Paper*, No. 1917.

Fernald, Lia C. H. 2007. "Socioeconomic Status and Body Mass Index in Low-Income Mexican Adults." *Social Science and Medicine*, 64: 2030–2042.

Forste, R., and E. Moore. 2012. "Adolescent Obesity and Life satisfaction: Perceptions of Self, Peers, Family, and School." *Economics and Human Biology*, 10: 385–294.

Hajizadeh, Mohammed, M. Karen Campbell, and Sisira Sarma. 2014. "Socioeconomic Inequalities in Adult Obesity Risk in Canada: Trends and Decomposition Analyses." *European Journal of Health Economics*, 15: 203–221.

Hatemi, H., et al. 2003. "Prevalence of Overweight and Obesity in Turkey." *Metabolic Syndrome and Related Disorders*, 1(4): 285–290.

Jia, H., and E. I. Lubetkin. 2005. "The Impact of Obesity on Health Related Quality of Life in the General Adult US Population." *Journal of Public Health*, 2: 156–164.

Kakwani, Nanak, Adam Wagstaff, and Eddy Van Doorslaer. 1997. "Socio-Economic Inequalities in Health: Measurement, Computation and Statistical Inference." Journal of Econometrics, 77(1):87–103.

Karaoğlan, Deniz, and Aysit Tansel. 2017. "Determinants of Obesity in Turkey: A Quantile Regression Analysis from a Developing Country." Bonn, Germany: Institute of Labor Economics (IZA) Discussion Paper No. 10491.

Renehan, Andrew G., Margaret Tyson, Matthias Egger, Richard F. Heller, and Marcel Zwahlen. 2008 "Body-Mass Index and Incidence of Cancer: A Systematic Review and Meta Analysis of Prospective Observational Studies." The Lancet, 331(9612):569–578.

Tansel, Aysit, and Deniz Karaoğlan. 2014. "Health Behaviors and Education in Turkey." Bonn, Germany: Institute for the Study of Labor (IZA) Discussion Paper No. 8262.

Tansel, Aysit, and Deniz Karaoğlan. 2016. "The Causal Effect of Education on Health Behaviors: Evidence from Turkey." Ankara, Turkey: Economic Research Center (ERC) Working Papers in Economics No. 16/06.

Turkey Demographic and Health Survey Data Set. 2013. Hacettepe University Institute of Population Studies. http://www.hips.hacettepe.edu.tr.

Van Doorslear, Eddy, Adam Wagstaff, Hein Bleichrodt, Samuel Calonge, Ulf G. Gerdtham, Michael Gerfin, Jose Geurts, Lorna Gross, Unto Hakinen, Robert E. Leu, Owen O'Donell, Carol Propper, Frank Puffer, Marisol Rodriguez, Gun Sandberg, Olaf Winkelhake. 1997. "Income Related Inequalities in Health: Some International Comparisons." Journal of Health Economics, 16(1):93–112.

Van Doorslear, Eddy, and Xander Koolman. 2004. "Explaining the Differences in Income Related Health Inequalities Across European Countries." Health Economics, 13(7):609–628.

Ventosa, Maria Merino, and Rosa M. Urbanos-Garrido. 2016. "Disentangling Effects of Socioeconomic Status on Obesity: A Cross-Sectional Study of the Spanish Adult Population." *Economics and Human Biology*, 22: 216–224.

Wagstaff, Adam. 2005. "The Bounds of Concentration Index When the Variable of Interest is Binary,with an Application to Immunization Inaquality." Health Economics, 14(4): 429–432.

Wagstaff, Adam. 2009. "Correcting the Concentration Index: A Comment." *Journal of Health Economics*, 28: 516–520.

Walsh, Brendan, and John Culinan. 2015. "Decomposing Socioeconomic Inequalities in Childhood Obesity: Evidence from Ireland." *Economics and Human Biology*, 16: 60–72.

Wang, C. Y., K. McPherson, T. Marsh, S. L. Gortmaker, and M. Brown. 2011. "Health and Economic Burden of the Projected Obesity Trends in the USA and the UK." *Lancet*, 378: 815–825.

Yumuk, V. D. 2005. "Prevalence of Obesity in Turkey." *Obesity Reviews*, 6 (1): 9–10.

Dinçer Dedeoğlu and Kaan Öğüt

Monetary Policy in Turkey

The Monetary Policy in Turkey after 2008: The Case of a Small Open Economy

Abstract: This chapter examines the monetary policy in Turkey since the 2008 global financial crisis. The impact of quantitative easing (QE) and tapering policies on monetary policy designation is considered. In the post-2008 period, the Central Bank of the Republic of Turkey (CBRT) tried to control capital inflows using innovative tools in QE episodes. However, during the subsequent 2013–2018 sub-period, in which Turkish Lira depreciated owing to capital outflows, CBRT followed a relatively simpler and more orthodox monetary policy.

Keywords: monetary policy, quantitative easing, Central Bank of Turkey

JEL: E44, E52, E58, F32, F41

1 Introduction

The history of the Turkish economy over the last four decades is replete with many examples of concepts taught in macroeconomics courses, such as debt monetization, the crowding-out effect, the impossible trinity, and exchange rate pass-through. Although this study mainly analyzes monetary policy in Turkey following the 2008 global financial crisis, as well as the developments in the money market, it also summarizes the fundamental structural characteristics of the pre-2008 period. The post-2008 period, which is the subject of the current analysis, is divided into 2008–2013 and 2013–2018sub-sections, to show how and in which direction the global financial conditions affected the monetary policy of a small open economy such as Turkey's. In the 2008–2013 sub-periods, the central banks of developed countries, in particular, the US central bank (FED), implemented expansionary policies known as quantitative easing (QE). Conversely, in the sub-period between 2013 and 2018, the QE policy was abandoned because it was thought that the criteria set for the US economy had been partially met. In the first sub-period, the Central Bank of the Republic of Turkey (CBRT) in Turkey struggled with the current account deficit and excess credit growth, whereas in the next sub-period the main issue was currency depreciation and high inflation rates. The CBRT monetary authority of Turkey developed appropriate policy tools to deal with those complications from both sub-periods.

From 2008 to 2013, during which there was excess credit growth and a high current account deficit as a result of intensive capital inflows, the CBRT tried to control capital inflows using innovative tools, whereas during the subsequent sub-period in which the Turkish Lira TL depreciated owing to capital outflows, the monetary authority followed a relatively simpler and more orthodox monetary policy.

2 The Monetary Policy During Pre-2008 Period

The main task of the CBRT until 1997 was to finance the budget. The fact that money was printed to finance the budget supports the Friedmanist view that inflation is a monetary phenomenon. As of 1993, direct monetization (short-term advances provided to the treasury) increased to 3% of national income and 42% of the budget deficit was financed by monetization (Fig. 1). During the period of 1994–1997, the monetization rate was partially reduced. In 1998, the use of short-term advances was terminated. Therefore, the rate of growth of the money supply decreased and the annual inflation rate decreased gradually, but there was no decrease in the monthly inflation rate. This has been suggested that this was because there were budget deficits underlying the inflationary process but the change in the method of financing these budget deficits did not

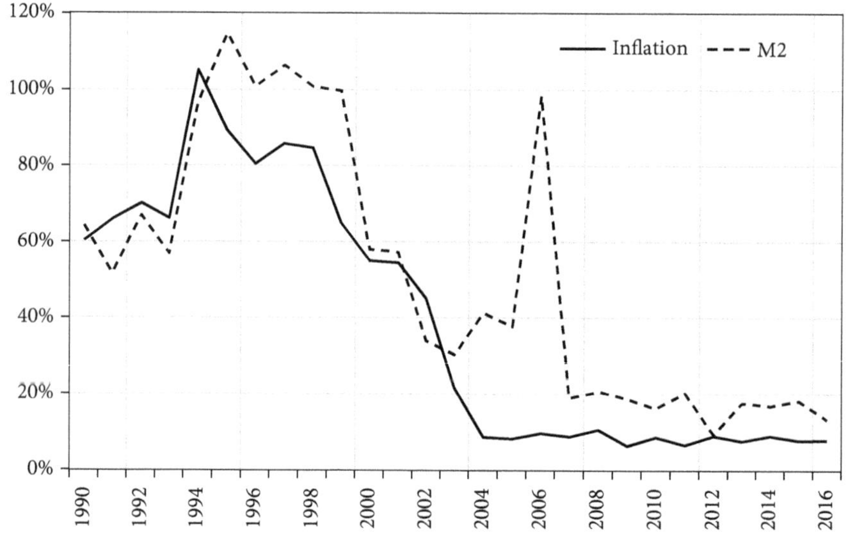

Fig. 1: Inflation and money supply (M2) growth. Source: CBRT

eliminate them (Yılmaz, Akçay, & Alper, 2002). In a sense, even though financing of budget deficits via monetization was abandoned, because Turkey was in a high inflationary environment at that time, the economic agents based their inflation expectations on the assumption that high inflation would continue, leading to inflation inertia (Özatay, 2011).

In 1999, Turkey started a stabilization program under the consultancy of the International Monetary Fund (IMF). One of the main determinants of this program was the crawling peg exchange rate regime, which resulted in twin (currency and banking) crises (Dedeoglu & Ogut, 2018). In the wake of the 2001 financial crisis, the CBRT responded by abandoning the fixed exchange rate regime and initiating a restructuring process in the economy. In May 2001, Turkey launched a new stabilization program called Turkey's Transition Program: Strengthening the Turkish Economy (STEP) (Özatay, 2005). The program also considered rescuing the collapsed banking sector.

One salient feature of the post-2001 period is that combatting inflation was made a central part of monetary policy. At the beginning of the restructuring process, significant institutional and legal changes were made. An article was included in Central Bank Law that gave the CBRT the primary objective of price stability. With this inclusion, the CBRT gained independence in its ability to select appropriate monetary policy instruments from the available instrument set. Operations that had previously been prohibited, such as directly providing advances to the treasury and other public institutions, purchasing debt instruments in the primary market issued by the treasury and public institutions, and financing public sector deficits using central bank resources were now permitted by the revised Central Bank Law (Kara, 2008). Moreover, in order to limit any increase in government debt, these measures were accommodated by the primary surplus policy of the government (Sener, 2011). Concurrently, an active communication policy was launched with the aim of enhancing the CBRT's credibility. Financial stability was defined in addition to price stability, thus enabling the CBRT to monitor and take necessary measures regarding the financial system. In line with the price stability objective, an inflation-targeting framework was adopted in 2002. From 2002 to 2006, implicit inflation targeting was implemented (Ersel & Özatay, 2008) and the monetary base was used as a nominal anchor (Keyder & Ertunga, 2012). As of 2006, a fully fledged formal inflation-targeting framework was adopted and the short-term interest rate was selected as the main policy instrument (Ozsuca & Akbostanci, 2013). Moreover, in order to decrease foreign exchange (FX) volatility and increase FX reserves, CBRT intervened to the FX market (Alper, Kara, & Yörükoğlu, 2013).

In this period of liquidity abundance on a global scale, capital inflows caused a potential accumulation of risk by causing local currencies to appreciate and speculative increases in asset prices in small open economies, such as Turkey's. Expectations for the abundance of liquidity to continue increased portfolio investments in these countries. It also increased the risk perception towards these countries, making them more sensitive to economic shocks. According to the IMF's September 2006 Financial Stability Report, the negative impacts of capital inflows triggered by a global abundance of liquidity on small open economies through the appreciation of the local currency are as follows:

- Speculative bubbles in asset prices, and the perception that these speculative bubbles will eventually burst, increase the country's vulnerability. The most appreciated local currency and the stock market with the highest increase will collapse first.
- An appreciated local currency supports the import of consumer and investment goods, which adversely affects the current account balance by reducing net trade. In addition, domestic banks increase the domestic credit supply by borrowing from abroad on favorable terms..

On the other hand, although its sustainability was doubtful, this process of injecting an abundance of liquidity allowed small open economies with low domestic savings rates to make investments using external savings. In countries where the money is overvalued and there was an expectation that this appreciation would continue in the medium term, imports of machinery, equipment, and capital goods increased. This also created a favorable environment for technology renewal in many sectors. The appreciated local currency combined with the expectation that this appreciation would continue gave firms access to external debt. This resulted in demand-led high growth rates, increased investments, and decreased value added owing to both the increase in the current account deficit and the increase in the use of imported capital and intermediate goods (Öğüt & Şahin, 2012). An example of this situation was experienced in 2007, immediately before the 2008 financial crisis. According to the IMF's Financial Stability Report of September 2006, in the first stage of the financial turbulence (the May–June correction), the most serious declines were experienced in the stock markets of Argentina, Hungary, India, Peru, Poland, Russia, and Turkey. The main feature of these countries was that they had experienced the largest increases in their stock markets. According to the IMF, the falls in the stock markets, especially in countries such as Brazil, Indonesia, and Turkey, where the currencies were overvalued and global capital could achieve the highest return, occurred in response to the devaluation of the local currency. These three countries are particularly important because they had the highest interest rates among emerging economies just before the turbulence. After 2001, although there was a declining trend in interest rates after the 2001 crisis, the treasury interest rate in Turkey only fell to 14%. Furthermore, the IMF claimed that in the second phase of the correction in June 2006, investors were more selective and so countries that were considered to be more vulnerable to external shocks remained under pressure. Thus, Hungary, South Africa, and Turkey experienced currency depreciations. The first period of turbulence in May arose from the idea that the speculative returns would not continue any longer and therefore profits should be realized. After it became clear that interest rates were going to increase in Japan and inflation was at a high level in the US, the realization process (a mass sell-off) began. In fact, interest rates did not immediately go up, nor did global liquidity immediately decrease. Rather, the events in June 2006 were mainly caused by the main economic indicators of some emerging countries. According to the IMF, Turkey was one of the countries worst affected by the fluctuation in May as a result of its overvalued currency. In June, Turkey exhibited the worst performance among these emerging countries in terms of main indicators, especially the current account deficit.

3 Developments in Global Money Markets in Post-2008 Era and Their Effects on Turkish Monetary Policy

After the 2008 crisis, in order to stimulate the economy, the central banks in advanced countries reduced their interest rate policy rates to nearly zero (Fig. 2). Since the central banks were unable to lower interest rates any further, they tried to stimulate the economy through unconventional monetary policies. While the policy interest rate fell to almost zero, other interest rates were still positive in proportion to the risk carried. In this context, central banks aimed to reduce the risk premiums by creating demand for financial assets based on the fact that financial assets' risk premiums are determined by supply and demand. According to Blanchard (2017), in this period, decreasing the premiums on those assets, and thus decreasing the corresponding borrowing rates with the aim of stimulating economic activity, was the main reason that central banks purchased financial assets other than short-term bonds. Blanchard and Summers (2017) indicated that the main feature of the macroeconomic environment was low interest rates. The real interest rate in the United States started to decline before the crisis, but the crisis further reduced interest rates and, until 2007, the real interest rates were expected to remain below the growth rate. These developments allowed the active use of fiscal policy. They also noted that the low interest rate on public debt would facilitate the servicing of the debt.

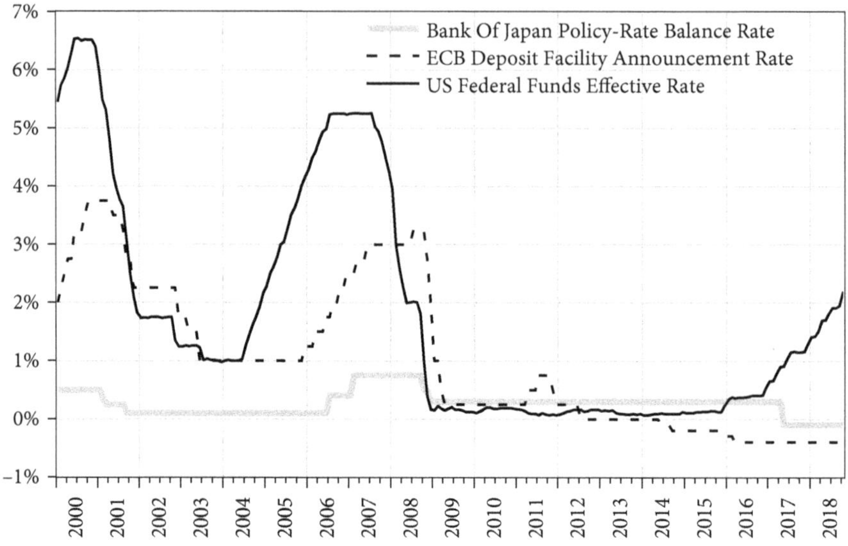

Fig. 2: Policy interest rates. Source: FRED

There were many factors behind this long-term decline in interest rates, such as low inflation rates, the aging of the population, the slowdown in productivity growth, and the global saving surplus (Bernanke, 2017). Bernanke (2017) identified forward guidance and QE as potentially effective and ancillary tools for loosening the zero lower bound (ZLB) constraint as well as the traditional interest rate reduction policy to overcome stagnation in the economy. However, he pointed out that for escaping recession, instruments such as negative interest rates and yield curve control do not seem to play an important role in the United States.

Before the start of the global financial crisis in 2007, it was generally accepted that in an environment of low inflation with a global liquidity glut, maintaining price stability was sufficient in terms of sustaining financial stability (Öğüt, Şahin, & Eren, 2014). However, after the financial crisis, it became clear that price stability was not sufficient to ensure financial stability (Öğüt, Şahin, & Eren, 2014) and low and stable inflation rates did not guarantee financial and macroeconomic stability (Borio, 2011).

Blanchard (2012) highlights that the pre-crisis orthodox inflation-targeting policy set a single objective (stable inflation) and tried to achieve it using a single tool, namely the policy rate. With the application of the correct interest rate rule, it was believed that a low and stable inflation rate could be achieved. Moreover, the credibility of the central bank also plays an important role in inflation targeting.

The implicit assumption of this orthodox approach was that the interest rate could simultaneously maintain a stable rate of inflation and the output gap. However, a temporary deviation from the inflation target was permitted to control the output gap. Blanchard (2012) suggests that price stability and general macroeconomic stability should be achieved through interest rate policy, as before the crisis, provided that the output gap is given more weight. Furthermore, Blanchard (2012) proposes the use of macroprudential policies to ensure financial stability.

In principle, however, Blanchard (2012) points out that these two separate policy instruments can affect the other objective transversely, even though each of the two separate objectives should have their own instruments. This potential cross-interaction played an important role in organizing the CBRT's policy toolkit in the post 2008 period. Empirical evidence suggests that low interest rates encourage excessive risk-taking, which requires the use of macroprudential instruments. Blanchard especially draws attention to the importance of the exchange rate in terms of developing countries implementing inflation targeting. He claims that in these countries the exchange rate is taken into account as an instability factor, in addition to its potential effect on inflation[1]. According to Blanchard (2012), sterilized exchange rate interventions can work particularly well with imperfect capital mobility. The sterilization of foreign currency buying and selling aims to ensure that the monetary policy is kept relatively independent. Otherwise, the impossible trinity of Mundell (impossible trilemma) occurs.

The concept of financial stability has been widely discussed in economics literature after the observation of speculative bubbles in asset prices. Excessive movements in asset prices were determined to hinder financial stability, and it is accepted that central banks have to take into account asset prices when determining interest rates.

Giese and Tuxen (2007) include an additional variable in the Taylor rule to represent the deviation of asset prices, including stock and property prices, from their target values. According to their model, central banks should try to burst asset bubbles by increasing the interest rate if the asset price goes above its target value. Nevertheless, there are studies that do not approve of financial stability as being used as one of the determinants of the direct interest rate through

1 Please refer to Calvo and Reinhart (2000) for details on the concept of fear of floating.

asset prices since this means overburdening the central banks. Svensson (2010) indicates that the interest rate policy would not be sufficient to ensure financial stability and that a more specific policy and appropriate tools would be required for this purpose. Furthermore, the low interest rates in 2001–2005 supported excessive credit growth and created a bubble in house prices by causing crisis conditions. However, he does not believe that higher interest rates would change the result because the interest rates, which can restrain credit growth and thus real estate prices, would have to be so high that they would adversely affect the real economy as a whole.

Over time, the number of studies showing a relationship between credit expansion and appreciation of domestic currencies began to increase. Mendoza and Terrones (2008) argue that macroeconomic data reveal the systematic relationship between credit booms and increasing asset prices. However, economic growth supported by credit and accompanied by increasing asset prices is generally followed by a financial crisis (Claessens et al., 2011). However, credit-driven economic growth, which is accompanied by increasing asset prices, is generally followed by a financial crisis (Claessens, Kose, & Terrones, 2011). The US, the UK, Spain, Ireland, and the Baltic Countries, which experienced the largest credit expansion rates in the 2000s, presented the slowest recovery after the 2008 crisis. Conversely, Germany, Switzerland, and developing countries, where relatively low leverage ratios were observed, were relatively unscathed by the collapse (Jorda, 2012). As a result of these developments, credit growth, leverage rates, and bubbles in asset prices (especially in house prices) are linked with financial crisis and hence financial stability.

In the aftermath of the financial liberalization process of the 1980s, constraints loosened, causing monetary policy to be focused only on inflation. In addition, during the period after the crisis period the length of business cycles doubled, increasing the importance of interactions between asset values and asset risks as well as economic agents' expectations about these assets. Furthermore, the fluctuations were not the result of unexpected shocks but were endogenous (Borio, 2012). According to Borio (2012), booms in financial cycles not only precede busts but also cause them and the fragilities accumulate in the growth phase of the business cycle. Borio (2013) also points out that private sector credits as a percentage of national income and the behavior of asset prices should be observed in order to monitor financial cycles.

Positive feedback dynamics between asset prices and credits play an important role in business cycle fluctuations (Öğüt, Şahin, & Eren, 2013). Rey (2014) points out that there is a positive feedback loop between asset price inflation and credit supply. In Rey's study, the endogenous money supply approach is adopted, in which the credit supply is mainly determined by the credit demand. In countries where financial markets are developed, mortgage-secured borrowing facilities have a positive impact on consumer credit demand from homeowners. In an environment where homes are used as collateral to secure loans, an increase in housing prices encourages more borrowing for consumption (Öğüt, Şahin, and Eren, 2014; Carlin and Soskice, 2015, p. 218, 225).

Gourinchas and Obstfeld (2012) emphasize that for 1973–2010, regardless of whether the countries were developed or not developed, the most powerful and meaningful predictors of financial crises were domestic credit growth and real appreciation of the local currency. The concept of financial stability in terms of developing countries, whose currency is mainly determined by capital movements and whose public and/or private sector debt is high, is different. Although these countries mostly adopted a floating exchange rate regime, instead of a freely floating system, they preferred a managed floating system in which the central bank intervenes in the exchange rate market through selling and buying currency to decrease the volatility in the exchange rates. In the literature, the practice of countries preventing the depreciation of their domestic currency, and hence the increase of the external debts in terms of local currency, is called "fear of floating". In their research on 154 countries, Calvo and Reinhart (2000) state that most of the countries that reported leaving the exchange rate to fluctuate freely did not actually allow this. A sudden depreciation in the exchange rate had the potential to cause companies with high foreign exchange liabilities and banks to fall into difficulties. Calvo and Reinhart (2000) show that the fluctuations in exchange rates in emerging markets are less than those in many developing countries that claim to implement a free-floating exchange rate regime. On the other hand, the fluctuations in international reserves and interest rates in emerging markets were more than those in developed countries. However, during the global liquidity glut period after 2001, many emerging economies realized that their local currency had appreciated, which led to domestic credit expansion, uncontrolled increases in asset prices, and deterioration of the current account balance. Generally, in countries with shallow financial and equity markets, price bubbles in the stock and/or real estate markets and the appreciation of the exchange rate (the overvaluation of the local currency) have been observed together. Thus, the valuation of the local currency may be regarded as a possible indicator for a speculative bubble. In fact, 13 years after the fear of floating study was conducted, a study of fear of appreciation was published by Levy-Yeyati et al. (2013), indicating that developing countries faced currency appreciation more often in the 2000s so exchange rate interventions were used to limit this currency appreciation.

Jorda, Schularick, and Taylor (2010) conducted an empirical study of 14 developed countries in the period of 1870–2008 and concluded that the strongest indicator of financial instability is credit growth. In addition, the correlation between credit booms and current account deficits has become more evident in recent years. Lane and McQuade (2013), in a working paper prepared by the European Central Bank (ECB), state that, especially during the 2003–2008 period, in European countries there was a strong relationship between net debt inflows and domestic credit growth, while there was no such relationship between portfolio (equity) inflows and domestic credit growth. One of the characteristics of the pre-crisis period in the European banking system was the differentiation between domestic deposit and credit growth rates. Banks funded credit growth above deposit growth by borrowing and issuing bonds on international banking and money markets. In addition, there was a negative correlation between domestic credit growth and the current account balance. Igan and Tan (2015) state that when the relationship between capital inflows and credit growth is examined, capital inflows that led to rapid expansion credit growth are indirect investments. Besides, regardless of whether the credit is household or business credit, other net capital inflows have been associated with credit growth in every period. In the same study, the researchers emphasize the empirical relationship between the current account deficit or capital inflow and asset prices. They also indicate that this relationship shed light on understanding the demand-side channel triggered by the credit boom.

Lane and McQuade (2013) assert that the current account balance can be thought of as an indicator for understanding the relationship between international capital movements and domestic credit growth. Besides, there was a close relationship between the variations in the magnitude of the recession in the 2008–2009 period and the growth in domestic loans in the 2003–2008 period. In Turkey, in a similar way to in the ECB report, the credit growth rate exceeded the deposit growth rate towards the year 2010 and in the summer of 2011 the total loan stock exceeded total bank deposits (Fig. 3). After this date, the deposit-to-credit ratio fell below 100%.

3.1 Effects of a Quantitative Easing Monetary Policy Strategy on Turkey's Monetary Policy: 2008–2013

In the aftermath of 2008, a ZLB interest rate and the QE policies of the US Federal Reserve (FED), the ECB, and the Bank of Japan (BOJ) (Fig. 7) triggered a new influx of capital to emerging market economies (Fig. 4 and Fig. 5).

In line with the literature on capital flows, capital inflow to Turkey after 2008 was mainly motivated by the interest rate differential. The CBRT, which

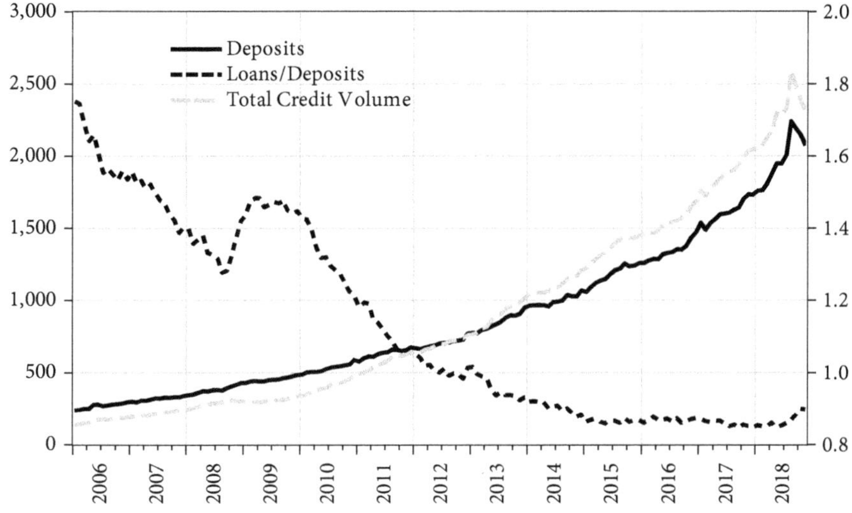

Fig. 3: Loans and deposits. Source: CBRT

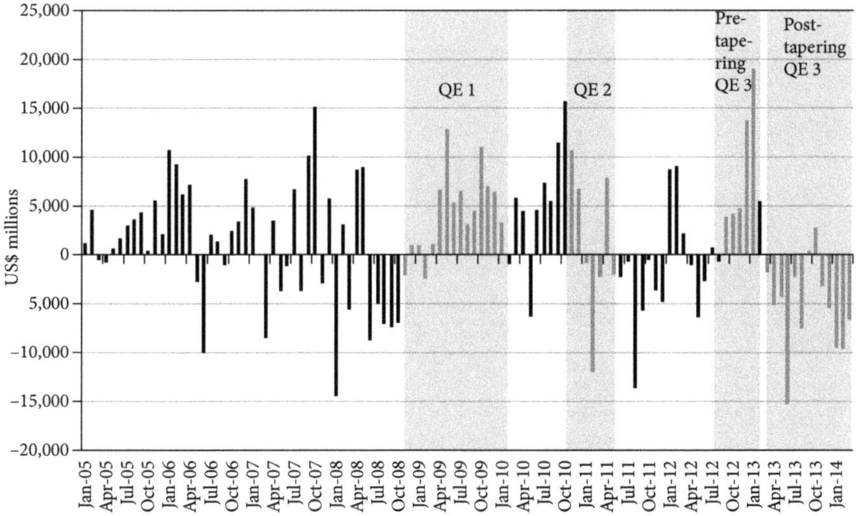

Fig. 4: Net equity inflows into emerging market economies. Note: Emerging market economies include 22 economies: Argentina, Brazil, Bulgaria, Chile, China, Colombia, Hungary, India, Indonesia, Malaysia, Mexico, Pakistan, Peru, Philippines, Poland, Romania, Russia, South Africa, Thailand, Turkey, Ukraine, and Venezuela. Source: Khatiwada (2017)

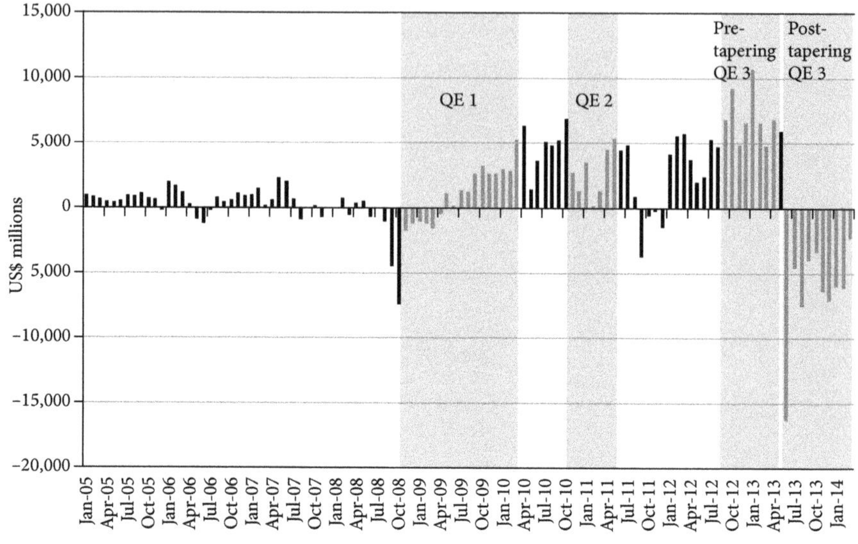

Fig. 5: Net debt inflows into emerging market economies. Source: Khatiwada (2017)

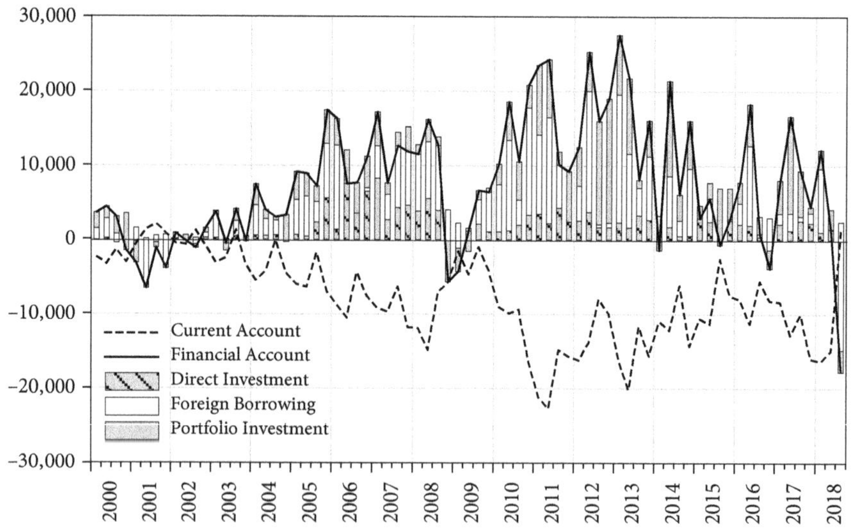

Fig. 6: Balance of payments. Source: CBRT, own calculations

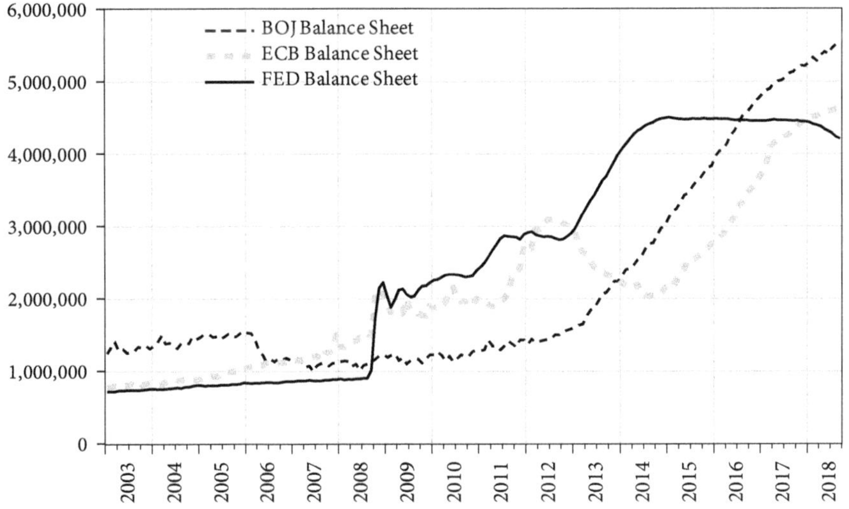

Fig. 7: The balance sheets of the FED, ECB, and BOJ. Source: FRED

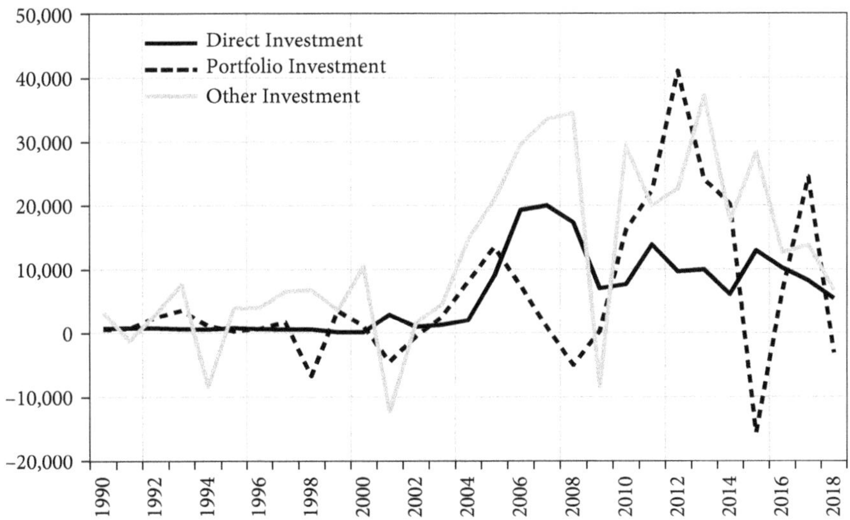

Fig. 8: Capital inflows to Turkey. Source: CBRT

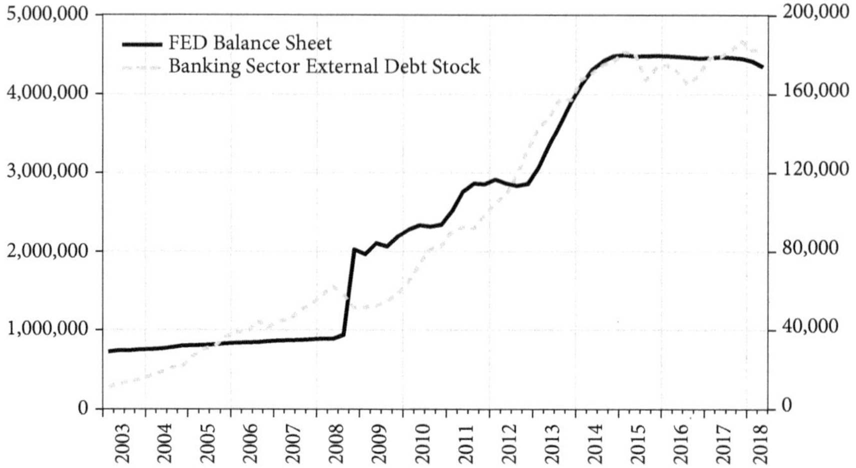

Fig. 9: FED balance sheet foreign debt of the Turkish banking sector.
Source: FRED, CBRT

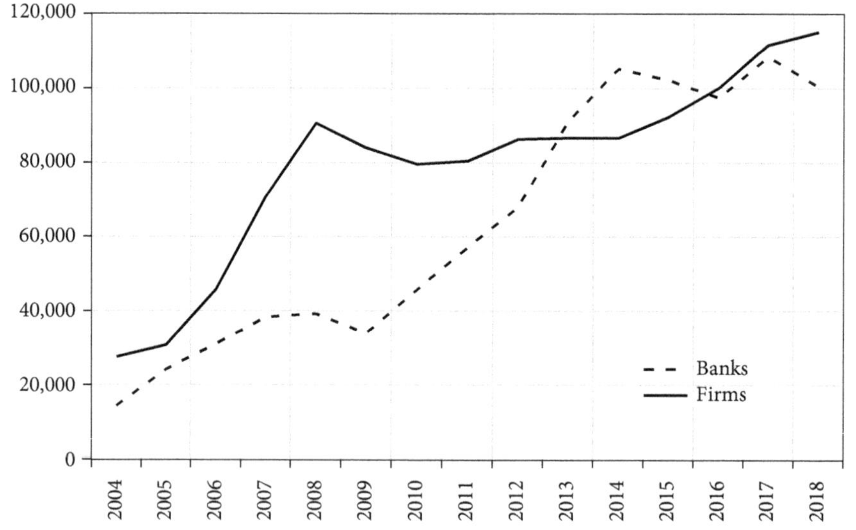

Fig. 10: Banking sector, non-banking sector, and firms' external debt (stock).
Source: CBRT

was relatively successful in inflation targeting but had difficulty in achieving its targets, was hesitant to lower interest rates after its turbulent experiences of 2006. Hence, foreign capital, aiming to benefit from high yields, entered the bond market, while Turkish banks increased their credit supply through cheap external sources (Fig. 9). The QE policies, which were introduced at the same time, became a guarantee of cheap and abundant external resources.

While there was an increase in foreign capital in Turkey in general, the proportion of portfolio investment and foreign debt began to increase and the composition of capital flows deteriorated. Lower credit interest rates also encouraged households and firms to demand more credit to finance their consumption and investment expenditure, which, in turn, led to an increase in the credit growth rate. In this low-interest environment, Turkish commercial banks preferred borrowing from foreign money markets and lending to the domestic market. This action, in turn, increased domestic credit growth (Dedeoglu & Öğüt, 2018). Consistent with the literature, the FED's asset purchases in this process had a significant positive impact on credit supply of commercial banks in Turkey (Altunok, Gümüş, Kapan, & Ongena, 2016). The increase in the external debts of Turkish banks since 2008 is remarkable (Fig. 9) and (Fig. 10).

From analyzing the flow data obtained through the balance of payments balance showing the periodic external borrowing of the banking and other sectors as well as the debt stock data, it can be seen that banks increasingly turned to external borrowing in the same period (Fig. 11). When we look at the flow data, obtained from the balance of payments, which shows the periodic external borrowings of the banking and other sectors, it is clear that banks increasingly turned to external borrowing in the same period.

It is clear that QE policies increased the flow of funds to developing countries. Although there was a significant increase in capital inflows to the bond/bill market in this period, no significant change was observed in inflows to the stock markets (Barlas & Kaya, 2013). Developed countries' QE policies led to lower bond yields, higher asset prices, and increased currency values in the rest of the world, where there was the opportunity to access large amounts of cheap liquidity (Özhan, Atiyas, & Keyman, 2013). A similar trend was observed in Turkey.

In line with the literature during this period, foreign capital inflows were mostly to the bond markets in Turkey. In Turkey, consistent with the ECB report by Lane and MacQuade (2013), late 2009 the credit growth rate exceeded the deposit growth rate and in the summer of 2011 the total credit stock exceeded total bank deposits (Fig. 3). This shows that banks were more likely to turn to other sources of funds as well as deposits to meet the demand for loans. The

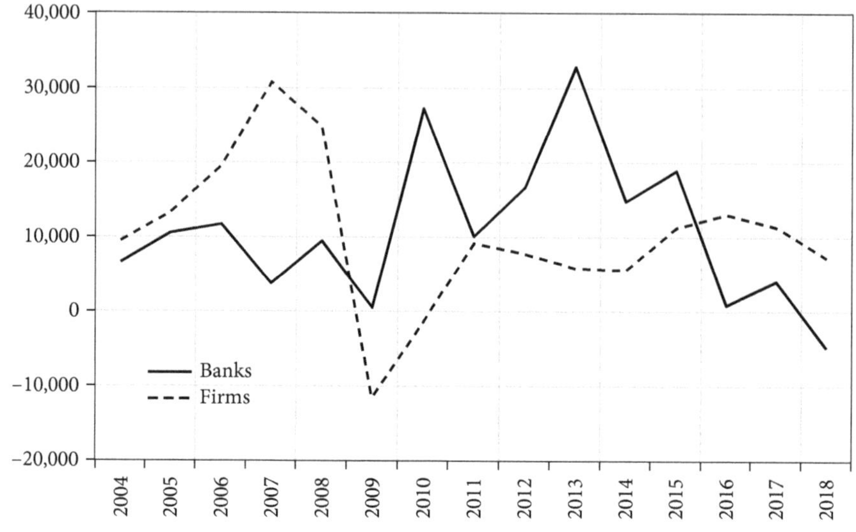

Fig. 11: Banking sector and firms' external debt (flow). Source: CBRT

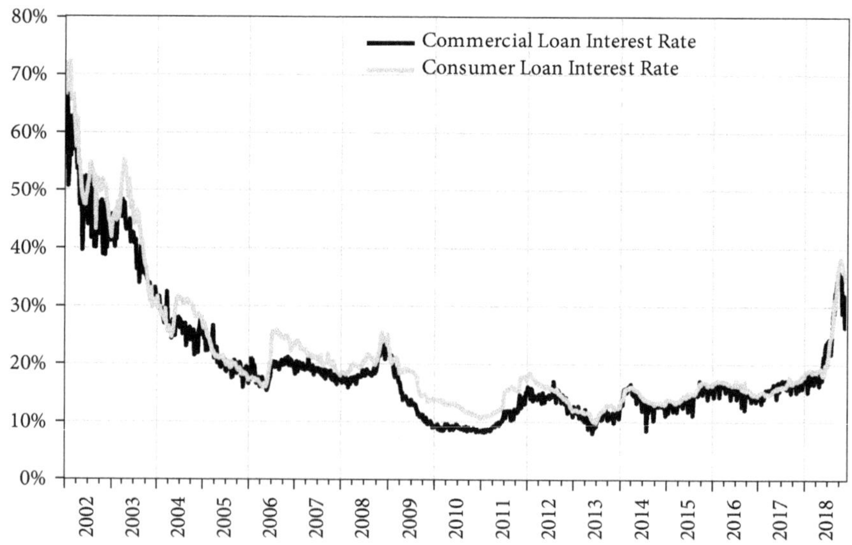

Fig. 12: Commercial loan interest rates and consumer loan interest rates. Source: CBRT

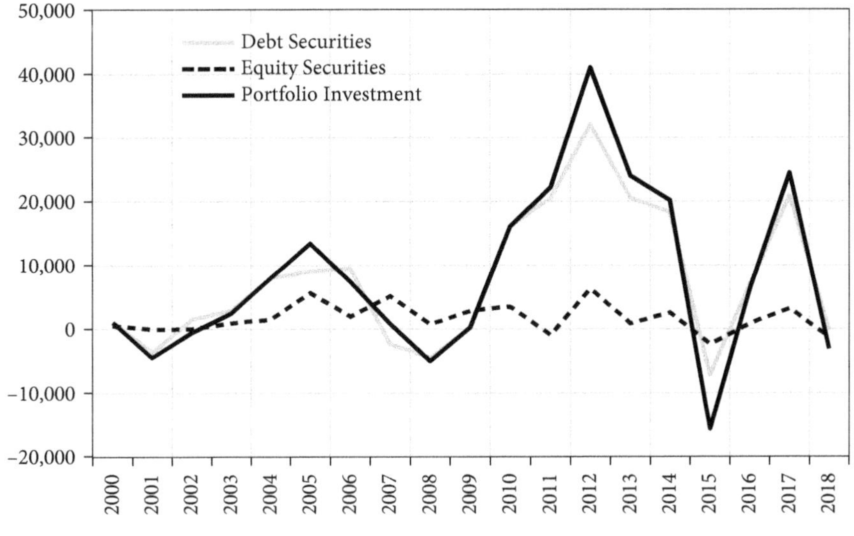

Fig. 13: Portfolio investment. Source: CBRT

most prominent alternative sources were borrowing from the central bank or external borrowing. In other words, the relationship between credit and deposits was weakened.

The ratio of non-financial private sector loans to national income reached 50% in 2010 and 85% by 2016 (Fig. 14). This means that the credit channel was becoming increasingly important in financing consumption and investments (Kara, 2012). In this context, the credit channel may also be a potential determinant of demand-driven inflation dynamics..

The total loan growth rate in 2010 exceeded 40% (Fig. 15). Indeed, a similar credit growth rate was achieved before 2006, but the ratio of credit to national income ratio was still at 25%. Moreover, the growth rate for fixed capital investments was much higher compared to that seen during the post-2008 period (Fig. 16).

In order to clearly reveal the relationship between domestic credit growth and the current account balance, instead of credit national income ratio or credit growth rate, the change in the ratio of credit stock to national income is used. This indicator shows how quickly indebtedness increases compared to income. The correlation between this variable and the current account balance is quite clear (Fig. 17). With reference to the credit and national income dynamics of countries around the world, the CBRT determined a 15% threshold for the credit

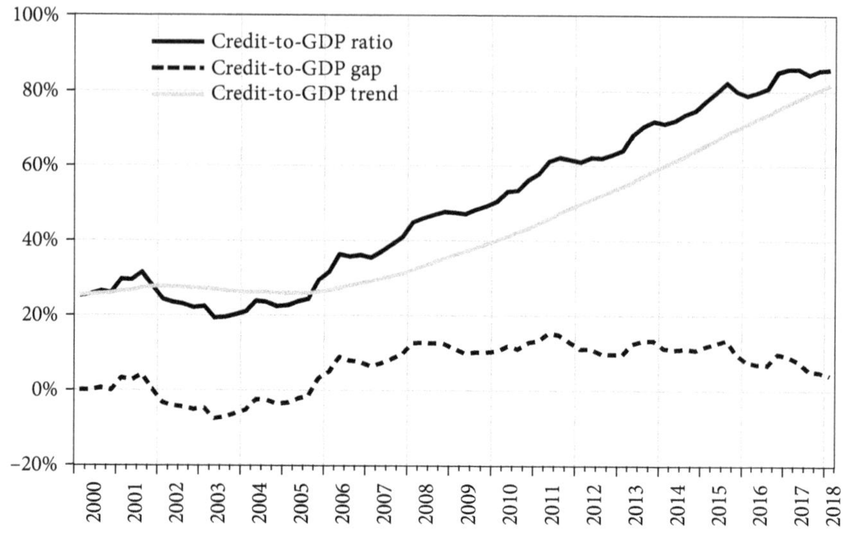

Fig. 14: Credit to Gross domestic product ratio. Source: CBRT

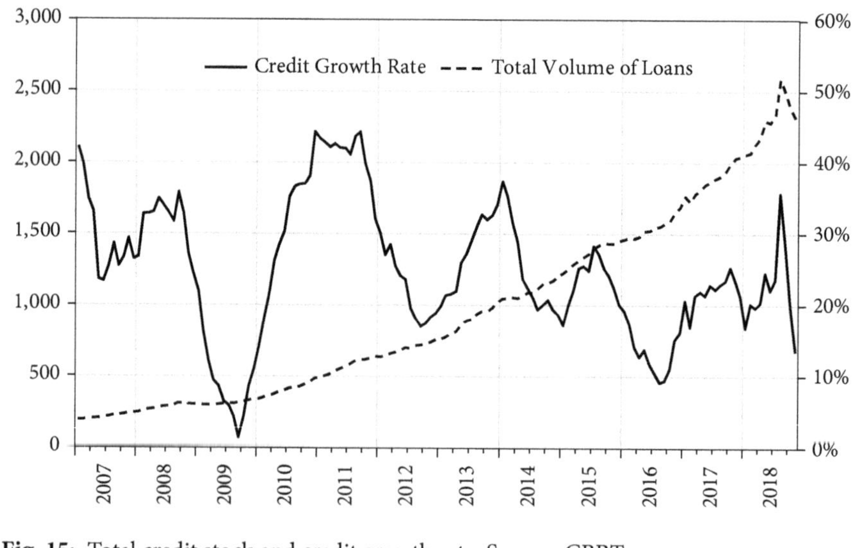

Fig. 15: Total credit stock and credit growth rate. Source: CBRT

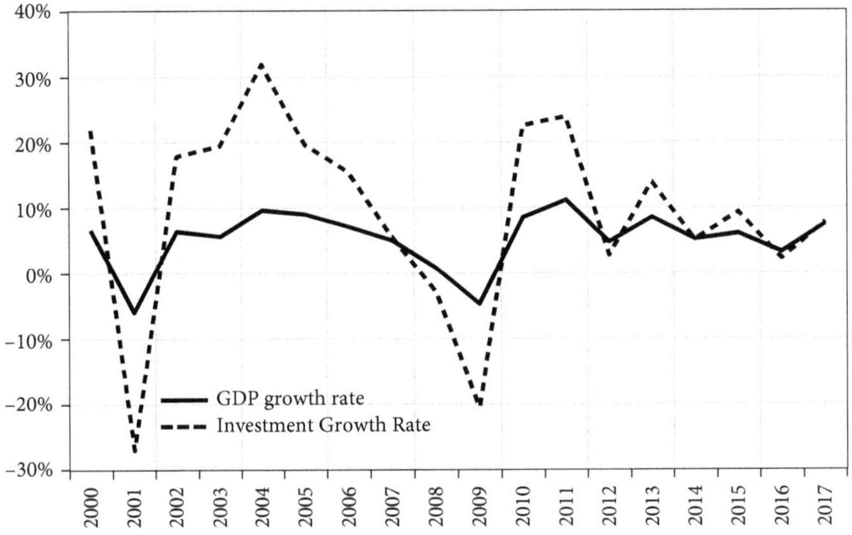

Fig. 16: GDP growth and investment growth. Source: CBRT, TURKSTAT

growth rate to achieve a sustainable current account deficit and avoid a potential increase in inflation (Kara, Tiryaki, & Yüksel, 2013).

Two important indicators of financial instability in the literature, namely credit growth and current account deficit, reached very high levels in Turkey as a result of an accelerating increase around 2010. At this point, with reference to the IMF report (2006), an appreciation in the exchange rate is expected, which is considered to be another indicator of financial instability.

In Fig. 18, the valuation of TL cannot be clearly observed around 2010. The Euro and dollar exchange rates seem to remain stable in the underlined period. However, the sterilized exchange rate interventions mentioned by Blanchard (2012) should be considered in this case. During this period, the CBRT purchased foreign currency to prevent the appreciation of TL (Fig. 19 and Fig. 20).

In fact, between mid-2009 and 2013 the CBRT has been increasing its FX reserves by buying foreign exchange, thus preventing the appreciation of the TL. In 2010, the CBRT, through its foreign exchange buying auctions, accumulated reserves of around $15 billion. In addition to the pre-announced foreign exchange auctions, the CBRT could also buy and sell foreign currency directly through interventions, but did not favor this method unless it was essential. The CBRT made direct intervention purchases in the 2003–2006 period when capital

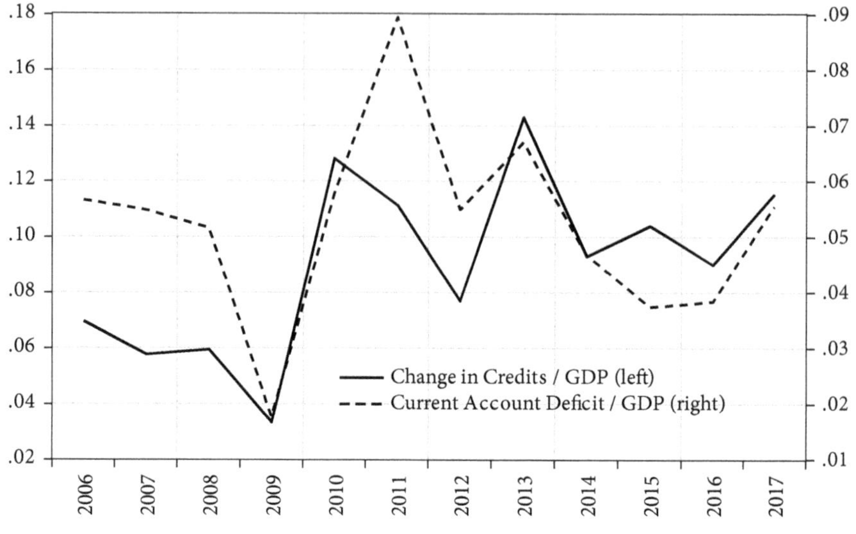

Fig. 17: Credit and current account deficit. Source: CBRT

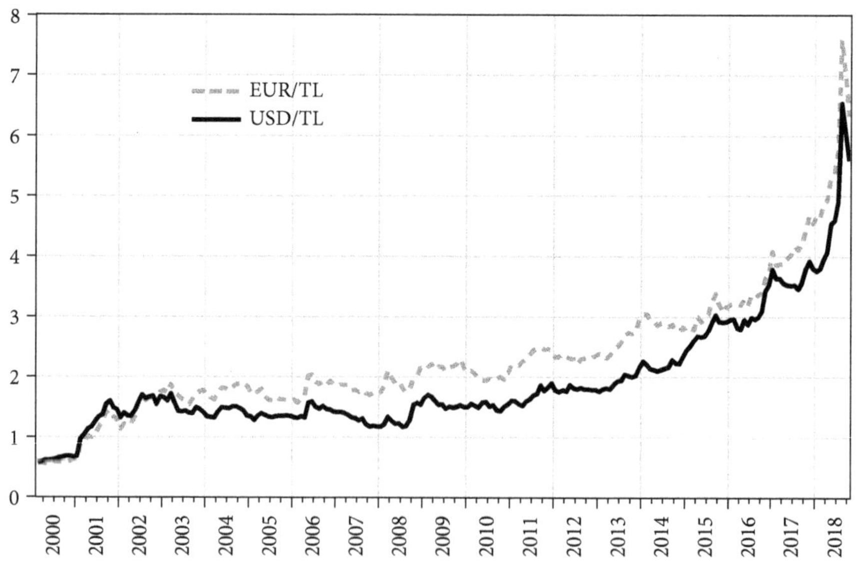

Fig. 18: Exchange rates. Source: CBRT

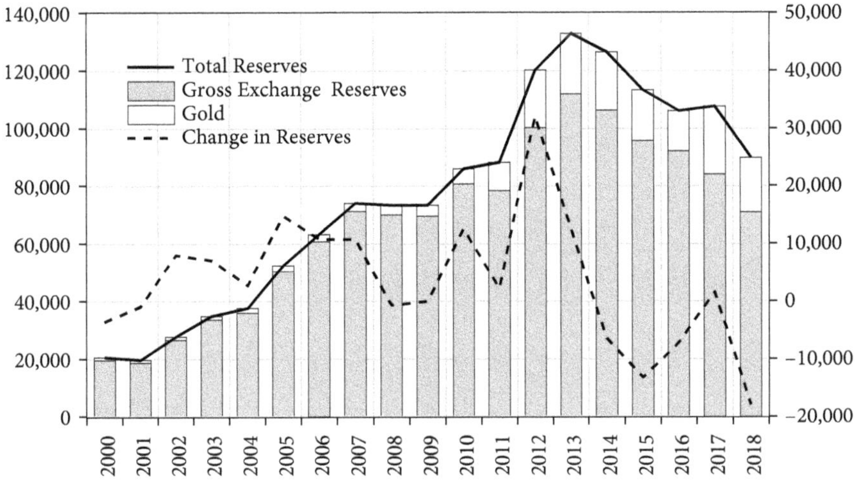

Fig. 19: Gross exchange reserves, gold, total reserves, and changes in reserves.
Source: CBRT

inflows to the foreign exchange market were intense and purchased foreign exchange through auctions in the post-2008 period (Fig. 20).

The CBRT intervened in the foreign exchange market, as Blanchard (2012) suggests, and partially sterilized these interventions. In this sense, CBRT adopted inflation targeting with a managed floating exchange rate regime. In addition, the CBRT, together with the reserve option mechanism (ROM), designed an instrument that combines the reserve policy with the exchange rate policy and acts as an automatic stabilizer.

At this point, it would be appropriate to look at how the literature examines the interventions of an inflation-targeting country in the exchange rate market. Inflation-targeting theory proposes that the monetary authority should choose the short-term interest rate as a policy instrument and that the exchange rate should be allowed to fluctuate as short-term capital flows will neutralize central banks' intervention in the foreign exchange market (Gersl & Holub, 2006). Following a series of monetary crises in the late 1990s and early 2000s, many developing countries abandoned their fixed exchange rate regimes, adopting various combinations of flexible exchange rates and inflation targeting (Edwards, 2006). Nevertheless, central banks have the means to intervene in the foreign exchange market in response to excessive fluctuations in the exchange rate and emerging trends.

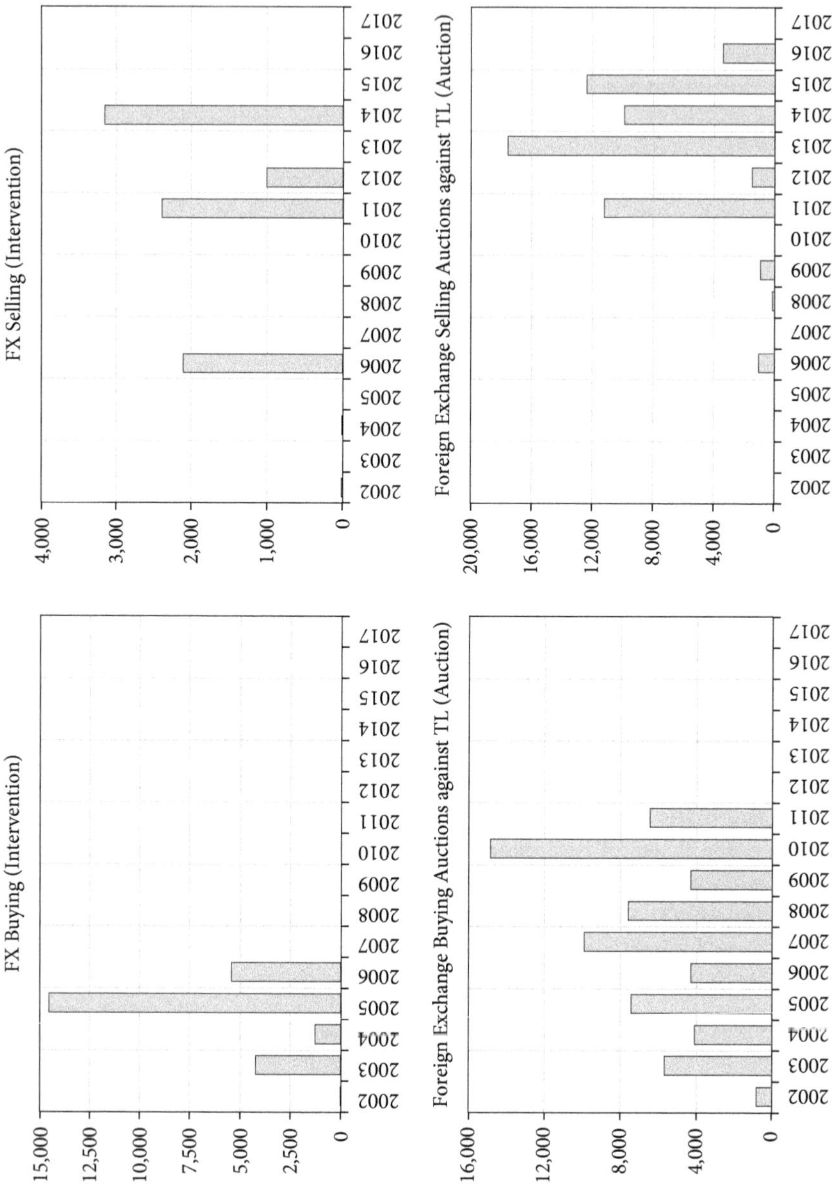

Fig. 20: Foreign exchange buying and selling (interventions and auctions). Source: CBRT

A country that implements the inflation-targeting regime to simultaneously determine the policy interest rate and the exchange rate should also sterilize the liquidity level, which is altered by foreign exchange buying and selling operations. Otherwise, foreign currency purchases have the potential to create inflationary effects.

Sterilization via open-market operations, by allowing the CBRT to keep the monetary base constant, makes it possible to control the interest rate. However, if the domestic interest rate is higher than the world interest rate, the cost of sterilization arises from this difference (Fischer, 2008; Bofinger & Wollmershauser, 2003).

In an economic system where the capital movement is free, the central bank, which wants to conduct an independent monetary policy, should leave the exchange rate to fluctuate freely. This hypothesis is called the impossible trinity. However, the ability of the monetary authority to determine the interest and exchange rates simultaneously allows it to mitigate a country's trilemma trade-offs. Bofinger (2011) states that the managed floating exchange rate regime could turn the impossible trilogy into a possible trilogy and that free capital movements, independent interest rate policy, and exchange rate targets could be achieved together. There is a similar expression in CBRT's May 2012 Financial Stability Report. It is stated that regulations on reserve requirements and reserve accumulation policies allow for mitigating Turkey's trilemma trade-offs and may enable the three objectives to be achieved.

In recent studies, it is also questioned whether inflation targeting should be implemented together with a flexible (floating) exchange rate regime in developing countries. Contrary to economic theory, it has been observed that developing countries that conduct inflation-targeting policy have intervened in the exchange rate market during both the appreciation and the depreciation periods. Some economists have also begun to propose a framework that consists of inflation-targeting policy and a floating exchange rate regime for developing countries (Kaltenbrunner and Painceria, 2012). Recently, the IMF has started to recognize these practices by the monetary authorities of the developing countries. By using these practices, while the monetary authorities of the developing countries are trying to achieve the target of low inflation, they attempt to prevent the deviation of exchange rates from a level that is compatible with a sustainable foreign trade balance. In line with these two objectives, a dual policy instrument set is recommended, including policy rate cuts as well as sterile interventions in the exchange rate market (Ostry et al., 2012a). This approach suggests that the macroeconomy, especially monetary policy, should be re-designed following the 2008 crisis. It is generally accepted with respect to the central banks of developed countries that it is sufficient to take into consideration consumer prices as well as asset prices. The most important asset price for developing countries is the exchange rate. It is therefore recommended that the monetary authorities of these countries take into account uneven exchange rate movements and use all of their available instruments to ensure price and exchange rate stability (Ostry et al., 2012b).

A central bank aiming at price stability should also put in place more than one policy instrument to monitor financial risks, especially during periods of rapid capital inflows (Başçı & Kara, 2011). The CBRT has identified two intermediate targets: first, ensuring the stability of the exchange rate by controlling the short-term capital inflows, thereby controlling the current account deficit, and second, slowing credit expansion. As proposed by Kara (2012), credit and foreign currency, which are easy to observe and serve as a transmission mechanism between instruments and final targets, have been determined as the two intervening variables. In this case, it was necessary for the monetary authority to develop a policy set that could affect credit growth and exchange rate channels separately.

In the same period, besides the sterilized interventions reported in the literature, the use of the required reserves to ensure financial stability also came to the fore. For example, in China, reserve requirements have been used as a policy instrument since 2007. In China, reserve requirements are increasingly being replaced by other open-market operations and used as an instrument to absorb liquidity in the banking system (Ma et al., 2011). Developing countries, including Latin America, Bolivia, Chile, Colombia, Peru, and Uruguay, have applied macroprudential policies, including reserve requirements in particular, to limit credit growth (Tovar et al., 2012). As expected, the CBRT used the required reserves as well as the sterilized foreign exchange market interventions in the same period. Moreover, in addition to these instruments, CBRT developed an innovative instrument (ROM) with the aim of indirectly guiding the exchange rate to stability by modifying the required reserves and letting them be held as foreign currency.

As of 2010, the fundamental problems with Turkey's economy were: (a) the TL, which is under appreciation pressure owing to capital inflows triggered by both the QE policies and interest rate differentials, (b) the credit boom, and (c) the increase in the current account deficit.

If the CBRT used the policy rate in line with the orthodox inflation-targeting policy, it would raise the policy interest rate to curb credit growth, leading to an increase in the short-term interbank interest rate. This would indirectly increase the funding costs of banks and increase interest rates on credit. However, increasing the policy interest rate causes the long-term (bond) interest rate to rise through the monetary transfer mechanism. This increase in the market interest rate then stimulates capital inflows, placing the TL under more appreciation pressure. In a sense, this means that increasing the policy interest rate has the potential to cause a trade-off between price stability and financial stability. That is why the monetary authority needs a tool that will not affect the market interest rate, while increasing the interest rate on credit. The required reserve ratio stands out as a potential monetary policy tool in this respect. The reserve requirement is the amount of funds that banks have to keep in central banks in exchange for their domestic and foreign currency liabilities. For the central bank to achieve financial stability and price stability simultaneously, the interest rates of the credit and bond markets should be differentiated. The reserve requirement, which enables differentiating the interest rates of credit and bond markets, allows for tightening monetary policy without accelerating capital flows (Alper & Tiryaki, 2011). Because of the required reserve ratio, banks do not convert all of the funds they collect into loans, thus the unit cost of deposits for the bank is higher than the interest rate paid by the bank to the deposit owner. However, in periods when the central bank pays interest on its required reserves, this cost decreases relatively (Ünalmış & Ünalmış, 2015). Banks tend to reflect this increase in the cost of deposits in their credit interest rates. Required reserves may help to control the increase in the credit demand and domestic demand by means of increasing the gap between the credit and deposit interest rates (Alper & Tiryaki, 2011). In an economy that adopts inflation targeting, altering the required reserve ratios is expected to directly affect market rates. However, this effect also depends on the degree of substitution between deposits and central bank loans (Vargas et al., 2010).

In an economy with an inflation-targeting regime, the effects of required reserves on the macroeconomy emerge from two channels, namely liquidity and cost. The liquidity channel works by altering the reserve requirements by affecting the lending behavior of banks by changing their requirements for short-term central bank resources. The cost channel affects the difference between the central bank's credit and deposit rates (Alper & Tiryaki, 2011). In the case when short-term central bank funds for banks are a perfect substitute for deposits, in response to an increase in the required reserve ratio, banks may reduce the interest rate on deposits, which becomes costlier, and replace the demand for deposits with central bank funds. In this case, they can reflect the additional cost as a result of the increase in the required reserve to deposit ratio instead of credit interest (Alper & Tiryaki, 2011).

In the period of October 2010–June 2011, this situation partially occurred in Turkey. The CBRT increased the required reserve ratios by considering that the banks would decrease the amount of credit. However, as the lender of last resort, the central bank is obliged to provide the short-term funds requested by the banks at the officially announced interest rate (the highest possible rate is the upper bound of the interest corridor). In this period, in response to the increase in the required reserve ratio, banks used more resources from the central bank through open-market operations (Özatay, 2012). When liquidity is withdrawn from the banking system through reserve requirements, banks have the opportunity to compensate for the liquidity deficiency through borrowing from the central bank, which will result in banks becoming more dependent on short-term central bank resources. If the perceived uncertainty regarding the central bank's policy rate is high, the increased dependence on short-term resources will make the interest rate risk of banks more visible. The CBRT's widening of the interest rate corridor, beginning from the last quarter of 2010, and the announcement that it would allow for some fluctuation in money market interest rates in line with the requirements of the conjuncture led to an increase in the interest rate risk of short-term resources (Alper & Tiryaki, 2011).

It is obvious that a strong substitution relationship between deposits and central bank funds reduces the effectiveness of the reserve requirement ratio as a policy instrument. At this point, we should mention the interest rate corridor that CBRT has been using effectively since 2010, instead of a single policy interest rate. In summary, the main objective of this policy is to weaken the substitution relationship between central bank funds and deposits. In fact, the interest rate corridor system has been used in Turkey since 2002. Since a net liquidity surplus was present in the banking system until mid-2010, the effective policy rate was the CBRT's borrowing rate, which is the lower bound of the interest corridor (Fig. 21).

In May 2010, the CBRT started 1-week repo auctions, a new liquidity instrument, which became the CBRT's primary funding tool; in other words, it became the policy interest rate. As of the end of 2010, the CBRT adopted financial stability as an additional supportive target besides its primary objective of price stability. In order to overcome the trade-off between price stability and financial stability, the CBRT, which needed new policy instruments, started to use the interest rate corridor and active liquidity policy in a coordinated way (Ünalmış, 2015). The CBRT has been a net lender to the market since 2010 so the funding rates of the central bank have played a more important role in monetary policy. Central banks determine the short-term interest rate by changing their balance sheet size. They can do this directly through the purchase and sale of bonds as well as by providing short-term debt (liquidity) to financial institutions, as the CBRT does. The CBRT provides liquidity supply through weekly repo and

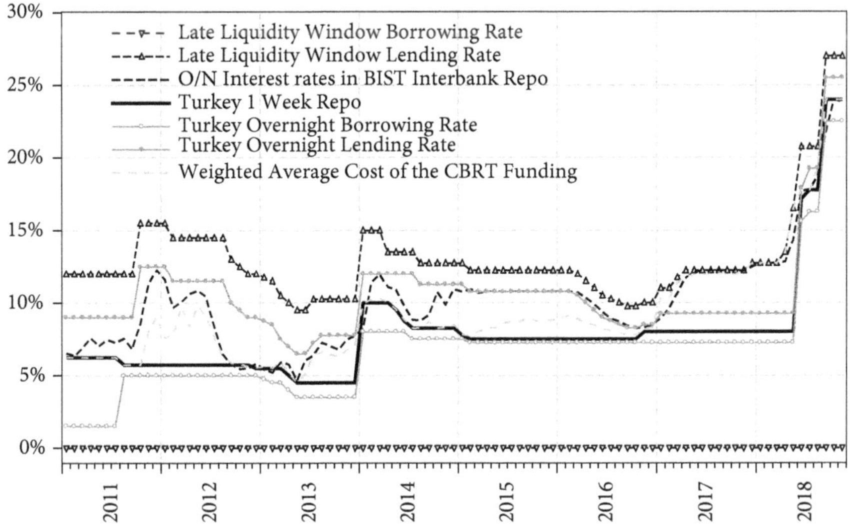

Fig. 21: Interest rates. Source: CBRT

overnight lending (marginal funding) opportunities. In this practice, the CBT determines the interest rate and size of the 1-week repo, and if additional liquidity is required, it meets this liquidity demand through the marginal funding (Kara, 2015). Thus, although CBRT does not change the interest rates, it ensures the establishment of the funding cost of banks, meaning that it will fall somewhere between the weekly repo rate and the upper limit of the corridor. Thus, CBRT started to use the policy interest rate and interest rate corridor together as a single policy instrument. As of the fall of 2012, the CBRT's average funding cost started to be used as the policy interest rate instead of the weekly repo rate. The CBRT's average funding cost became the most important determinant of the short-term market interest rate, then the interbank money market, and then TRLIBOR. In this way, the central bank has the opportunity to determine the funding rate on a daily basis by considering the global liquidity conditions.

The fact that the policy rate and the upper limit of the interest rate corridor are different allows the CBRT to set the cost of short-term funds that it provides to the banking sector. The central bank decides how much of the bank's liquidity demand will be funded overnight and how much of it will be funded weekly. This will make the interest rate corridor an important instrument in determining short-term market interest rates. By changing the liquidity composition provided to banks, the central bank is able to direct the cost of access to liquidity.

ROM, which is an additional reserve requirement tool, allows banks to hold a part of their required reserves in FX or gold. The amount of FX or gold that is held in exchange for one unit of TL reserve is called the reserve option coefficient (Aslaner et al., 2014). In a different sense, the ROM, whose main aim is to reduce excessive capital flows, functions like an automatic stabilizer or an alternative FX intervention strategy. Because the opportunity cost of holding TL reserves is relatively high during periods of strong capital inflows, banks would prefer to use the ROM. An increase in the ROM utilization rate would be considered as a sign of an increase in capital inflows, thereby more FX holdings in the central bank accounts facilitate preventing the appreciation of the domestic currency. On the contrary, because the cost of borrowing FX would be relatively higher than the cost of borrowing domestic currency during periods of capital outflow, banks would rather decrease the portion of FX that is held at the central bank, which then brings out additional FX supply and allows for releasing the depreciation pressure on the domestic currency. The new instruments enabled the CBRT to control the effects of excess capital flows, reduce the impact of credit growth, and reduce the effects of excess capital flows and credit growth on the current account balance.

3.2 Effects of a Quantitative Easing Monetary Policy Exit Strategy on Turkey's Monetary Policy: 2013–2018

The Chicago Federal Reserve chairman, Charlie Evans, said he hoped the FED would not undergo a tightening monetary policy before the unemployment rate fell to 6.5% and the inflation rate rose to 2.5%. In 2014, the unemployment rate target could be achieved but the inflation rate target could not be achieved. Following this, the FED began to increase the federal funding rate.

After the FED's QE program was accompanied by high capital inflows to developing countries, the FED mentioned for the first time that in May and July 2013, it will reduce its monthly asset purchases (tapering). The FED announced in December that, as of January 2014, it would reduce its monthly $85 billion purchases within the QE3 program by $10 billion every month. With this gradual reduction, asset purchase, that is, the QE program, was concluded in October 2014(Rai & Suchanek, 2014). Thus, the process, which started in 2008 when the FED's balance sheet was $900 billion, ended when the balance sheet had reached $4.5 trillion. After that the FED commenced balance sheet reduction operations. The FED reduces its balance sheet by returning the matured bonds to the institutions that issued them and getting their money back. At the same time, the ECB continued its QE policy but started to decelerate it; however, the FED started to reduce its balance sheet as of October 2017 (Fig. 7).

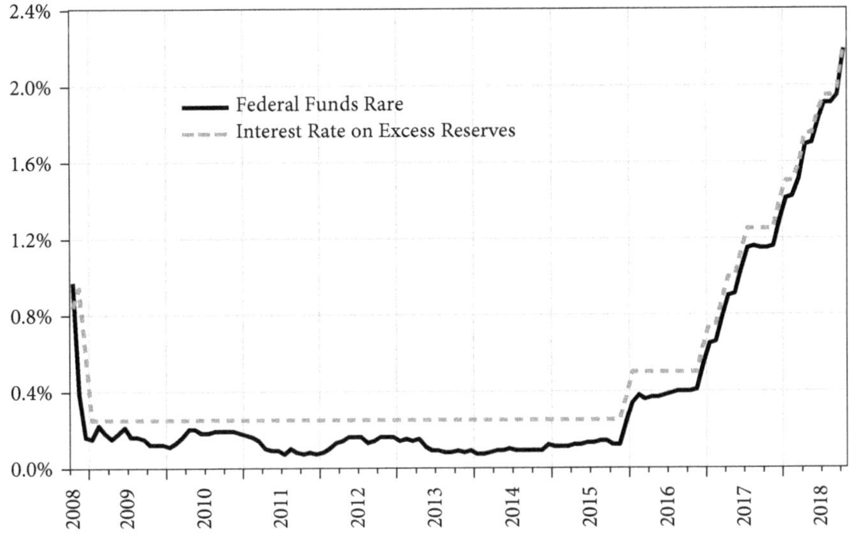

Fig. 22: Federal funds rate and interest rate on excess reserves. Source: FRED

The 2013 taper announcement led to a reduction in capital inflows to developing countries, including Turkey. After 2010, direct foreign capital inflow to the bond market decreased. In 2015, this decrease turned to capital outflow. In addition, in 2013 there was a net outflow of capital from the stock market. In 2015, net capital outflows were observed in developing countries, Turkish banks became net external debt payers, and their external debt stock decreased. In this period, the funding needs of Turkish banks increased by 53 billion TL and they turned to central bank resources to meet this need. When external resources were reduced, the need for funding from the CBRT increased and thus the need for collateral increased. While open-market transactions increased, government debt securities held by banks decreased (Er & Güney, 2016).

The decrease in capital inflows put pressure on the exchange rate and the TL at times depreciated in an accelerating manner. The CBRT increased its FX selling auctions. In 2013, the total foreign exchange reserves of the central bank decreased from $132 billion to $126 billion, the most significant decrease in foreign exchange reserves since the 2001 crisis. The reserves continued to decrease until 2018 and unfortunately the CBRT's efforts failed to prevent the depreciation of the TL.

Another effect of this acceleration in the exchange rate depreciation was increasing inflation. In particular, producer prices, which are sensitive to exchange rates, exhibited a rapid upward trend in 2016.

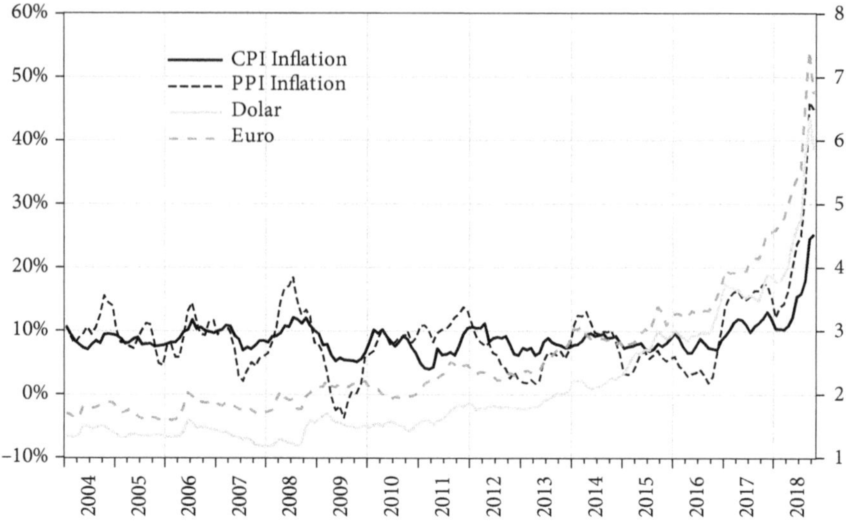

Fig. 23: Inflation and exchange rates. Source: CBRT

The rise in exchange rates also affected consumer prices through producer prices via the pass-through effect. The fear of floating literature states that central banks that adopt inflation targeting and want to direct the exchange rate put forward the exchange rate pass-through to inflation as the reason for their exchange interventions. In the period after 2015, exchange rate pass-through in Turkey was clearly observed. Therefore, after 2015, the CBRT tried to direct the exchange rate through interventions (Fig. 23).

The instruments used for achieving financial stability developed between 2010 and 2012 did not operate symmetrically, except for ROM. In other words, these instruments, which were relatively successful in managing capital inflows, remained ineffective against capital outflows. Thus, the CBRT turned to the orthodox inflation-targeting regime within the framework of policy simplification[2]. However, owing to the high growth rate and the government's low unemployment targets, the interest rate could not be increased. Therefore, almost all of the funding was made at the upper limit of the interest rate corridor so the policy rate became meaningless. Later, the CBRT used the late liquidity window, which is an exceptional penal treatment, as a normal funding tool (CBRT, 2018). The CBRT, which stated that it did not raise the policy rate, increased the cost

2 ROM could be used partially

of banks' funding and pushed the interbank overnight interest rate towards the upper limit of the late liquidity corridor. In other words, the CBRT implemented a clear-cut tight monetary policy but gave the government a message that the policy rate had not increased. Thus, the independence of the CBRT again became a prominent subject. The CBRT was unable to explain its strategy with economic motives.

In June 2018, as a requirement of the simplification policy, the CBRT started to provide all of its funding through weekly repo auctions. However, owing to the sudden increase in the exchange rate, for which the political tension with the USA was one of the causative factors, the weekly repo auction was not carried out between August 13 and September 14, 2018, and the funding was instead issued through the CBRT lending at the overnight maturity rate. Despite the simplification claims, the CBRT explained this policy preference as being based on the sudden and severe increase in the exchange rate. Despite the CBRT's claims that it was following a simplification process, the reason for these contrary actions is that the rise in the exchange rate is very sudden and severe. In the September 13 Monetary Policy Committee meeting, the policy rate was increased from 17.75% to 24% and it was decided that all funding was again to be provided by weekly repo auctions. By the end of 2018, the CBRT had designed a monetary policy based on the policy interest rate, but under this policy it could also respond to sudden exchange rate movements by using the upper limit of the interest rate corridor (Fig. 24).

4 Conclusion

The 2008 economic crisis affected Turkey negatively, as with most developing countries. Turkey was affected negatively through two channels, namely the deterioration of its current account balances and currency appreciation. In response to this situation, the CBRT implemented several measures. Since the traditional interest rate policy failed to simultaneously achieve price and financial stability, the CBRT diversified its policy tools and adopted an unconventional approach (Kara, 2012). In addition to the main policy tool of policy rate, for the inflation-targeting Turkish economy, complementary instruments were utilized. These additional complementary instruments comprise the reserve requirement ratio, an interest rate corridor, and foreign exchange intervention. The aim of using these instruments was to promote growth without increasing inflation and maintain a sustainable current account deficit. For this purpose, the CBRT tried to prevent excessive movements in the exchange rates. In order to do so, the CBRT adjusted the width of the interest rate corridor in response

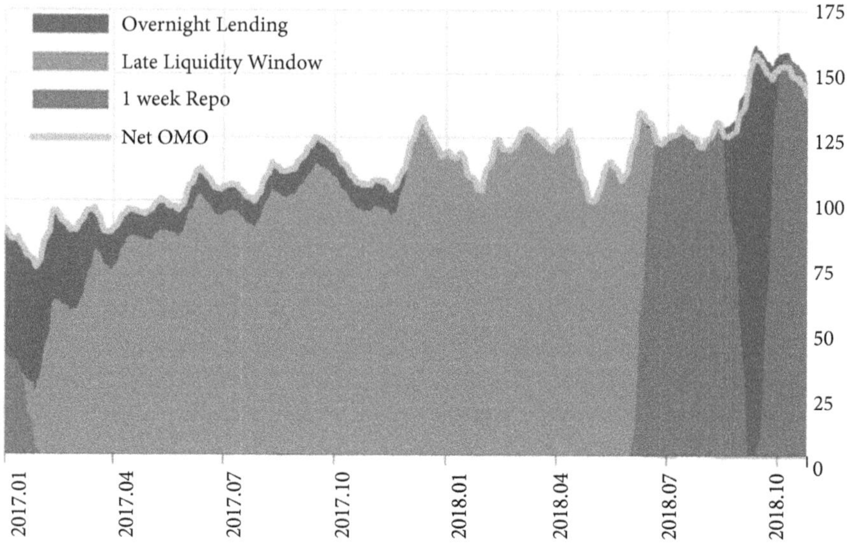

Fig. 24: CBRT funding (2-week moving average, billion TL). Source: CBRT

to the intensity of capital flows, which enabled the CBRT to change the short-term interest rate quickly without changing the policy interest rate. The CBRT supported this action through foreign exchange interventions to release appreciation or depreciation pressure on the Turkish lira. Furthermore, to control the credit growth rate, the CBRT preferred to use the required reserve ratio instead of altering the policy interest rate, which has the potential to affect capital flows. In the same period, to reduce the need for FX intervention, the CBRT employed an additional policy instrument, namely the ROM (Alper et al., 2013).

Bibliography

Alper, K., & Tiryaki, T. (2011). Zorunlu Karşılıkların Para Poitikasındaki Yeri. Working Paper No.11/8. Central Bank of the Republic of Turkey (CBRT). Ankara.

Alper, K., Binici, M., Demiralp, S., Kara, H., & Özlü, P. (2014). Reserve Requirements, Liquidity Risk and Credit Growth. Working Paper No.14/24. Central Bank of the Republic of Turkey (CBRT). Ankara.

Alper, K., Kara, H., & Yrükoğlu, M. (2013). Alternative Tools to Manage Capital Flow Volatility. Working Paper No.13/31. Central Bank of the Republic of Turkey (CBRT). Ankara.

Altunok, F., Gümüş, İ., Kapan, T., & Ongena, S. (2016). The Effects of US Unconventional Monetary Policies on Bank Lending in Emerging Markets: Evidence from Turkey. www.efmaefm.org/.../EFMA2016_0212_fullpaper.pdf.

Aslaner, O., Çıplak, U., Kara, H., & Küçüksaraç, D. (2014). Reserve Option Mechanism: Does it Work as an Automatic Stabilizer. CBRT Working Paper No. 14/38. Ankara.

Barlas, Y., & Kaya, N. (2013). Parasal genişleme Politikalarının Gelişmekte Olan Ülke Portföy Akımları Kompozisyonuna Etkisi. CBRT Working Paper No. 13/01. Ankara.

Başçı, E. & Kara, H. (2011). Finansal İstikrar Politikası ve Para Politikası. İktisat İşletme ve Finans. 26 (302). 9–25

Bernanke, B. S. (2017). Monetary Policy in a New Era. PIIE.

Blanchard, O. (2012). Monetary Policy in the Wake of the Crisis. O. J. Blanchard, D. Romer, A. M. Spence, & J. E. Stiglitz. In the Wake of the Crisis (s. 7–14). The MIT Press. Cambridge, Mass., United States.

Blanchard, O., & Johnson, D. (2013). Macroeconomics. Pearson. New York.

Blanchard, O., & Summers, L. (2017). Rethinking Stabilization Policy. Back to the Future. PIIE.

Bofinger, P. (2011). The Scope for Foreign Exchange Market Interventions. United Nations Conference on Trade and Development .

Bofinger, P., & Wollmershauser, T. (2003). Managed Floating: Theory, Preactice and ERM II. CEPR/Deutsche Bank Research Workshop. Kronberg.

Borio, C. (2011). Central Banking Post-crisis: What Compass for Uncharted Waters? BIS Working Papers.

Borio, C. (2012). The Financial Cycle and Macroeconomics: What We Have Learnt? BIS Working Paper No. 395.

Borio, C. (2013). Macroeconomics and the Financial Cycle: Hamlet without the Prince. VOX.

Calvo, G. A. & Reinhart, C. M. (2000). Fear of Floating, NBER Working Paper No.7993.

Carlin, W., & Soskice, D. M. (2015). Macroeconomics. Oxford University Press.

Claessens, S., Kose, A., & Terrones, M. (2011). Financial Cycles: What? How? When? Working Paper, IMF.

Dedeoğlu, D. & Öğüt, K. (2018). Examination of Money Supply Endogeneity in Turkey: Evidence from Asymmetric Causality Test. Cogent Economics & Finance, 6 (1), 1–18.

Edwards, S. (2006). The Relationship Between Exchange Rates and Inflation Targeting Revisited. National Bureau of Economic Research, Working Paper, 12163.

Er, H. & Güney, İ. E. (2016). Para Politikasında Kaldıraç Etkisi: Likidite Kanalı. Working Paper No.16/20. Central Bank of the Republic of Turkey (CBRT). Ankara.

Ersel, H., & Özatay, F. (2008). Fiscal Dominance and Inflation Targeting: Lessons from Brazil. Emerging Markets Finance and Trade, 44(6), 38–51. doi:10.2753/REE1540-496X440603

Fischer, S. (2008). Mundell Fleming Lecture: Exchange Rate Systems, Surveliance and Advice. IMF Staff Papers, 55 (3).

Giese, J., & Tuxen, C. G. (2007). Global Liquidity and Asset Prices in a Cointegrated VAR. Manuscript.

Gersl, A., & Holub, T. (2006). Foreign Exchange Interventions Under Inflation Targeting: The Czech Experience. Contemporary Economic Policy, 475–491.

Gourinchas, P., & Obstfeld, M. (2012). Stories of the Twentieth Century for the Twenty-First. American Economic Journal: Macroeconomics, 4(1), 226–265.

Gray, S. (2011). Central Bank Balances and Reserve Requirements. IMF.

Igan, D., & Tan, Z. (2015). Capital Inflows, Credit Growth, and Financial Systems. IMF.

Jorda, O. (2012). Credit: A Starring Role in the Downturn. FRBSF Economic Letter.

Jorda, O., Schularick, M., & Taylor, A. M. (2010). Financial Crises, Credit Booms, and External Imbalances: 140 Years of Lessons. National Bureau of Economic Research.

Kaltenbrunner, A., & Painceria, J. P. (2012). The Impossible Trinity on Steroids: Inflation Targeting and Exchange Rate Management in Emerging Markets. V Encontro da AKB / V Conference of the Brazilian Keynesian Association.

Kara, H. (2008). Turkish Experience with Implicit Inflation Targeting. Central Bank Review, 8 (1). 1–16.

Kara, A. H. (2012). Monetary Policy in Turkey After the Global Crisis. Working Paper No.12/17. Central Bank of the Republic of Turkey (CBRT). Ankara.

Kara, A. H. (2015). Faiz Koridoru ve Para Politikası Duruşu. Working Paper No.15/13. Central Bank of the Republic of Turkey (CBRT). Ankara.

Kara, H. K., Tiryaki, S. T., & Yüksel, C. (2013). In Search of a Reasonable Credit Growth Rate for Turkey. Central Bank Review. Central Bank of the Republic of Turkey, vol. 14(1), 1–14.

Keyder, N., & Ertunga, E. İ. (2012). Para: Teori, Politika, Uygulama. Seçkin Yayıncılık. Ankara.

Khatiwada, S. (2017). Quantitative Easing by the Fed and International Capital Flows. Working Paper No. HEIDWP02-2017. Graduate Institute of International and Development Studies' International Economics Department. Geneva.

Lane, R. L., & McQuade, P. (2013). Domestic Credit Growth and International Capital Flows. European Central Bank.

Levy-Yeyati, E., Sturzenegger, F., & Gluzmann, P. A. (2013). Fear of Appreciation. Journal of Development Economics. 101(C). 233–247.

Ma, G., Xiandong, Y. & Xi, L. (2011). China's Evolving Reserve Requirements. BIS Working Papers No.360.

Mendoza, E. G., & Terrones, M. E. (2008). An Anatomy of Credit Booms: Evidence from Macro Aggregates and Micro Data. IMf Working Paper No. 08/226.

Ostry, J. D., Ghosh, A. R., & Chamon, M. (2012.a, February). Two Targets, Two Instruments: Monetary and Exchange Rate Policies in Emerging Market Economies. IMF Staff Discussion Note .

Ostry, J. D., Ghosh, A. R., & Chamon, M. (2012.b, May). On Inflation Targeting and Forex Intervention: are Two Targets Better Than One . Vox.

Ozsuca, E. A., & Akbostanci, E. (2013). An Empirical Analysis of the Bank Lending Channel in Turkey. Iktisat Isletme ve Finans, 28(328), 33–50. doi:10.3848/iif.2013.328.3749

Öğüt, K., & Şahin, S. (2012). Türkiye'de Finansal İstikrar Sorununa Sistem Dinamiği Yaklaşımı. Turkish Economic Association 3. International Conference on Economics. İzmir.

Öğüt, K., Şahin, S., & Eren, E. (2013). Asset Price and Credit Cycles in a Financialized Economy. 1st World Keynes Conference, (s. 191–204). İzmir.

Öğüt, K., Şahin, S., & Eren, E. (2014). Para Politikası Etkinliğine Sistem Dinamiği Yaklaşımı. A. Arı içinde, Prof. Dr. İlker Parasız'a Armağan, Bir Duayen ile İktisat ve Finansı Çok boyutlu Düşünmek 273–312. Efil Yayınevi. Ankara.

Özatay, F. (2005). High Public Debt, Multiple Equilibria and Inflation targeting in Turkey - BIS Papers No 23.

Özatay, F. (2011). Parasal İktisat Kuram ve Politika. Efil Yayınevi. Ankara.

Özatay, F. (2012). Para Politikasında Yeni Arayışlar. Iktisat Isletme ve Finans, 27(315), 51–75.

Özhan, K. G., Atiyas, İ., & Keyman, E. F. (2013). Unconventional Monetary Policy and Its Reflections on the Global Economy. Think Tank 20: The G-20 and Central Banks in the New World of Unconventional Monetary Policy. içinde Brookings Institution.

Rai, V. Suchanek, L. (2014). The Effect of the Federal Reserve's Tapering Announcements on Emerging Markets. Bank of Canada. Working Paper. No.14/50

Rey, H. (2014). Capital Account Management. G. Akerlof, O. Blanchard, D. Roomer, & J. Stiglitz içinde, What Have We Learned? The MIT Press.

Sener, U. (2011). Turkish Monetary Policy in a Post-Crises Era: A Further Case of 'New Consensus'? In C. Gnos & L.-P. Rochon (Eds.), Credit, Money and Macroeconomic Policy a Post-Keynesian Approach. 289–312. Cheltenham: Edward Elgar Publishing. doi:10.4337/9781849808729.00023

Svensson, L. E. (2009). Flexible Inflation Targeting – Lessons from the Financial Crisis. Speech at the Workshop, Towards a New Framework for Monetary Policy. Amsterdam: Netherlands Bank.

Svensson, L. E. (2010). Monetary Policy After the Financial Crisis. https://www.frbsf.org/economic-research/files/Svensson2.pdf

Tovar, C. E., Mercedes, G. E. & Martin, M. V. (2012). Credit Growth and the Effectiveness of Reserve Requirements and Other Macroprudential Instruments in Latin America. IMF Working Paper No.142.

Ünalmış, D. & Ünalmış, İ. (2015). Zorunlu Karşılıklara Faiz Ödenmesi, Working Paper No.15/1. Central Bank of the Republic of Turkey (CBRT). Ankara.

Vargas, H., Varela C., Betancourt, Y. R. & Rodríguez N. (2010). Effects of Reserve Requirements in an Inflation Targeting Regime: the Case of Colombia. Banco de la República I Colombia Working Paper No.587

Yılmaz, K., Akçay, C. O. & Alper, E. (2002). Inflation and Growth Dynamics: An Analysis of Turkey in the Light of Developing Country Experiences. TÜSİAD Working Paper (No.2002-12/341), İstanbul.

Hüseyin Kaya and Özer Selçuk

Internal Migration and Wages
Internal Migration and Wages in Turkey

Abstract: This chapter considers earning difference between internal migrants and natives in Turkey and investigates the effect of the length of the residence on this earning difference. Conflicting with the most of the existing results in the literature, we find that internal migrants in Turkey are earning significantly more compared to demographically similar natives. We also find that the relation between the wages of migrants and the duration of migration is U-shaped. This means that the wages of migrants decrease with the duration of migration up to a point and then start to increase. Moreover, by using Oaxaca-Blinder decomposition method, we find that 83 percent of this earning difference is explained by differences in the productivity characteristics and 17 percent arises from differences in returns to covariates.

Keywords: internal migrant, native, wage gap

JEL: J31, J61

1 Introduction

Internal migration has always been an important and influential socio-economic phenomenon in Turkey. Since 1950, Turkey has experienced a rapid and mass migration period mainly from eastern villages of Anatolia to western cities of the country. According to Turkish Statistical Institute's 2015 survey, 31 percent of the whole population lives in a province different from their birthplaces. As a result of this inflow, although only 38 percent of the population was living in the cities in 1970, this figure increased to 65 percent in 2000, and to 92 percent in 2016 (Bostan, 2017). Together with several other reasons like security concerns, public service opportunities, and geographic conditions, socio-economic motivations like the desire for a better life are the driving force behind the migration decision. On the other hand, the amount of research in Turkey aiming to find out whether the internal migrants are successful in finding better life, especially better income, in their new destinations is quite limited.

Different than other countries experiencing internal migration, in Turkey, migrants are generally choosing their new destinations in accordance with previously migrated family members and people from the same town. Hence, after migrating they are able to join to already existing social networks in their new destinations that were formed by the fellow countryman. In Turkey, having the same village or town of origin is considered as an important tie between people and promotes solidarity with each other. According to the Turkish Department of Associations,[1] 15,755 charities (around 14 % of all charities) in Turkey are established to support the solidarity and cooperation of individuals who migrated from the same town or village. Hence, the question whether migrants are experiencing wage discrimination or they are able to overcome this possibility with the help of social networks among fellow countryman deserves consideration.

In the literature, earning differences between immigrants and native-born people in case of international immigration is excessively studied. On the other hand, the amount of research for internal migration is relatively limited. As quite common result of this limited amount of research considering the wage differentials in case of internal migration, it is found that natives are earning significantly more compared to the income of the migrants.

As a country experiencing mass internal migration like Turkey, most of the research on this topic is conducted for China. Mang and Zhang (2001) study the wage differentials between urban residents and rural migrants in Shanghai. They find a significant difference in wages between rural migrants and urban residents where urban residents are favorably treated, while their migrant counterparts are discriminated against. Zhigang, Shunfeng (2006) study rural-urban migration and wage determination in Tianjin and find that urban workers earn more than migrant workers. Similarly, Zhu (2016) examines wage differentials between urban residents and rural migrants in China's labor market and finds that the wage differential is higher at the top end compared to the bottom part of the wage distribution. By using Chinese Household Income Project 2002 survey data, Demurger, Gurgand and Yue (2009) find that 70 percent of rural migrants experience discrimination in terms of wage paid for equal work where urban residents earn 1.3 times more than rural migrants.

Danzer, Dietz, Gatskova and Schmillen (2014) study welfare consequences of internal migration to big Kazakh cities by using 2010 household survey belonging to four urban centers. Contrary to the previous findings in the literature, they find that the subjective socio-economic status of migrant households exceeds that of local residents while their incomes are not significantly different. Similarly, Gagnon, Xenogiani, and Xing (2011) investigate discrimination in urban labor markets against rural migrants by using the data from a random

1 https://www.dernekler.gov.tr/en/home-links/Distribution-Fellow-Countrymen.aspx

draw of the 2005 Chinese national census survey. They find no earnings discrimination between rural migrants and urban residents in China.

Borjas, Bronars and Trejo (1992) investigate the difference between the wages of young interstate migrants and natives in the US and the effect of the number of years spent in the destination state on this difference. They find that internal migrants initially earn 10 percent less than demographically comparable natives and this difference decreases over time.

This chapter studies the wage difference between internal migrants and natives in Turkey by using Household Labor Force Survey[2] for the years 2014, 2015 and 2016.

The rest of the chapter is organized as follows. Section 2 presents the data and summary statistics. Section 3 introduces the econometric model and discusses the empirical findings. Section 4 provides the robustness analysis. Section 5 is the conclusion.

2 Data

This paper is about earning difference between internal migrants and natives. We study the effect of the length of the residence in their new destination on the earnings of migrants. For this purpose, we use the data from the Household Labor Force Survey of Turkey for the years 2014, 2015 and 2016 which contains 1,163,577 observations. Together with a set of questions about personal characteristics, this survey also contains questions about migration status, like whether the individual is an internal migrant and for how long the individual is living in the current place.

Descriptive statistics for our sample including the individuals who are not in labor market are given in Tab. 1. According to our dataset, 420,811 individuals, around 36 percent of the whole sample, are internal migrants, hence living in a place different than their birth places. 49.3 percent of these migrants are female and 50.7 percent are male. The data indicates that the level of education is higher for the internal migrants compared to the natives. On the other hand, the unemployment rate among the natives is 4.12 percent and among the migrants it is 5 percent. In Turkey, the average wage for public sector is higher compared to the private sector and there is a significant difference in the participation rates of migrants and natives in public and private sectors. 23.5 percent of migrants are working in public sector, while for natives this figure is only 7.8 percent. The

2 In accordance with the European Union standards, Household Labor Force Survey data is collected by Turkish Statistical Institute.

Tab. 1: Prevalence (%)

		Native %	Migrant %	Total %
Gender	**Male**	47.92	49.33	48.43
	Female	52.08	50.67	51.57
	N	742,755	420,811	1,163,566
Labor Force Status	**Employed**	44.43	45.17	44.70
	Unemployed	4.12	5.00	4.44
	Out of Labor Force	51	50	51
	N	742,755	420,811	1,163,566
	No School	21	13.57	18.12
	Primary School	35	32.85	34.07
Education	**Secondary School**	23	14.19	19.67
	High School	15	17.98	16.22
	University or College	6.20	19	11
	Masters/PhD	**0**	2.20	1.01
	N	742,755	420,811	1,163,566
	Private	90.70	75.36	85.09
Public/Private Sector	**Public**	7.80	23.50	13.54
	NGO	1.50	1.14	1.37
	N	330,041	190,100	520,141
Job type	**Full Time**	83.62	90.56	86.16
	Part Time	16.38	9.44	13.84
	N	330,041	190,100	520,141
	Agriculture and Mining	40.72	12.40	30.37
Sector	**Manufacturing**	14.76	19.62	16.54
	Construction	6.30	7.50	6.74
	Service	38	60	46
	N	330,041	190,100	520,141

reason for this difference is the countrywide central exam that is used to hire public officers. Moreover, 40.72 percent of natives working in the private sector are in agriculture and mining sector where wages are significantly lower than other sectors. As a final remark, part-time working is more common for natives compared to migrants with rates 16.38 and 9.44 percent, respectively.

Our data set also contains the declared income of the employed individuals. Tab. 2 shows the average hourly real income in Turkish lira (TL) for natives and migrants. According to this table, the average real earnings for migrants is around

Tab. 2: Average Hourly Real Income

	Average Hourly Real Income	
	Native	**Migrant**
2014	7.337355	12.35289
2015	7.463544	12.31544
2016	8.189057	12.90682
	Average Hourly Real Income (Public Sector Excluded)	
2014	6.085496	8.465943
2015	6.301455	8.812249
2016	7.061758	9.229442
	Average Hourly Real Income (Public and Agriculture Sectors excluded)	
2014	6.318497	8.618052
2015	6.533145	8.959219
2016	7.332552	9.367344

57 percent higher compared to the average real earnings for migrants when all sectors are considered. Note that in Turkey, the average wage in public sector is higher compared to private sector and the average wage in agriculture and mining sectors is lower compared to the other sectors. The wage gap between migrants and natives, which is 57 percent in favor of migrants, is also stable but smaller when public sector and agriculture/mining sectors are excluded.[3]

3 Empirical Framework and Results

In this chapter, we employ the similar methodology of Borjas et al. (1992) which is originally used as the wage equation for internal young migrants when investigating if young internal migrants in the United States experience economics assimilation.

Specifically, we use a regression equation of the form

$$Ln(w_i) = X_i\alpha + \beta_1 E_i + \beta_2 E_i^2 + \gamma_1 M_i + \gamma_2 M_i.T + \gamma_3 M_i.T^2 + Z_i\lambda + \varepsilon_i,$$

3 The reason for the sharp rise in the average earnings from 2015 to 2016 is the increase in minimum wage in Turkey. In accordance with the election campaign promise, the minimum wage has increased by 30 % in 2016, which is 21.2 % higher than the inflation in 2015.

where w represents the hourly real wage, X is a vector of personal characteristics like age, gender, education and marital status. M is the dummy variable for being a migrant (M = 1 means the individual is a migrant which means he/she is residing in a place different than the one he/she was born in and $M = 0$ means the individual is residing in the place he/she was born in). E measures the job experience which is the number of years the individual has been working for his/her current job. T stands for the years spent as a migrant and Z is a collection of control variables including regional, sectoral and year dummies. The coefficient γ_1 captures the earning difference between natives and migrants, and the coefficients γ_2 and γ_3 measures the effect of the length of residence of the migrants on their earnings. The model is estimated with OLS and the results are provided in Tab. 3.

The first column of Tab. 3 stands for the regression results where the explanatory variables are female dummy, age, age squared, marital status dummy, education dummy, experience, experience squared, migrant and interaction terms such as migrant times, time spent as a migrant and migrant times square of time spent as a migrant. On top of these explanatory variables, Model 2 considers sectoral dummies (agriculture/mining sector, manufacturing sector, services and construction). Model 3 includes public sector, private sector and non-profit sectors. Finally, Model 4 takes into account the regional dummies.

For all of the models presented in Tab. 3, migrant dummy and the interaction terms (M.T and $M.T^2$) are all significant at 1 percent level. Moreover, for all of these models we find $\gamma_1$to be positive, which means that the earnings of migrants are significantly higher compared to the natives. More specifically, if $T = 0$ (which means the migrant has just migrated) the results from Model 1 and Model 2 suggest that the migrants are earning almost 28 percent ($= e^{0.25}-1$) more compared to demographically similar natives. When we include the sectoral and regional dummies, estimate for the coefficient of migrant dummy decreases to 0.169. When T = 0 this estimation suggests 18.5 percent ($= e^{0.17}-1$) higher earnings for the migrants compared to the natives. This result is quite interesting and conflicting, to the best of our knowledge, with the results already existing in the literature. According to us, the main reason behind this finding is the existence of strong connections and solidarity among the migrants who migrated from the same town or village. We think that with the help of strong solidarity among fellow countrymen, migrants are able to overcome the possibility of being discriminated.

The coefficient of the interaction term of migration dummy (M) and migration duration (T) is found to be significantly negative. In contrast, the coefficient of interaction term of migration dummy (M) and squared migration duration

Tab. 3: Estimation Results

	Model 1	**Model 2**	**Model 3**	**Model 4**
Migrant Dummy	0.254***	0.249***	0.178***	0.169***
	(72.37)	(71.05)	(52.59)	(50.20)
Migrant x T	−0.0141***	−0.0137***	−0.00819***	−0.0106***
	(-37.09)	(-36.27)	(-21.97)	(-28.60)
Migrant x T^2	0.000257***	0.000249***	0.000177***	0.000203***
	(27.56)	(26.85)	(19.15)	(22.09)
Age	0.0680***	0.0620***	0.0705***	0.0719***
	(166.15)	(140.16)	(172.92)	(154.58)
Age Squared	−0.000785***	−0.000716***	−0.000812***	−0.000823***
	(−132.75)	(−115.39)	(−135.51)	(−124.48)
Experience	0.0243***	0.0262***	0.0176***	0.0177***
	(61.40)	(65.68)	(45.29)	(45.71)
Experience Squared	−0.000110***	−0.000156***	−0.000186***	−0.000189***
	(-8.16)	(−11.58)	(−14.21)	(−14.48)
Gender				
Male	Reference	Reference	Reference	Reference
Female	−0.0765***	−0.0761***	−00619***	−0.0542***
	(-34.98)	(-34.31)	(-28.49)	(-24.90)
Marital Status				
Single	Reference	Reference	Reference	Reference
Married	0.0468***	0.0568***	0.0255***	0.0292***
	(16.72)	(20.30)	(9.60)	(11.19)
Divorced	0.00639	0.0210***	−0.00248	−0.00535
	(1.06)	(3.48)	(−0.42)	(−0.93)
Widow	−0.0225	−0.0175	−0.000223	0.00652
	(−1.80)	(−1.41)	(−0.02)	(0.53)
Education				
No School	Reference	Reference	Reference	Reference
Primary School	0.209***	0.191***	0.179***	0.162***
	(36.09)	(33.44)	(31.23)	(28.45)
Secondary School	0.380***	0.349***	0.334***	0.323***
	(67.09)	(62.11)	(58.72)	(56.94)
High School	0.543***	0.520***	0.483***	0.472***
	(93.61)	(90.47)	(83.06)	(81.42)
College/University	1.021***	1.000***	0.862***	0.844***
	(168.46)	(165.89)	(139.39)	(137.13)

(continued on next page)

Tab. 3: (continued)

	Model 1	Model 2	Model 3	Model 4
Masters/PhD	1.519***	1.499***	1.312***	1.278***
	(181.61)	(180.24)	(147.63)	(145.04)
Year Dummy				
2014	Reference	Reference	Reference	Reference
2015	0.0255***	0.0237***	0.0291***	0.0302***
	(11.08)	(10.37)	(13.13)	(13.91)
2016	0.117***	0.115***	0.122***	0.123***
	(51.75)	(51.13)	(56.20)	(57.97)
Sectors				
Agriculture and Mining		Reference		Reference
Manufacturing		0.126***		0.174***
		(26.93)		(37.84)
Services		0.230***		0.283***
		(41.60)		(52.09)
Construction		0.127***		0.105***
		(27.72)		(23.43)
Public/Private				
Private Sector			Reference	Reference
Public Sector			0.384***	0.452***
			(128.10)	(145.54)
Non-Profit Sector			−0.276***	−0.221***
			(-37.59)	(-29.94)
Regional Dummies	No	No	No	Yes
N	278496	278496	278496	278496
R^2	0.951	0.952	0.955	0.957

(T^2) is positive. This means the relation between the wages of migrants and the duration of migration is U-shaped. These results indicate that the wages of migrants decrease with the duration of migration up to a point and then start to increase. For example, when we consider the results of Model 4, the wages of migrants are decreasing during the first 26.1 years of migration $\left(= \frac{-\widehat{\gamma_2}}{2\widehat{\gamma_3}} \right)$ and beyond this point additional years of migration duration causes an increase in migrants' wage.

The relationship between the wages and other considered determinants are found to be in line with the existing literature. Age and experience have inverse U-shape relation with the earnings. Moreover, our results indicate that females are earning less compared to males, which reveals the existence of gender pay gap in favor of males in Turkey. More specifically, according to the results of Model 4, a woman earns 5 percent (= $e^{-0.054}-1$) less than a demographically comparable man. The results also suggest that education pay-off is quite significant in Turkey. Especially having a university degree or more leads to an enormous increase in earnings. According to the results of Model 4, having a high school degree causes 60 percent (= $e^{0.47}-1$) but having a college/university degree causes 130 percent (= $e^{0.84}-1$) higher earnings compared to no-schooling. Moreover, service sector workers are paid more than those of other production sectors and public sector workers are paid more compared to people working in private and non-profit sector.

4 Estimation Results When Different Sub-Samples Are Considered

Together for the whole sample, for robustness check the model presented above is estimated for a collection of subsamples. The first one of these subsamples is obtained by excluding the agricultural and mining sector. The reason behind this choice is the fact that the average hourly earnings are lower in agricultural/mining sector compared to the other and most of the migrants are not working in this sector. Since the average earnings in private and public sectors are also different in Turkey and public employees are appointed by central government according to the results of a nation-wide exam, the model is also estimated for private and public sectors separately. The same equation is also estimated for males and females separately to see if the wage difference is affected by gender. The results of these estimations are presented in Tab. 4. In order to save space, we only present the estimation results of migrant dummy and interaction terms.

When the model is estimated for different subsamples, the results turn out to be similar to the previous results presented in Tab. 3. Again we find that migrants are earning significantly more than natives. Also, the earnings of migrants are decreasing with the migration duration up to a point and then start to increase. Hence, our results are quite robust to different subsamples.

The reason behind the higher earnings for migrants can be related to some unobserved characteristics that make the migrants more productive than natives who are the people decided not to migrate. For example, a person who decides to migrate can be more adaptive, more flexible or has self-confidence which

Tab. 4: Estimation Results for Subsamples

	Subsample Containing only Male	**Subsample only Containing Female**	**Subsample containing only Public Sector**	**Subsample containing only Private Sector**	**Subsample where Agriculture/ mining excluded**
Migrant Dummy	0.244***	0.270***	0.242***	0.124***	0.259***
	(60.14)	(39.22)	(45.26)	(28.66)	(72.61)
Migrant x T	−0.0151***	−0.0166***	−0.0153***	−0.00757***	−0.0164***
	(-34.37)	(-22.33)	(-28.21)	(−15.64)	(-42.51)
Migrant x T^2	0.000253***	0.000297***	0.000291***	0.000155***	0.000284***
	(23.66)	(16.02)	(22.27)	(12.94)	(29.99)
Regional Dummies	Yes	Yes	Yes	Yes	Yes
Sectoral Dummies	Yes	Yes	Yes	Yes	Yes
N	203316	75180	63499	208037	263828
R^2	0.955	0.948	0.980	0.945	0.954

Tab. 5: Results for the Subsample of People Who Migrated Younger Than 16

	Model 1	**Model 2**	**Model 3**	**Model 4**
Migrant Dummy	0.641***	0.550***	0.642***	0.722***
	(16.42)	(13.26)	(16.61)	(17.94)
Migrant x T	−0.00546***	−0.00507***	−0.00465**	−0.00529***
	(-3.58)	(-3.34)	(-3.09)	(-3.60)
Migrant x T^2	0.0000848**	0.0000820**	0.0000679*	0.0000815**
	(3.07)	(2.98)	(2.50)	(3.06)
N	30075	30075	30075	30075
R^2	0.953	0.953	0.956	0.958

in turn makes him/her more productive. On the other hand, being a migrant may have nothing to do with productivity but it forces people to work hard or it provides the opportunity to benefit from the established fellow countrymen networks which in turn leads to a higher income. To control for the effect of the unobserved characteristics, we consider only the people for whom migration decision is not his/her own decision but their parents'. Hence, we consider the people who migrated under the age of 16 and Tab. 5 presents the results of all four models that are estimated by using this subsample. In order to save space, we report the estimation results for only migration dummy and the interaction terms.

According to our results migrants, who migrated under the age of 16 earn significantly more than the natives. Besides, the wage difference between these migrants and natives is found to be even higher in this case. Given that $T = 0$, the results of Model 4 indicate that the migrants earn 105 percent (= $e^{0.72}-1$) more than the demographically comparable natives. Moreover, migrants' wages tend to decrease up to a point (until T reaches to 32.4 years) and beyond that point additional migration duration leads to higher earnings for migrants.

5 Oaxaca-Blinder Decomposition

In the literature of the labor economics, the Oaxaca-Blinder decomposition (Blinder, 1973; Oaxaca, 1973) is often employed to investigate the wage gap between two groups. This method decomposes the wage gap into two parts, "explained" part and "unexplained/discrimination" part. Explained part is the part of the wage gap due to the differences in the averages of the determinants of wage. On the other hand, unexplained part refers to the part of the wage gap due to differences in the effects of these determinants.

Suppose that the mean log wage function for migrants (M) and locals (L) is described by following equations:

$$\text{for migrants: } E\left[Y_M | X_M\right] = X_M B_M$$
$$\text{for locals: } E\left[Y_L | X_L\right] = X_L B_L$$

where Y is the log hourly real wage, X is the vector of determinants including constant, and B is the vector of coefficients. The mean log wage gap between migrants and locals can be written as

$$\bar{Y}_M - \bar{Y}_L = \left(\bar{X}_M - \bar{X}_L\right)\hat{B}_M + \bar{X}_L\left(\hat{B}_M - \hat{B}_L\right)$$

where $\hat{B}$ is the OLS estimate of the B. The first term at the right hand side of the equation is the "explained" part and the second term is the "unexplained/discrimination" part. While the fractions of explained part and unexplained part are not affected by the use of categorical variables, contributions of the categorical predictors to wage structure depend on the choice of the omitted category (Oaxaca and Ransom, 1994; Gardeazabal and Ugidos. 2004). We follow Yun (2005) and compute decomposition based on normalized effects, which is a solution to omitted category problem.

Tab. 6 above shows the overall results of the decomposition. The average wage gap between migrants and locals is 0.4 TL per hour. A total 83 percent of the

Tab. 6: Oaxaca-Blinder Decomposition. Detailed Estimation Results of Decomposition Are Provided in Appendix.

	Mean Log Wage
Migrants	1.915***
	(1188.48)
Locals	2.315***
	(1151.94)
Wage Gap	−0.399***
	(−155.09)
Explained Part	−0.332***
	(−160.30)
Unexplained Part	−0.0670***
	(-42.21)

t statistics in parentheses * $p < 0.05$, ** $p < 0.01$, *** $p < 0.001$

wage gap is explained by differences in the productivity characteristics. On the other hand, 17 percent of the wage gap is due to the discrimination effect, which arises from differences in returns to covariates.

6 Conclusion

In this note, we provide an analysis of wage difference between natives and internal migrants in Turkey. Moreover, we study the effect of the length of residence on the wages of migrants. Different than other countries and conflicting with already existing results in the literature, for Turkey we found that migrants are earning significantly more compared to the natives with the same demographics. We think that strong ties and solidarity among the fellow countrymen is the main reason behind this result. For robustness check, we estimate our model by using several subsamples and we find that the still internal migrants are earning significantly more. Additionally, we employed Oaxaca-Blinder decomposition method and find that 17 percent of the wage gap is due to the discrimination effect, which arises from differences in returns to covariates.

Hence, the results of this paper show a significant productivity difference between the natives and the migrants. The areas attracting migrants are in fact receiving more productive labor than their existing residents which is quite beneficial for their local economies. Also the migrants are moving to places where they can utilize their productive skills more. So, the transfer of population as a result of migration is a win-win case for both migrants and the areas attracting migrants. On the other hand, the decision to migrate is a hard one because of the transaction costs associated with it. Together with the financial costs like cost of moving, the transaction costs may also include the non-financial ones like cost of leaving friends and family behind. In order to increase the overall productivity in the country, policy makers should try to minimize these transaction costs which act as barriers in front of migration.

Appendix

Tab. A1: Oaxaca-Blinder Decomposition Results

	Migrant	Local	Explained	Unexplained
Age	0.0314***	0.0491***	−0.124***	0.650***
	(25.71)	(55.12)	(-45.07)	(11.78)
Age Squared	−0.000361***	−0.000570***	0.0926***	−0.305***
	(-23.55)	(-50.06)	(39.34)	(−11.04)
Experience	0.0227***	0.0169***	−0.0386***	−0.0412***
	(39.84)	(31.34)	(-40.53)	(-7.27)
Experience Squared	−0.000382***	−0.000107***	0.0121***	0.0296***
	(-21.44)	(-5.55)	(19.34)	(10.24)
Female	−0.0871***	−0.0967***	0.00370***	0.00701*
	(-28.26)	(-31.64)	(20.71)	(2.22)
Marital Status				
Single	Reference	Reference	−0.00713***	0.00133
			(−15.37)	(0.70)
Married	0.103***	0.0764***	−0.00474***	−0.0176***
	(24.25)	(21.70)	(−12.47)	(-3.82)
Divorced	0.0970***	0.0517***	−0.000294***	−0.00129***
	(11.49)	(6.44)	(-5.49)	(-4.36)
Widow	0.00298	0.0691***	−0.00000308	0.000515***
	(0.17)	(4.43)	(−0.66)	(3.92)
Education				
No School	Reference	Reference	−0.00537***	0.00335***
			(−16.60)	(9.21)
Primary School	0.131***	0.0499***	−0.0183***	0.00201
	(15.31)	(6.77)	(-30.38)	(1.62)
Secondary School	0.222***	0.155***	−0.0286***	0.00488***
	(25.40)	(20.53)	(-62.81)	(5.28)

(*continued on next page*)

Tab. A1: (continued)

	Migrant	**Local**	**Explained**	**Unexplained**
High School	0.412***	0.339***	−0.00410***	0.00362***
	(47.12)	(44.93)	(-24.86)	(3.45)
College/University	0.847***	0.664***	−0.0656***	−0.0206***
	(92.68)	(82.47)	(-91.23)	(−17.18)
Masters/PhD	1.265***	1.149***	−0.0314***	−0.000249
	(111.20)	(73.57)	(-55.30)	(−0.95)
Year Dummy				
2014	Reference	Reference	−0.000313***	−0.00541***
			(-3.91)	(-6.54)
2015	0.0145***	0.0226***	0.0000286	−0.00275***
	(4.49)	(7.83)	(0.64)	(-3.31)
2016	0.0913***	0.132***	−0.000409**	0.00808***
	(29.07)	(46.56)	(-3.29)	(10.17)
Sectors				
Agriculture and Mining	Reference	Reference	−0.00376***	−0.00174***
			(-24.38)	(-5.48)
Manufacturing	0.0697***	0.122***	0.000284***	0.00167
	(8.19)	(21.94)	(6.74)	(1.76)
Services	0.151***	0.243***	0.00340***	0.00347***
	(15.58)	(36.71)	(22.99)	(7.86)
Construction	0.0156	0.0516***	0.00378***	−0.00547*
	(1.87)	(9.59)	(22.17)	(-2.25)
Public/Private				
Private Sector	Reference	Reference	−0.0109***	−0.0139**
			(-27.91)	(-3.23)
Public Sector	0.457***	0.467***	−0.0618***	−0.000514
	(100.58)	(110.01)	(-77.99)	(−0.31)
Non-Profit Sector	−0.274***	−0.222***	−0.00517***	0.000827***
	(−19.71)	(-26.49)	(-25.55)	(3.49)
Constant	1.011***	0.751***	0.00370***	−0.378***
	(44.65)	(43.55)	(20.71)	(−13.25)
Regional Dummy	Yes	Yes	Yes	Yes
N	127829	150667	278496	278496
R^2	0.592	0.481		

t statistics in parentheses * $p < 0.05$, ** $p < 0.01$, *** $p < 0.001$

References

Blinder, A. S. (1973). Wage discrimination: Reduced form and structural estimates. *Journal of Human resources*, 436–455.

Borjas, G. J., Bronars, S. G., & Trejo, S. J. (1992). Assimilation and the earnings of young internal migrants. *The Review of Economics and Statistics*, 170–175.

Bostan, H. (2017). Türkiye'de iç göçlerin toplumsal yapıda neden olduğu değişimler, meydana getirdiği sorunlar ve çözüm önerileri. *Coğrafya Dergisi*, 35, 1–16.

Danzer, A. M., Dietz, B., Gatskova, K., & Schmillen, A. (2014). Showing off to the new neighbors? Income, socioeconomic status and consumption patterns of internal migrants. *Journal of Comparative Economics*, 42(1), 230–245.

Demurger, S., Gurgand, M., Li, S., & Yue, X. (2009). Migrants as second-class workers in urban China? A decomposition analysis. *Journal of Comparative Economics*, 37, 610–628.

Gardeazabal, J., & Ugidos, A. (2004). More on identification in detailed wage decompositions. *Review of Economics and Statistics*, 86(4), 1034–1036.

Gagnon, J., Xenogiani, T., & Xing, C. (2011). Are all migrants really worse off in urban labour markets: New empirical evidence from China. *IZA Discussion Paper* No. 6268.

Glaeser, E. L., & Maré, D. C., (2001). Cities and skills. *Journal of Labor Economics*, 19, 316–342.

Meng, X., & Zhang, J. (2001). The two-tier labor market in urban China: Occupational segregation and wage differentials between urban residents and rural migrants in Shanghai. *Journal of Comparative Economics*, 29(3), 485–504.

Oaxaca, R. (1973). Male-female wage differentials in urban labor markets. *International Economic Review*, 693–709.

Oaxaca, R. L., & Ransom, M. R. (1994). On discrimination and the decomposition of wage differentials. *Journal of Econometrics*, 61(1), 5–21.

Yun, M. S. (2005). Hypothesis tests when decomposing differences in the first moment. *Journal of Economic and Social Measurement*, 30(4), 295–304.

Zhigang, L., & Shunfeng, S. (2006). Rural–urban migration and wage determination: The case of Tianjin, China. *China Economic Review*, 17(3), 337–345.

Zhu, R. (2016). Wage differentials between urban residents and rural migrants in urban China during 2002–2007: A distributional analysis. *China Economic Review*, 37, 2–14.

Kıvanç Karaman and Seçil Yıldırım-Karaman

Anchoring of Inflation Expectations

Anchoring of Inflation Expectations in Turkey between 2013 and 2018

Abstract: In this chapter, we investigate the anchoring of inflation expectations in Turkey from 2013 to 2018, which is the period after the recovery from the global financial crisis. First, we calculate the far-ahead forward interest rates to measure the long-run inflation expectations using high-frequency bond yield data. Next, we analyze how the volatility of forward interest rates changes over time. Finally, we test how forward interest rates react to monetary policy announcements by using event study approach. The results show that long-term bond returns and far-ahead forward interest rates move in the opposite direction with the monetary policy stance in the sample period. Hence, we conclude that the policy decisions of the CBRT were not consistent with the long-term inflation target and inflation expectations were not well-anchored.

Keywords: Turkey, CBRT, monetary policy, forward interest rates, inflation expectations, event study

JEL: E2, E31, E52, E58, E5

1 Introduction

As part of the IMF stabilization program, Central Bank of the Republic of Turkey adopted inflation-targeting regime in 2001. With this program, CBRT started to use the inflation target as a nominal anchor to manage the expectations of the agents.[1] This policy became successful and the inflation rate in Turkey decreased significantly after 2001. Fig. 1 displays the inflation rate in Turkey after the CBRT adopted inflation-targeting regime.

In 2009, central banks in advanced economies adopted extraordinary policy tools to mitigate the negative consequences of the global financial crisis. This, in turn, caused massive capital inflows to developing countries, which increased current account deficit and threatened financial stability in these economies. As Fig. 2 shows, the current account deficit in Turkey increased to above 10 % of GDP in 2010.

---

1 Bernanke et al. 1999; Bernanke and Mishkin, 1997; Svensson, 1997; Gurkaynak et al., 2010 discuss that inflation targeting helps anchoring inflation expectations.

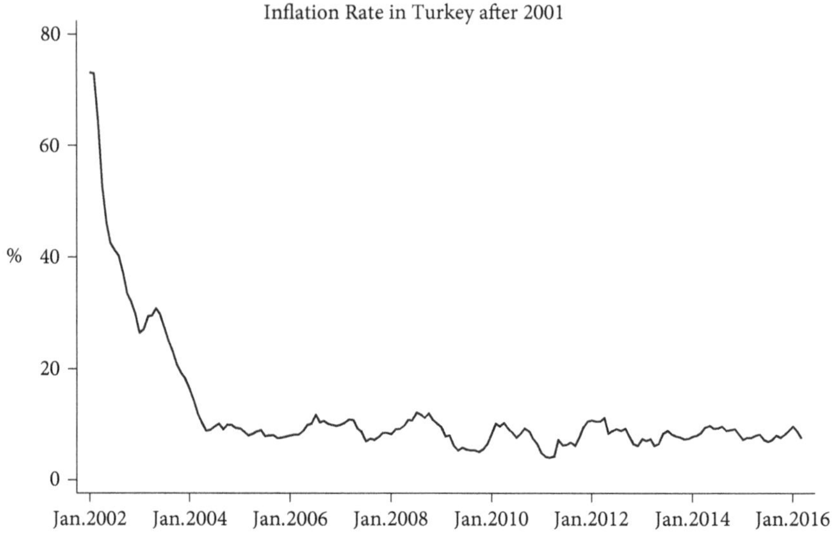

Fig. 1: Inflation Rate in Turkey after 2001

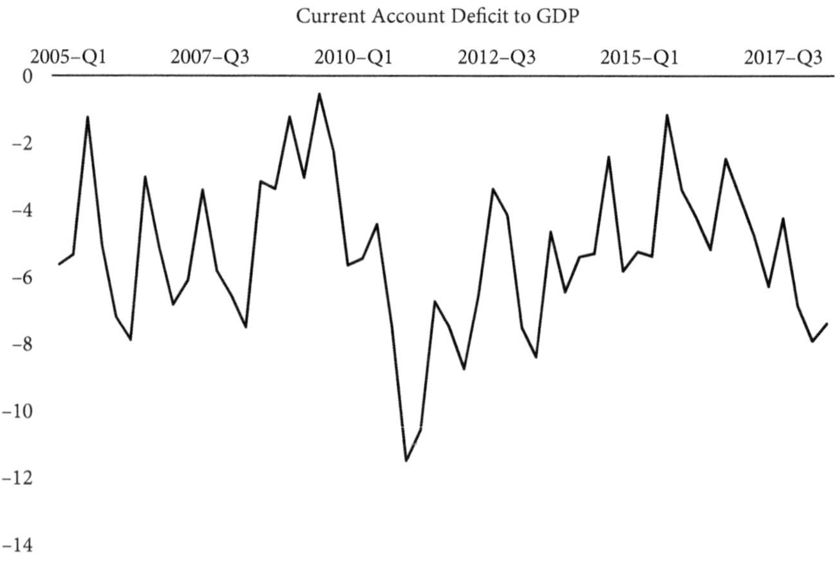

Fig. 2: Current Account Deficit to GDP

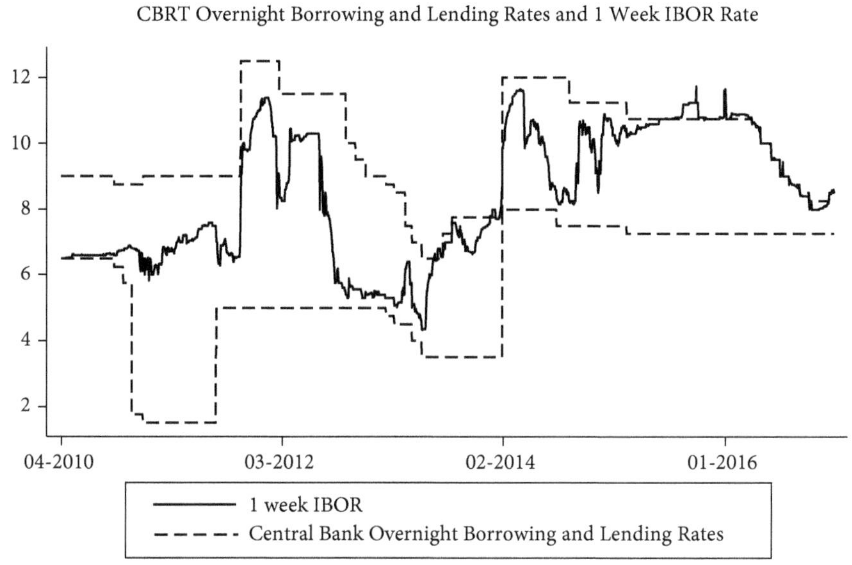

Fig. 3: CBRT Overnight Borrowing and Lending Rates and One Week|BOR Rate

Due to the concerns about the financial stability, the CBRT adopted alternative policy tools, which aimed to stabilize financial markets in addition to maintaining price stability.[2] In particular, the CBRT used the reserve requirements to control the loan growth and then used the volatility of the overnight interest rate as a policy tool to decrease the short-term currency inflows and contain the current account deficit. As Fig. 3 shows, one-week interbank borrowing rate fluctuated within the band between the overnight borrowing and lending rates. The CBRT increased the volatility of the market rate to increase the risk of financial assets in Turkey to reduce capital inflows.

The CBRT continued to implement the new policy mix even after the recovery from the financial crisis, which raised concerns about the anchoring of inflation expectations. Gürkaynak et al. (2015), Acemoğlu and Üçer (2015), Akkaya and Gürkaynak (2012), Karaman and Yıldırım-Karaman (2017) argue that the economic policy in Turkey moved towards a discretionary framework in the late 2000s and therefore macroeconomic uncertainty increased and the management of the expectations weakened. As Fig. 4 shows, inflation rate was consistently

2 See Akçelik et al., 2013; Kara, 2013

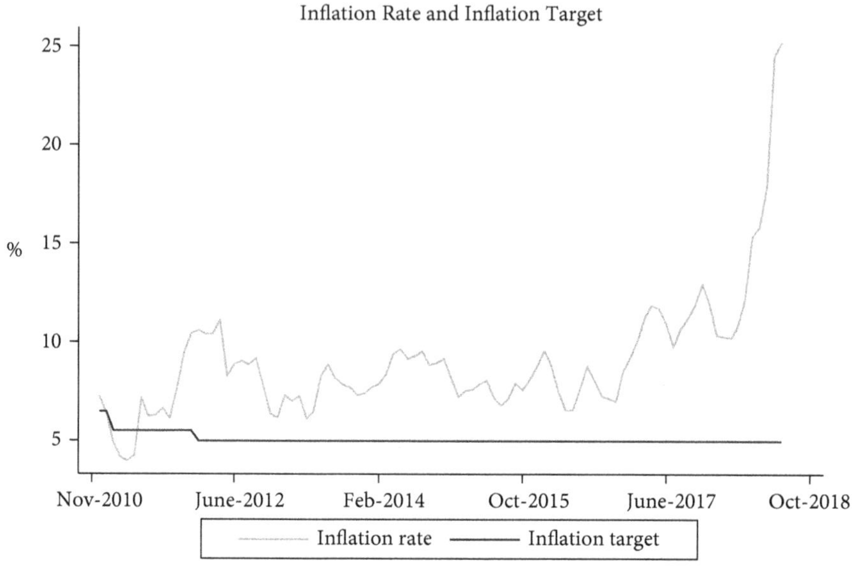

Fig. 4: Inflation Rate and Inflation Target

above from its target level (5 %) between 2012 and 2018 and increased to above 20 % in 2018.

In the beginning of 2017, the CBRT started monetary tightening due to the deterioration in the inflation outlook and used the weighted average funding cost as a policy tool. Fig. 5 establishes that the CBRT responded to the significant increase in the inflation rate by increasing the weighted average funding cost and stopped providing cheap funding to the banks. From January to September 2018, USD/TRY exchange rate depreciated by around 78 % and the inflation rate increased to above 20 %. In response to this deterioration in the inflation outlook, the CBRT increased the policy rate by 625 basis points on September 2018 and announced that the tight stance in monetary policy would be maintained decisively until inflation outlook improved.

This study investigates the anchoring of inflation expectations in Turkey from 2013 to 2018, which is the period after the recovery from the global financial crisis. Building on Ehrmann et al. 2011, we calculate far-ahead forward interest rates to measure the long-run inflation expectations using high-frequency bond yield data. Next, we analyze how the volatility of forward rates changed over time. Evolution of the volatility of forward rates establishes whether the inflation expectations are well-anchored. Finally, we test how long-term bond returns

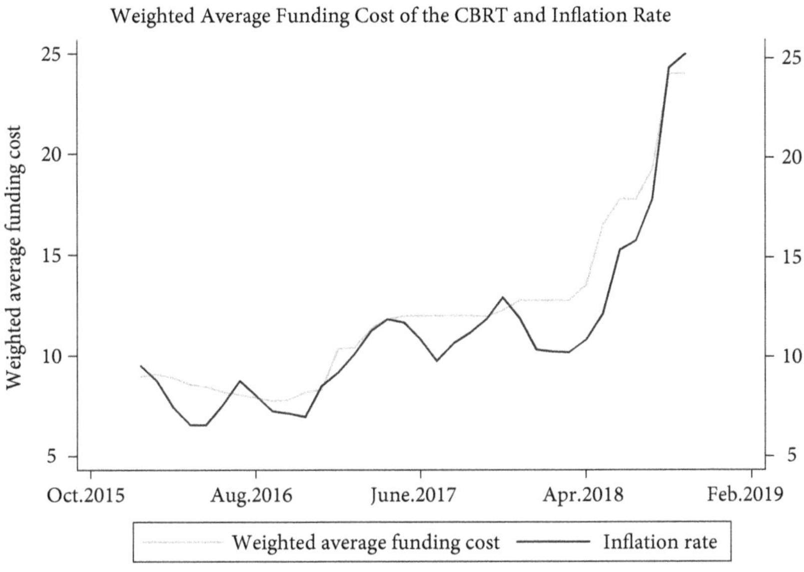

Fig. 5: Weighted Average Funding Cost of the CBRT and Inflation Rate

and forward interest rates reacted to monetary policy announcements to analyze whether monetary policy announcements were effective in anchoring long-run inflation expectations in the sample period.

The results show that both the long-term bond returns and far-ahead forward interest rates moved in the opposite direction with the monetary policy stance in the sample period. Namely, if a policy decision was expansionary, it induced an increase in both the long-term bond returns and far-ahead forward interest rates. Intuitively, if an expansionary policy decision was not consistent with the long-term inflation target, it created uncertainty about the future inflation rates which, in turn, caused the agents to expect higher interest rates in the future. Consequently, the term premium for the long-term bond returns increased. This finding suggests that the inflation expectations were not well-anchored in Turkey in the sample period.

This study contributes to the literature on the effectiveness of monetary policy in Turkey. Demiralp et al. (2012) find that the CBRT could manage the expectations and control the long-term interest rates before 2010 whereas it could not do so after 2010. They suggest that adopting multiple policy objectives in the post-2010 period might have weakened the control of the CBRT over the long-term interest rates. Duran et al. (2012) and Aktaş et al. (2009) find that the

CBRT policies had significant impact on asset prices before 2009. Çiçek and Akar (2014), in their analysis for the period between 2002 and 2013, show that inflation expectations have been anchored to inflation targets. Karaman and Yıldırım-Karaman (2017) find that inflation rate in Turkey would have been lower by around 3 percentage points if the CBRT continued to strict inflation targeting after 2010. Eroğlu and Yıldırım-Karaman (2017) show that policy decisions of the CBRT after 2010 made the yield curve steeper. Different from these papers, we investigate the anchoring of inflation expectations using forward interest rates for the period after the recovery from the global financial crisis. Our results also relate to the literature that investigates the impact of inflation targeting on the management of inflation expectations. Our findings suggest that inflation expectations were not well-anchored between 2013 and 2018, which is the period in which CBRT did not implement strict inflation targeting. This finding is consistent with Bernanke et al. (1999), Bernanke and Mishkin (1997), Svensson (1997), Svensson and Woodford (2003), Johnson (2002), Levin, Natalucci and Pieger (2004), and Gürkaynak, Levin and Swanson (2010) which argue that inflation targeting helps anchoring of inflation expectations.

The rest of the chapter proceeds as follows: Section 2 presents the bond yield data and the calculation of forward rates. Section 3 discusses the reaction of bond returns to monetary policy shocks. Section 4 presents the reaction of the far-ahead forward interest rates to monetary policy shocks and discusses whether the inflation expectations are well-anchored and the last section concludes.

2 Zero Coupon Bond Yields and Forward Interest Rates

In this section, we use zero-coupon bond yields to calculate far-ahead forward interest rates for Turkey. 1-year, 2-year, 3-year, 5-year and 10-year zero-coupon bond yield data is obtained from Global Financial Database. Fig. 6 shows the evolution of zero-coupon bond yields in Turkey between 2012 and 2018. As the figure displays, in 2017, bond yields started to increase significantly and spiked in 2018 along with the increase in the inflation rate.

Fig. 7 displays 1-week interbank rate, 5-year and 10-year bond returns between 2016 and 2018. We observe that when the short-term interest rates were low (high), long-term bond returns were higher (lower) than short-term rates by around 5 percentage points. After the CBRT increased the policy rate by 625 basis points in September 2018, bond yields declined by around 500 basis points. This pattern is consistent with the expectations hypothesis. In particular, when there is a decline in the short-term interest rates, which is not consistent with the

Fig. 6: Zero-Coupon Bond Yields in Turkey

long-term inflation target, inflation expectations increase and in turn increase the term premium and long-term interest rates.

Following Gürkaynak et al. (2007) and Ehrmann et al. (2008), we use far-ahead forward interest rates to investigate whether the inflation rate is well-anchored. Forward rate is defined as the expected future zero rate implied by today's term structure of interest rates. Suppose that r_t^k is the return from k-year maturity zero-coupon bond and r_t^m is the return from m-year maturity zero-coupon bond. M-year ahead (k-m)-year forward interest rate is calculated as follows:

$$f_m^{k-m} = \frac{\left(k * r_t^k - m * r_t^m\right)}{k-m}$$

The intuition for using forward rates is that they are proxies for the future interest rate expectations. When the central bank has a long-term credible inflation target, we expect macroeconomic shocks to have transitory effects on the future path of the interest rates and forward interest rates do not react to these shocks as Ehrmann et al. (2008) note.

For Turkey, one-year, two-year, three-year, five-year and ten-year zero-coupon bond yield data is available after 2010. Using this data, we can calculate one-year

Fig. 7: One-Week Interbank Rate and Long-term Bond Returns

ahead one-year forward interest rate, two-year ahead one-year forward interest rate, three-year ahead two-year forward interest rate and five-year ahead five-year forward interest rate. Fig. 8 displays the calculated far-ahead forward interest rates for Turkey for the years between 2016 and 2018. Forward interest rates increased along with the depreciation of the Turkish lira and the increase in the inflation rate in the second half of 2017. They spiked in 2018 when the inflation rate increased above 20 % and started to decrease after the CBRT hiked its policy rate to 24 % on September 2018. The intuition behind this pattern is that the CBRT kept short-term interest rates at low levels despite the high-inflation rate until the beginning of 2018. In turn, the inflation expectations for the future, long-term interest rates and forward interest rates increased.

Fig. 9 shows one-, two- and three-year ahead forward rates, USD/TRY exchange rate and inflation rate between January 2017 and October 2018. We observe that far-ahead forward interest rates move in the same direction with the exchange rate and inflation rate. In 2018, inflation rate increased and USD/TRY exchange rate depreciated significantly. In turn, uncertainty increased raising concerns about the future path of the inflation rate and increasing forward interest rates.

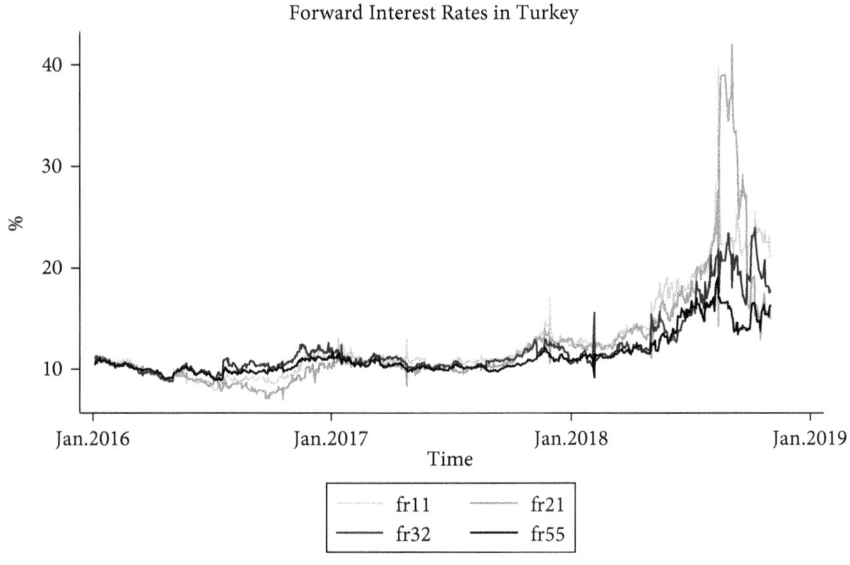

Fig. 8: Forward Interest Rates in Turkey

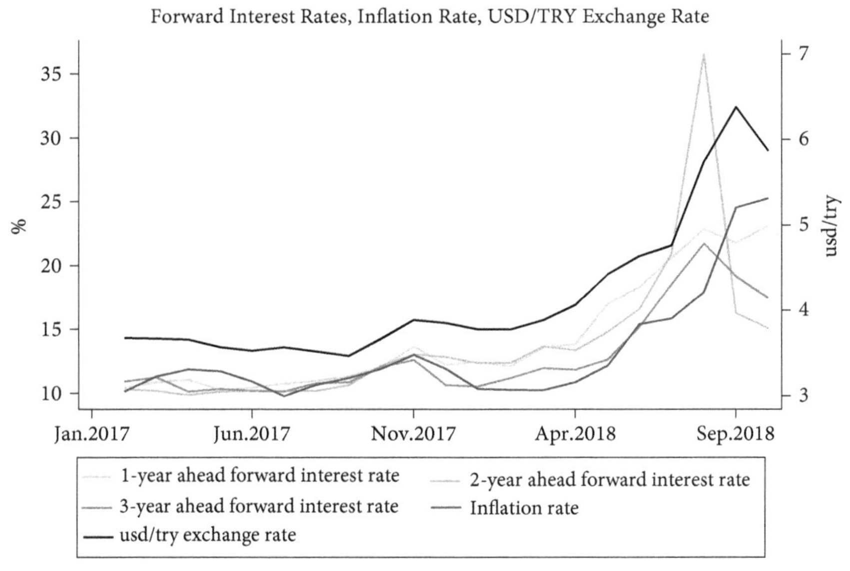

Fig. 9: Forward Interest Rates, Inflation Rate, USD/TRY Exchange Rate

3 Reaction of Bond Returns to Monetary Policy Shocks

Monetary authority uses short-term policy rate as policy instrument and targets the long-term interest rates which, in turn, affects the inflation rate and economic growth. If a reduction in the policy rate is consistent with the long-term inflation target, bond returns move in the same direction with the short-term interest rates because policy actions are transmitted to financial markets efficiently. If not, policy decisions induce uncertainty about the future inflation rate which, in turn, causes long-term interest rates to increase despite the low level of short-term interest rates. In order to measure the impact of monetary policy decisions on the bond returns, we measure the surprise component of the monetary policy shocks. Surprise component of a policy decision is the difference between the actual policy change and the market expectation. Because the expectations are priced in the market before the actual decision is made, we calculate the monetary policy surprises by taking the difference between one-week interbank borrowing rates before and after the policy meetings. We estimate the following OLS equation to investigate the response of bond returns to monetary policy shocks using event study approach:

$$\Delta y_{it} = \alpha + \beta S_t + \varepsilon_t$$

S_t is the monetary policy surprise at time t, Δy_{it} is the daily change in the government bond return with maturity i. The regression results are presented in Tab. 1:

Regression results show that the responses of one, two and three-year bond returns to monetary policy shocks are insignificant, while those of five and ten-year bonds are significant and negative. A 100 basis points monetary policy

Tab. 1: Responses of Bond Returns to Monetary Policy Surprises Between January 2013 and November 2018

	Change in the One-Year Bond Return	**Change in the Two-Year Bond Return**	**Change in the Three-Year Bond Return**	**Change in the Five-Year Bond Return**	**Change in the Ten-Year Bond Return**
Constant term	0.005	0.009	0.004	−0.002	0.005
	(0.009)	(0.009)	(0.008)	(0.006)	(0.006)
Monetary Policy Surprise	0.45	−0.18	−0.58	−0.86***	−0.78***
	(0.43)	(0.48)	(0.38)	(0.31)	(0.29)

(Standard deviations are in parenthesis)

surprise causes respectively 86 and 78 basis points decrease in the 5-year and 10-year bond returns. These findings provide evidence that long-term bond returns do not move in the same direction with the short-term interest rates. If a policy shock is expansionary,[3] it induces an increase in the five- and ten-year bond returns rather than a decrease. The intuition behind this finding is that expansionary policy decisions which are not consistent with the long-term inflation target generate uncertainty about the future price level and hence increase the long-term interest rates. Since monetary policy stance in Turkey was expansionary in the sample period, this result suggests that the CBRT did not have control over the long-term interest rates. Expansionary policy decisions induced an increase in the expected inflation rate and generated macro-level uncertainty. Hence, we conclude that monetary transmission was not efficient in the sample period. This finding is consistent with Karaman and Yıldırım-Karaman (2017) which show that monetary policy decisions increased the inflation rate but did not have any impact on the growth performance of Turkey after 2010.

4 Anchoring of Inflation Expectations

In this section, we investigate whether inflation expectations are well-anchored in the sample period using far-ahead forward rates. First, we analyze how the volatility of forward rates changed over time. Next, we test how forward rates reacted to monetary policy announcements. If the inflation expectations were well-anchored, we expect no change in the volatility of forward rates and no reaction of forward rates to monetary policy shocks.

Fig. 10 displays the volatility of one-year, two-year and three-year ahead forward interest rates between January 2017 and October 2018. If long-run inflation expectations were well-anchored, then we expect forward interest rates to be stable over time. The graph shows that the volatility of far-ahead forward interest rates increased significantly in 2018 along with the deprecation of Turkish lira and significant increase in the inflation rate. This pattern suggests that inflation expectations are not well-anchored in Turkey in the sample period.

In order to investigate how monetary policy decisions affected long-run inflation expectations in the sample period, we estimate the responses of far-ahead forward interest rates to monetary policy surprises in Turkey between 2013 and 2018. If long-run inflation expectations were well-anchored, then we expect

3 Most of the policy decisions of the CBRT were expansionary in the sample period.

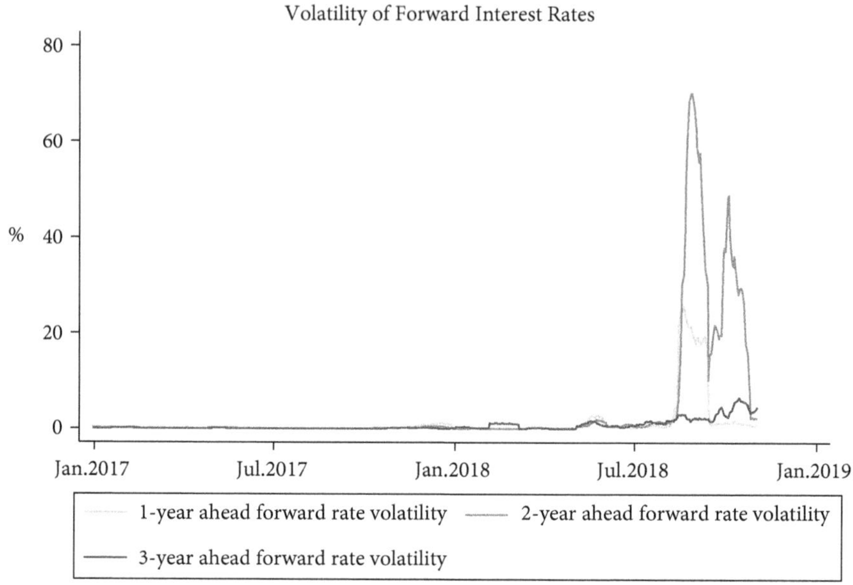

Fig. 10: Volatility of Forward Interest Rates

forward interest rates not to respond to monetary policy shocks. We estimate the following OLS equation:

$$\Delta f_{ikt} = \alpha + \beta S_t + \varepsilon_t$$

where S_t is the monetary policy surprise at time t, Δf_{ikt} is the daily change in the i year ahead k year forward interest rate at time t.

The regression results are presented in Tab. 2. The results show that the responses of three-year ahead two-year, two-year ahead three-year and five-year ahead five-year forward interest rates to monetary policy shocks were negative and significant at 95 % confidence level. Far-ahead forward interest rates moved in the opposite direction with the monetary policy stance. This finding suggests that expansionary policy decisions of the CBRT were not consistent with the long-term inflation target in the sample period and raised concerns about the future inflation rate which, in turn, increased the expected interest rates. We conclude that inflation expectations were not well-anchored in the sample period.

This finding is in line with Karaman and Yıldırım-Karaman (2017) and Demiralp et al. (2012). Karaman and Yıldırım-Karaman (2017) present a counter-factual estimation for the inflation rate and economic growth for the

Tab. 2: Responses of Far-Ahead Forward Interest Rates to Monetary Policy Shocks Between January 2013 and November 2018

	Change in the one-year ahead one-year forward interest rate	**Change in the two-year ahead one-year forward interest rate**	**Change in the three-year ahead two-year forward interest rate**	**Change in the two-year ahead three-year forward interest rate**	**Change in the five-year ahead five-year forward interest rate**
Constant term	0.013	−0.006	−0.005	−0.005	0.01
	(0.02)	(0.03)	(0.013)	(0.010)	(0.008)
Monetary Policy Surprise	−0.82	−1.37	−1.29**	−1.32**	−0.69*
	(1.02)	(1.39)	(0.655)	(0.52)	(0.40)

(Standard deviations are in parenthesis)

period after the global financial crisis. They show that inflation rate would have been three percentage points lower and economic growth rate would have been the same had the CBRT continued to implement strict inflation-targeting policy after 2010. Demiralp et al. (2012) show that the response of long-term yields to the communication of the CBRT was stronger before 2010 which suggests that the CBRT could manage the expectations before 2010 whereas it could not do so after 2010. In this study, we cannot compare these two periods because the data for daily bond returns is not available for the period before 2010. Nevertheless, our results imply that quitting strict inflation targeting hurt the credibility of the CBRT and weakened the management of long-term inflation expectations.

In a broader sense, our results are consistent with the argument that if central banks focus on objectives other than the inflation rate, it has negative consequences for economic performance. In this vein, Issing (2004) argues that sustaining long-term growth is possible if only the inflation rate is kept at low levels. Orphanides (2013) states that if central banks focus on multiple objectives, monetary policy will be overburdened. Davig and Gürkaynak (2015) build a model that shows that focusing mandates other than price level causes welfare losses in the economy because there are other policy makers in the economy with more appropriate policy tools for cyclical issues.

5 Conclusion

This chapter investigates whether the inflation expectations are well-anchored in Turkey after the recovery from the global financial crisis using high-frequency data and event study approach. What was peculiar about this period is that the CBRT adopted multiple policy objectives such as maintaining financial stability and stabilizing the price level. The results show that expansionary policy decisions in the sample period caused an increase in the long-term bond returns and far-ahead forward interest rates. This finding suggests that monetary policy decisions generated uncertainty about the future price level and inflation expectations were not well-anchored in the sample period.

In the broader context, our findings relate to the debates in the literature on the impact of inflation targeting on the anchoring of long-run inflation expectations. In this debate, the empirical evidence we find supports that adopting multiple objectives weakens the central banks' management of expectations and strict inflation targeting helps anchoring of inflation expectations.

References

Acemoglu, D. & Ucer, M. (2015). "The Ups and Downs of Turkish Growth, 2002–2015: Political Dynamics, the European Union and the Institutional Slide", *National Bureau of Economic Research*, No. w21608.

Akçelik, Y., Başçı, E., Ermişoğlu, E. & Oduncu, A. (2013). The Turkish Approach to Capital Flow Volatility. *CBRT Working Paper*, No. 13/06.

Akkaya, Y., & Gurkaynak, R. (2012). "Cari açık, bütçe dengesi, finansal istikrar ve para politikası: Heyecanlı bir dönemin izi", *İktisat İşletme ve Finans*, 27(315), 93–119.

Aktaş, Z., Alp, H., Gürkaynak, R., Kesriyeli, M. and Orak, M. (2009). "Türkiye'de Para Politikasının Aktarımı: Para Politikasının Mali Piyasalara Etkisi" İktisat İşletme ve Finans 24(278), 9–24.

Bernanke, B. S., & Mishkin, F. S. (1997). Inflation Targeting: A New Framework for Monetary Policy? *Journal of Economic perspectives*, 11(2), 97–116.

Bernanke, B. S., Laubach, T., Mishkin, F. S., & Posen, A. S. (1999). *Inflation Targeting*. Princeton: Princeton University Press.

Cicek, S., & Akar, C. (2014). Do Inflation Expectations Converge Toward Inflation Target or Actual Inflation? Evidence from Expectation Gap Persistence. *Central Bank Review*, 14(1), 15–21.

Davig, T., & Gürkaynak, R. S. (2015). "Is Optimal Monetary Policy Always Optimal?", *International Journal of Central Banking*, 11, 353–384.

Demiralp, S., Kara, H., & Özlü, P. (2012). Monetary Policy Communication in Turkey. *European Journal of Political Economy*, *28*(4), 540–556.

Duran, M., Özcan, G., Özlü, P., & Ünalmış, D. (2012). Measuring the Impact of Monetary Policy on Asset Prices in Turkey. *Economics Letters*, 114(1), 29–31.

Ehrmann, M., Fratzscher, M., Gürkaynak, R. S., & Swanson, E. T. (2011). Convergence and Anchoring of Yield Curves in the Euro Area. *The Review of Economics and Statistics*, 93(1), 350–364.

Eroglu, B., & Yildirim-Karaman, S. (2017). Responses of Term Structure of Interest Rates and Asset Prices to Monetary Policy Shocks: Evidence from Turkey. *METU Studies in Development*.

Gürkaynak, R. S., Levin, A., & Swanson, E. (2010). Does Inflation Targeting Anchor Long-run Inflation Expectations? Evidence from the US, UK and Sweden. *Journal of the European Economic Association*, 8(6), 1208–1242.

Gürkaynak, R. S., Kantur, Z., Taş, M. A., & Yıldırım-Karaman, S. (2015). Monetary Policy in Turkey after Central Bank Independence. *Iktisat Isletme ve Finans*, 30(356), 9–38.

Gurkaynak, R. S., Levin, A. T., Marder, A. N., & Swanson, E. T. (2007). Inflation Targeting and the Anchoring of Inflation Expectations in the Western Hemisphere. *Economic Review-Federal Reserve Bank of San Francisco*, 2007, 25.

Issing, O. (2004). "Inflation Targeting: A View from the ECB", *Federal Reserve Bank of St. Louis Review*, 86(4), 169–179.

Johnson, D. R. (2002). The Effect of Inflation Targeting on the Behavior of Expected Inflation: Evidence from an 11 Country Panel. *Journal of Monetary Economics*, *49*(8), 1521–1538.

Kara, A. H. (2013). Monetary Policy after the Global Crisis. *Atlantic Economic Journal*, 41(1), 51–74.

Karaman, K. K., & Yıldırım-Karaman, S. (2017). The Monetary Policy Change in Turkey in 2009 and Its Implications for Inflation and Growth. *Bogazici Journal, Review of Social, Economic and Administrative Studies*, 31(1), 1–21.

Levin, A. T., Natalucci, F. N., & Piger, J. M. (2004). "The Macroeconomic Effects of Inflation Targeting", *Federal Reserve Bank of St. Louis Review*, July–August, pp. 51–80.

Orphanides, A. (2013). "Is Monetary Policy Overburdened?", *BIS Papers*, No. 435.

Svensson, L. E. (1997). Inflation Forecast Targeting: Implementing and Monitoring Inflation Targets. *European Economic Review*, 41(6), 1111–1146.

Svensson, Lars E. O., & Michael Woodford. (2003). "Implementing Optimal Policy Through Inflation-Forecast Targeting". In: *The Inflation Targeting Debate*, Ben S. Bernanke and Michael Woodford, eds. Chicago: University of Chicago Press.

M. Celalettin Baykul and Hakan Acaroğlu

Flat-Plate Solar Collectors

An Economic Inquiry about Flat-Plate Solar Collectors (FPSCs) for Turkey: A Case Study for a Mid-Size Anatolian City, Eskisehir

Abstract: Solar energy systems supply energy saving according to conventional systems by considering ecological balance. In this chapter, we focus on one of the most frequently used solar energy systems: Flat-Plate Solar Collectors (FPSCs). The main function of FPSCs is turning solar energy into heat energy. Hot water is supplied by absorbing solar energy on collectors in FPSCs. We propose manufacturing this device with domestic possibilities and consuming energy with national and natural resources. In line with this proposal, Eskisehir and Turkey have convenient potential for utilizing solar energy. It is known that the most accepted expenditure in a Turkish household's energy consumption was found to be heating and Turkish households preferred natural gas with higher ratios against solar energy. This ratio can be gradually changed in favor of solar energy usage by preferring solar energy utilization in Turkey in the near future.In this chapter, the regional economical analysis of solar systems is made considering Eskisehir. After introducing the device technically, the need for the device will be discussed and the barriers will be explained for the region. At the end, not only the consumers and the producers will have an investment decision idea, but also the government will have an encouragement policy for the society about these devices.

Keywords: solar energy, FPSCs, economic policy, Eskisehir, Turkey

Jell classification: D240, J380, O210

1 Introduction

Renewable energy sources can be an alternative solution for Turkey about providing her energy demands. Solar energy is one of the candidates for both production and utilization of this energy demand which has an environmentally friendly feature. As being a developing country that is targeting to be a developed country, Turkey should apply to use more of this clean alternative. We know that the annual average total insolation is 2,623 hours (≈7.2 h/day) and the average annual solar radiation is 1,303 kWh/m^2 per year (≈3.6k Wh/m^2 day) in Turkey which corresponds to a potential of 304,707 million kWh, annually. The data about solar energy potential of Turkey is shown in Tab. 1 which shows the

Tab. 1: Sunshine hours and solar radiation in the regions of Turkey. Source: Çapık et al. (2012)

Region	Sunshine hours (h/d)	Solar radiation (cal/cm²d)
Southeast Anatolia	8.2	344.8
Mediterranean	8.1	328.3
East Anatolia	7.3	322.4
Central Anatolia	7.2	310.3
Aegean	7.5	308.0
Marmara	6.6	275.9
Black Sea	5.4	264.5
Average	7.2	309.6

Tab. 2: Monthly average solar potential of Turkey. Source: Demirbas & Bakıs (2004), Çapık et al. (2012)

Months	Solar energy kcal/cm²-month	Solar energy kWh/m²-month	Sunshine-period h/month
January	4.45	51.75	103
February	5.44	63.27	115
March	8.31	96.65	165
April	10.51	122.23	197
May	13.23	153.86	273
June	14.51	168.75	325
July	15.08	175.38	365
August	13.62	158.40	343
September	10.60	123.28	280
October	7.73	89.90	214
November	5.23	60.82	157
December	4.03	46.87	103
Total	112.74	1311	2640
Average	308 cal/cm²-d	3.6kWh/m²-d	7.2 h/d

sunshine period and solar radiation in regions of Turkey and Tab. 2 shows the monthly average solar potential of Turkey.

Besides, Turkey's total primary energy supply (TPES) was equivalent to around 124 million tons of oil (MTOE) in 2014. While natural gas, coal, oil and Renewable Energy Sources (RES) had a share of 32 %, 29 %, 28 % and 10 % of this total, respectively. The domestic production of this TPES had around 25 %

with around 31 MTOE in the same year. The fact is that Turkey is faced with difficulties in meeting its energy demands through domestic needs. The estimated total primary energy demand (TPED) will be around 218 MTOE in 2023 (MENR, 2013–2014; Ozcan, 2018).

Since Turkey has a solar energy potential, it can solve the increased energy deficits by obtaining heat energy from solar energy. This can be achieved, first of all, by developing national and regional plans about RES. Solar energy usage strategy is one of these plans. By producing solar energy systems with domestic resources, in particular, obtaining heat from solar insolation through a recycling action can be given as an example for this strategy. In line with this strategy, Republic of Turkey Ministry of Energy and Natural Resource (RTMENR) agreed on a "supply security" and "energy efficiency and saving" policy on the side of energy in the strategical plan of 2015–2019 (RTMENR, 2017). The plan objects to agree on some strategic targets for reaching a well-designed energy policy under some new concepts such as reliability, sustainability, environment-friendly and affordability by 2023 (Ervural et al., 2018).

According to UCTEA (2012), Turkey's foreign energy dependency has increased for the reason of the government's privatization policies, which reduces the effectiveness of public uses and leads to higher energy prices. The Turkish Government has an aim of decreasing the share of natural gas in the electricity generation sector, firstly replacing it with domestically produced renewable energy and then with the other energy resources (Austvik & Gülmira, 2017). The Turkish Government can change the low share of renewable energy in total energy utilization by (1) creating economic activities for the energy needs and make use of Turkey's geopolitical location (to create an energy corridor between Europe and Asia), (2) mitigating environmental problems, protecting environment and public health, and (3) reducing the energy dependency and current account imbalances (Çapık et al., 2012), (Bulut & Muratoglu, 2018).

An FPSC is a relatively well-known solar thermal technology in Turkey. Solar radiation is converted to heat and transmitted through a transfer such as water. FPSCs are often applicable for the replacement of fossil fuels and utilized for water heating. However, there exist definite technological, economic, political and social barriers in developing countries related to FPSCs (Sovacool et al., 2011). Although FPSCs have some costs such as installation, annual maintenance and repairs, these solar energy systems generate many ecological benefits that surpass indicated costs after their installation. These benefits contain long-term fuel savings and exemptions from tax fees for the energy generated that also benefits the region and the nation.

There are various studies related to renewable energy and solar energy systems and the suitable policies that may be applied in Turkey. These studies are Baris and Kucukali (2012), Çapık et al. (2012), Simsek and Simsek (2013), Toklu (2013), Kilickaplan et al. (2017), Benli (2016), Bulut and Muratoglu (2018), Ediger et al. (2018), Ervural et al. (2018), Ozcan (2018). But this study basically conducts an economic inquiry about a technological device: FPSC, in a mid-size Anatolian city, Eskisehir. The purpose of the study is to suggest an alternative key for the energy requirement by using solar energy and converting it to heat and by concentrating on the city of Eskisehir and extending this to the entire country.

2 FPSC Device and Its Utilization in Economics

2.1 Technical Characteristics of FPSC Device

The most popular collector for hot water is the FPSC in Turkey, which has a rectangular box with a cover, can be installed on a building's roof as it is seen from Fig. 1 which is installed on a house's roof. A typical FPSC contains two collectors which have totally 4–6 m^2 surface area and a 160–200 liter capacity water storage tank. Such an FPSC system's cost is approximately $1,000, which is accounted for by the installer's overheads and marketing costs (Benli, 2016).

Technically, an FPSC system consists of a flat-plate collector, a hot water storage tank, and connection pipes between the collector and the storage tank, as the pictures can be found in Acaroğlu and Baykul (2016). An FPSC consists of a cover system, an absorber system, insulation, a working fluid, and the structure needed to hold the various components in the appropriate positions. A cover system generally includes two layers of glass, which reduces the loss of heat

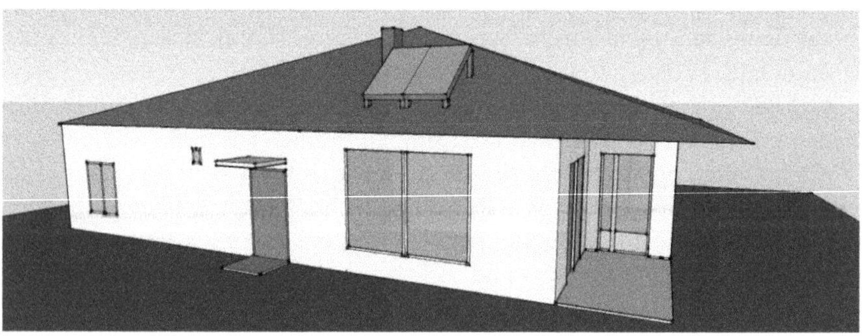

Fig. 1: An FPSC installed on a house's roof. Source: The figure is drawn originally with Autocad software by its authors.

from the absorber. The cover transmits sunlight, and the FPSC serves to capture the incident solar energy. An absorber is a flat black plate, and metal tubes are connected to this plate. The captured incident solar energy is turned into heat in the absorber. This heat is firstly transferred to the tubes by heat conduction, and after that it is transferred into the water by the tubes by heat convection. Since the density of hot water is less than the density of cold water, this difference makes the natural convection possible. After adequate circulation is achieved, the hot water can be stored in the storage tank. If this circulation is made with the use of a water pump, the circulation is called forced convection (Acaroğlu & Baykul, 2016).

2.2 The Domestic Production of FPSCs in Eskisehir

FPSCs can be utilized effectively in Eskisehir eight months/year because of its geographical alternatives: Eskisehir is positioned to collect enough solar insolation and it is characterized by low levels of moisture. The building design in Eskisehir should be established in accordance with the solar energy potential of Eskisehir. So the domestic production of FPSCs in Eskisehir would be a rational decision for producers. Besides, consumers demand could be encouraged by this production. Fig. 2 and Tab. 3 show Eskisehir's solar energy potential map and total solar radiation levels of each districts. In addition to this, Fig. 3 shows Eskisehir's global radiation values and Fig. 4 shows Eskisehir's sunshine hours bi-monthly. The researchers found that the most convenient district for setting

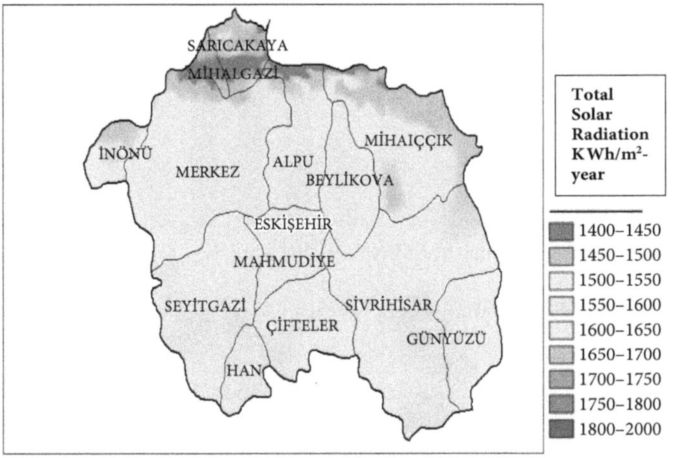

Fig. 2: Solar energy potential map and total solar radiation level of Eskisehir by KWh/m^2-year. Source: General Directorate of Renewable Energy (GDRE-a)

Tab. 3: Sunshine hours of Eskisehir's districts in 2016 (hours/year). Source: Esgazete (2017)

Districts	**hours/year**
Alpu	2454 hours
Beylikova	2506 hours
Çifteler	2553 hours
Günyüzü	2640 hours
Han	2540 hours
İnönü	2454 hours
Merkez	2357 hours
Mihalgazi	2374 hours
Mihalıççık	2502 hours
Sarıcakaya	2391 hours
Seyitgazi	2376 hours
Sivrihisar	2594 hours
Mahmudiye	2499 hours

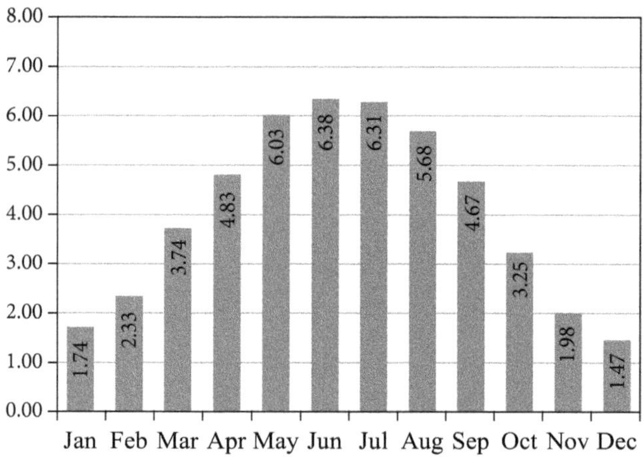

Fig. 3: Eskisehir's global radiation values (KWh/m^2-day). Source: GDRE-a

up a solar energy system in Eskisehir was Sivrihisar. Günyüzü took the second place, Çifteler took the third place and Mahmudiye took the forth place (Esgazete, 2017). The same research points out that Turkey has the highest potential for renewable energy sources in the world. There are facilities in Turkey; however, the applications are not enough and they are not made judiciously.

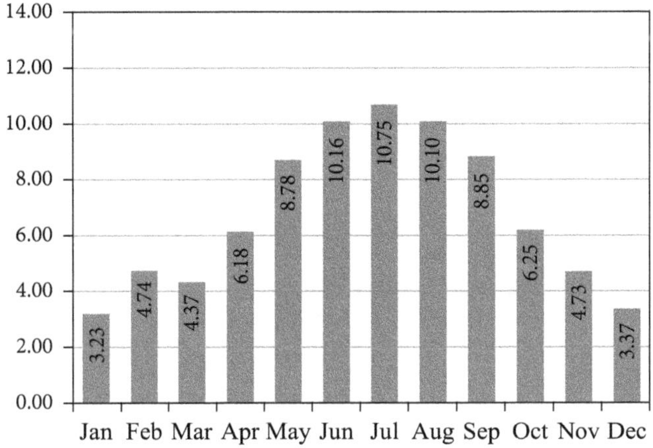

Fig. 4: Eskisehir's sunshine hours (h). Source: GDRE-a

2.3 Economics of FPSC Production

If one wants to set up an FPSC manufacturing firm, he or she needs to conduct an economic production function. This function has to include independent variables such as labor, capital and technological progress (this variable can be taken as exogenous and can be assumed as stable for short term) and a dependent variable such as output (the number of manufactured FPSCs). After the necessary assumptions according to the conditions of the location and economic constraints, the relationship between the production and the cost can be set up. A profit function can be written in this concept. The maximization conditions for the labor and the capital variables can be set up and after that the total revenue can be calculated in the condition of profit maximization (i.e., by calculating the marginal productivity of the labor and the marginal productivity of the capital and equating both of them to "zero" for the maximization condition). The detailed information about this phenomenon can be found in the study of Acaroğlu and Baykul (2016).

3 The Current and Near Future of FPSCs Market in Eskisehir, Turkey and in the World

3.1 The Current Status of the FPSC Device and Its Market in the World

Globally speaking, 35 GW_{th} of capacity of glazed (flat plate and vacuum tube technology) and unglazed collectors were recently installed in 2017, carrying

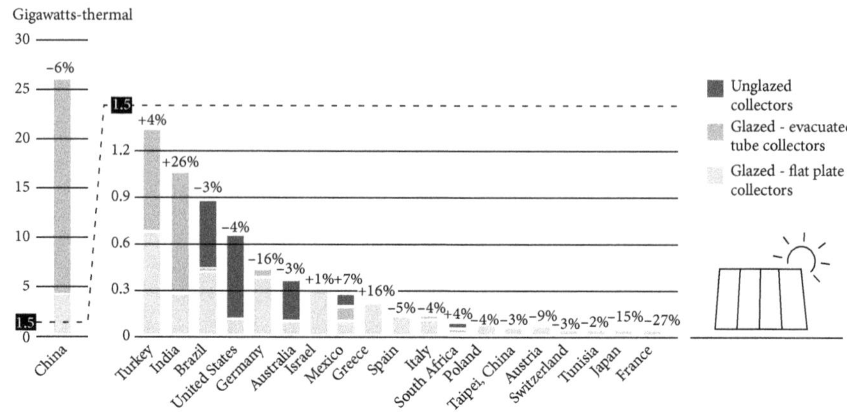

Fig. 5: Solar water heating collectors for top 20 countries for added capacity, 2017. Source: Ren21, Global Status Report (2018)

the total capacity to an estimated 472 GW_{th} by the end of 2017. Fig. 5 shows that the six leading countries for new installations in 2017 were China, Turkey, India, Brazil, the United States and Germany. The top 20 countries for solar thermal installations (both glazed and unglazed collectors) corresponded for 93 % of the whole global market in 2017.

In most of the top 20 countries, FPSCs dominated the market. Considering all new installations in the top 20 markets, FPSCs accounted for 23 % (up from 21 % in 2016). China was the world's largest solar thermal market without a doubt. As we understand from Fig. 5, new collector installations in 2017 totaled 26.1 GW_{th} (37.26 million m^2) in China, 19 times greater than the total additions in the second largest market, Turkey. The capital cost and energy price, architectural type of buildings and household composition are the important factors in the widening of the market for FPSCs (Chang et al., 2009).

3.2 The Current Status of FPSC Device and Its Market in Eskisehir and in Turkey

Turkey was the second largest market for new installations, adding 1.35 GW_{th} (1.93 million m^2) in 2017, up 4 % over 2016. Solar water heater sales remained high, even without direct investment subsidies, as a result of a strong construction market. Nearly 60 % of new solar thermal capacity was installed in new buildings, mainly in the south and west of the country. This was accelerated by Turkey's urban transformation program, which encompasses replacing multi-family houses in urban areas with new earthquake-resistant high-rise buildings.

Tab. 4: Installation trends of solar water heathers (FPSC and Vacuum) over the years in Turkey. Source: Benli (2016)

	1990	1995	2000	2005	2010	2012
FPSC (m^2)	$1.5*10^6$	$2.8*10^6$	$3.99*10^6$	$4.99*10^6$	$7.39*10^6$	13,685,943
Vacuum (m^2)	-	-	150	4000	110,000	1,811,970
					Total =	15,479,913 m^2

The fact is that, as it can also be understood from Tab. 4, vacuum tube collectors gained a market share in Turkey's colder regions, like middle and eastern Anatolia, corresponded to half of the country's additions in 2017. Natural circulation systems dominated Turkey's residential market, while on the contrary, forced circulation systems made up the majority of commercial installations in hospitals, hotels, military bases and stadiums [Ren21, 2018].

The FPSCs with metal absorbers and glass cover are widely used in Turkey as it is understood from Tab. 4. Another point of view from Tab. 4 is that the market share was around 99 % in 2005. The annually installation seemed to reach the saturation point in 2010, but the market share started to decline (Benli, 2016).

3.3 Renewable Energy Support Policies for Turkey

Turkey is an emerging economy, and its energy demand is growing with its young population. It has a remarkable potential in renewable energy sources. However, the utilization of these sources depends not only on the economic factors but also the environmental impacts and barriers. Turkey is importing its energy needs. In other words, it has an energy dependency on other countries. On the other hand, there have been an increasing consciousness in the last decade in Turkey about renewable energy sources on environment after the introduction of many power plants in the country, especially after the enactment of the Renewable Energy Law (Law No. 5346), since it promotes the utilization of renewable energy sources (Baris & Kucukali, 2012). Renewable energy (especially the solar energy) can be a solution for preventing this dependency, because renewable energy is both environmentally friendly and has an economical sustainability. Turkey's geographical location is convenient for producing renewable energy (i.e., solar energy). This can be understood from the solar energy potential map of Turkey that is given in Fig. 6. As a result of this potential, a policy priority should be given on developing and implementing renewable energy and its technologies. In this manner, energy conversation and efficiency policies are also very crucial. In this concept, there needs to be a collaboration and a consensus

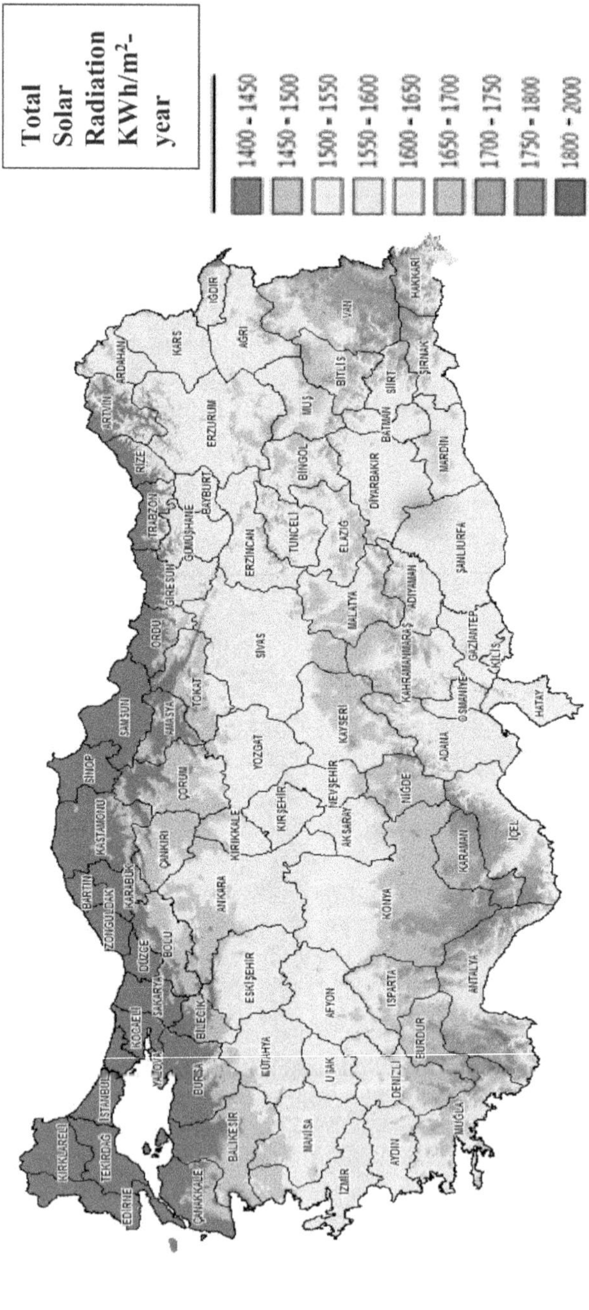

Fig. 6: Solar energy potential map of Turkey. Source: GDRE-b

between the government, the consumers, and the producers for decreasing the energy costs (Simsek & Simsek, 2013). Tab. 5 shows the current implemented renewable energy support policies for Turkey, in the sub-categories of "regulatory policies" and "fiscal incentives and public financing."

4 Factors Affecting the Production and Consumption of FPSCs in Eskisehir and in all of Turkey

4.1 Technical Features, Optimization Characteristics and Efficiency Calculations about FPSC (Its Investment and Utilization in Turkey)

FPSCs are devices used to produce solar thermal energy and use it for heating utilizations such as water and room heating and other industrial appliances. FPSCs are trendy for low- and medium-heating applications, and there are some improvements in terms of size reduction and enhanced efficiency (Pandey & Chaurasiya, 2017).

According to Ma et al. (2018), who made a face-to-face questionnaire survey that are selected randomly for 12 representative Chinese provinces, it was found that (1) socio-demographic variables of residents' had a significant effect on preferring FPSC in the first-stage choice (for buying or not buying); (2) information spillover had a facilitate effect on the usage of FPSCs; (3) the electricity prices had no effect on the choice of FPSCs; and (4) government subsidies had an effect for the first stage but had no effect on the decision about choosing the device for the following stage. These issues can be a guideline for Turkish Government, producers and consumers in the country. More technically, a simple example can be given for setting up a FPCS in Eskisehir as follows:

A simple example for Eskisehir:
In line with Elginkan (2009), but this time for Eskisehir, let's say we have a 160 ltr capacity boiler and 2,30 m^2 collector area. How much does this collector warm up through a day in the summer months?

(Let's consider, **q**Eskisehir-summer = 25,4 MJ/m^2 * day, collector efficiency 0,71, system efficiency 0,90, region heat 25 ^{0}C and heat of tap water 24 ^{0}C.)

qproduced = **q**Eskisehir-summer * collector efficiency * system efficiency

qproduced = 25,4 * 0,71 * 0,90 **q**produced = 16,200 MJ/m^2*day

(our 2,3 m^2 collector produces 16200 kJ energy through a day.)

mwater * cp * (Twater - Ttap) = **q**produced * collector area

(Now, we can calculate how much we can heat up our water with the collector's produced energy through a day.)

160 * 4,18 * (Twater - 24) = 16200 * 2,30

Twater = 79 ^{0}C.

Tab. 5: Renewable energy support policies for Turkey. Source: Ren21, Global Status Report (2018)

	Regulatory Policies							**Fiscal Incentives and Public Financing**			
Country	**Feed-in tariff/ premium payment**	**Electric utility/ quota obligation/ RPS**	**Net metering/ billing**	**Transport obligation/ mandate**	**Heat obligation/ mandate**	**Tradable REC**	**Tendering**	**Investment or production tax credits**	**Reductions in sales, energy, CO2, VAT, or other taxes**	**Energy production payment**	**Public investment, loans, grants, capital subsidies or rebates**
Turkey	·			·			**O**	**O**			·

Note: Renewable energy targets (P), Renewable energy in INDC or NDC (·) P: Power, **O**: National tender held in 2017: Existing national policy or tender framework(could include sub-national) INDC: Intended nationally determined contribution NDC: Nationally determined contribution

Our FPSC on the roof heat up our water 55 C^0. If we heated up with electricity, we would consume 8,2 kWh of electricity and our cost would be (1kWh electricity's price is 0,46 TL) 3.77 TL. During summer season, 3.77 TL would stay in our pocket and we would also have an environmentally friendly system. In general, these systems have 3–4 years pay-back periods.

4.2 A Reasonable Scenario for Eskisehir and a Practical Vision for Turkey

There are about 100,000 residences in Eskisehir. We can make an approximation that the FPSCs that are needed in Eskisehir can be around 200,000. If an FPSC's cost is between €300 and €700 (let's assume €500 and €1 = 6 TL), the set-up cost would be 3,000TL. Therefore, 600,000,000 TL of revenue will be needed to install FPSCs for the hot water demand in Eskisehir.

According to Acaroğlu and Baykul (2016), a firm that produces FPSCs could produce 30 collectors per day in an optimal case. If this condition is satisfied, then 10,950 collectors would be manufactured per year in Eskisehir. If we add the periodic maintenance and repair costs that would be incurred automatically. We will be faced with 1,100,000 TL (the maintenance and repair cost are assumed to be 100 TL for one collector) revenue at the end of one year. Each year, the same 1,100,000 TL would be added to the following year. After the end of the 30-year lifespan of an FPSCs firm, 33,000,000 TL of income would have been obtained.

5 Conclusion

This chapter makes an economic inquiry about a technological device: FPSC, in a mid-size Anatolian city, Eskisehir. The aim of the study is to offer an alternative solution for the energy need by using solar energy and converting it to heat and by focusing on the city of Eskisehir and applying this in the whole country.

With its young and increasing population rates, the energy needs of Turkey increase day by day. A reasonable solution to that problem seems to be to produce the energy needed individually or not importing totally from other countries. To increase the use of renewable energy sources with solar energy and FPSCs and to produce FPSCs within the sources of private sector would open the way for Turkey. However, Turkey should be careful on adjusting the market conditions. Both the producers and consumers should be cared for by government regulations. Competitiveness in the energy markets should be increased but the infant firms need to be supported. Patent numbers on new technological developments should be awarded and scientists should be encouraged.

Using solar energy and producing the necessary devices with domestic resources will also help solve the unemployment problem in the cities and in the country at the end. Since FPSCs are technological devices, the employed workers in this field would automatically be qualified. Thus, the quality level of the labor force increases and Turkey will become a country such that has an efficient labor force in the long term. Expansion of producing and consuming FPSCs throughout the country could be a rational target in the following years for Turkey. If this can be achieved, the development would be possible. Not only the development but also security problems would be solved in a certain amount by decreasing the energy dependency from foreign countries. Besides, conventional fossil fuels have the effect of carbon dioxide (CO_2) emissions that can have a potential impact for climate change. Solar energy does not give any harm to environment as mentioned above. The residents of Eskisehir would have an opportunity to find both high-quality employment alternatives and the positive externalities that accompany by beating the problems of negative environmental externalities caused by the consumption of conventional energy by utilizing FPSCs.

Saving energy seems possible by setting up an effective insulation for residences. Because the energy need for residents mostly stems from heating purposes. The wide use of FPSCs in residences in line with a redesign of architecture will be a good strategy for reducing the energy deficit in the country. For instance, provinces could plan so that they supply their energy need individually, and consume it efficiently. Geometrically, if buildings would be designed to benefit from solar energy by using FPSCs at the most convenient angle, this will be a practical approach in energy saving. Besides, fossil fuels are giving harm to the environment. Pollution of soil, pollution of the air, and pollution of the water are the expected side effects.

The Turkish Government should be careful on this issue and should redesign the related tax and subsidization policies in the domestic energy markets. For instance, the tax ratios could be decreased on producing and consuming FPSCs and necessary subsidization for producers and consumers could be rearranged. Specifically, buildings which prefer to set up these devices could be exempt from property taxes or environmental taxes. For the last words, if the consumption and production of these devices could be increased in Turkey, this will help the country to solve its energy problems without damaging the environment. So society and government should be in consensus and they should also be conscious of this subject.

References

Acaroğlu, H. and Baykul, M. C. 2016. Economic analysis of flat-plate solar collectors (FPSCs): A solution to the unemployment problem in the city of Eskisehir. *Renew Sustain Energy Rev* 64, 607–617.

Austvik, O. G. and Gülmira, R. 2017. Turkey in the geopolitics of energy. *Energy Policy* 107, 539–547.

Baris, K. and Kucukali, S. 2012. Availability of renewable energy sources in Turkey: Current situation, potential, government policies and the EU perspective. *Energy Policy* 42, 377–391.

Benli, H. 2016. Potential application of solar water heaters for hot water production in Turkey *Renewable and Sustainable Energy Reviews* 54, 99–109.

Bulut, U. and Muratoglu, G. 2018. Renewable energy in Turkey: Great potential, low but increasing utilization, and an empirical analysis on renewable energy-growth nexus. *Energy Policy* 123, 240–250.

Çapik, M., Yılmaz, A. O., and Çavuşoğlu, I. 2012. Present situation and potential role of renewable energy in Turkey. *Renewable Energy* 46, 1–13.

Chang, K. C., Lin, W. M., Lee, T. S., and Chung, K. M. 2009. Local market of solar water heaters in Taiwan: Review and perspectives. *Renewable and Sustainable Energy Reviews* 13, 2605–2612.

Demirbas, A. and Bakıs, R. 2004. Energy from renewable sources in Turkey: status and future direction. *Energy Sources* 26, 473–484.

Ediger, V. Ş., Kirkil, G., Çelebi, E., Ucal, M., Kentmen-Çin, Ç. 2018. Turkish public preferences for energy. *Energy Policy* 120, 492–502.

Elginkan. 2009. E.C.A Güneş Enerjisi Sistemleri. Link: http://www.elginkan.com.tr/assets/media/mediaFile_52f889fc17d27.pdf (Accessed on: November 25, 2018).

Ervural, B. C., Zaim, S., Demirel, O. F., Aydin, Z., Delen, D. 2018. An ANP and fuzzy TOPSIS-based SWOT analysis for Turkey's energy Planning. *Renewable and Sustainable Energy Reviews* 82, 1538–1550.

Esgazete (2017). Link: https://www.esgazete.com/roportaj/iste-eskisehir-in-uygun-gunes-enerji-santrali-kurulum-yeri-haritasi-h121213.html (Accessed on: November 25, 2018).

Kilickaplan, A., Bogdanov, D., Peker, O., Caldera, U., Aghahosseini, Arman, Breyer, C. 2017. An energy transition pathway for Turkey to achieve 100 % renewable energy powered electricity, desalination and non-energetic industrial gas demand sectors by 2050. *Solar Energy* 158, 218–235.

Ma, B., Yu, Y., and Urban, F. 2018. Green transition of energy systems in rural China: National survey evidence of households' discrete choices on water heaters. *Energy Policy* 113, 559–570.

MENR (Republic of Turkey Ministry of Energy and Natural Resources). 2014. National renewable energy action plan for Turkey.

MENR (Republic of Turkey Ministry of Energy and Natural Resources). 2013. MENR budget presentation of the year 2014 to the Grand National Assembly of Turkey.

Ozcan, M. 2018. The role of renewables in increasing Turkey's self-sufficiency in electrical Energy. *Renewable and Sustainable Energy Reviews* 82, 2629–2639.

Pandey, K.M. and Chaurasiya, R. 2017. A review on analysis and development of solar flat plate collector. *Renewable and Sustainable Energy Reviews* 67, 641–650.

Republic of Turkey Ministry of Energy and Natural Resources. General Directorate of Renewable Energy (GDRE-a). Link: http://www.yegm.gov.tr/MyCalculator/pages/26.aspx (Accessed on: October 18, 2018).

Republic of Turkey Ministry of Energy and Natural Resources. General Directorate of Renewable Energy (GDRE-b). Link: http://www.yegm.gov.tr/MyCalculator/Default.aspx (Accessed on: October 18, 2018).

Republic of Turkey Ministry of Energy and Natural Resources (RTMENR). 2017. 2015–2019 Strategical Plan. Link: https://sp.enerji.gov.tr/sp-2015-2019.html (Accessed on: October 18, 2018).

REN21. 2018. Renewables 2018 Global Status Report.

Simsek, H. A. and Simsek, N. 2013. Recent incentives for renewable energy in Turkey. *Energy Policy* 63, 521–530.

Sovacool, B. K. and D'Agostino, A. L. et al. 2011. The socio-technical barriers to solar home systems (SHS) in Papua New Guinea: "Choosing pigs, prostitutes, and poker chips over panels". *Energy Policy* 39, 1532–1542.

Toklu, E. 2013. Overview of potential and utilization of renewable energy sources in Turkey. *Renewable Energy* 50, 456–463.

UCTEA (Union of Chambers of Turkish Engineers and Architects). 2012. Türkiye'nin Enerji Görünümü. Oda Raporu, MMO/588, Genişletilmiş İkinci Baskı. Link: http://www.mmo.org.tr/resimler/dosya_ekler/dd924b618b4d692_ek.pdf). (Accessed on: October 18, 2018).

Pınar Deniz and Erhan Aslanoğlu

Determinants of Interest Rates

Decomposing the Determinants of Interest Rates under Inflation Targeting

Abstract: This chapter investigates the monetary policy rule of the Central Bank of the Republic of Turkey under a structural VAR (vector autoregression) model, structurally decomposes the variations of the determinants of the monetary policy, and compares the findings with a set of inflation-targeting emerging market economies. Structural VAR methodology is used for time series analysis for Turkey whereas GMM (generalized method of moments) based panel VAR is employed for the panel of eight emerging countries. Empirical findings suggest the dominance of inflation rate in the long-term model whereas inflation rate loses its priority in the short-term model for Turkey. A group of emerging countries are observed to keep inflation as priority in the short-term model contrary to the findings for Turkey.

Keywords: inflation targeting, emerging market economies, structural VAR, variance decomposition

Jel: C32, E52, E58

1 Introduction

One of the main challenges inside macroeconomic topics is that governments often contradict with central banks since the objective of most central banks worldwide is to maintain price stability whereas it is mainly achieving high-growth rate and low-unemployment levels for the government. The disharmony between fiscal and monetary policy is so crucial that there have been several theories available. High public expenditure is justified and even advised during stagnant periods which takes place under a school of thought referred as Keynesian policies. On the other hand, it is criticized when the government applies populist policies especially during election periods since the redundant expenditures may lead to inflation, rise in government bond rates in the case of deficit and harm the long-term objectives in return for short-term gains. Even more exaggerated version for public finance is the seigniorage since it provides a walk-through for excessive expenditures which is also criticized to bring about inflation. At this point, *central bank independence* comes as a crucial term in here. Fiscal and monetary policies should be coherent so as to prevent disadvantages of one's dominance over the other one. As always, there are optimal positions which are under the responsibilities of researchers and policy-makers to evaluate and decide. Taking into account the fact that maintaining price stability is open to many outside shocks and its importance is not well understood since it is not very visible, an effective communication with public through announcements of "drawbacks of overexpansionist policies" may help central banks resist such pressures coming from the government side. Another important way to enable monetary discipline and prudence is inflation targeting.

Inflation targeting (IT) policy is adopted by many countries after its first implementation by New Zealand (1990) as the gains are observed through time. Bernanke and Mishkin (1997) explain that IT is characterized as follows: (i) an announcement of a target for inflation, (ii) an increase in the communication with the public so as to share the policy objective, (iii) generally an improvement in the credibility of the central bank. Even if the economic benefits of IT are significant, unwillingness to adopt the policy can be explained under two cases: (i) transition to inflation-targeting policy requires some preparations in the form of improvements in the fiscal performance, financial system, credibility in the institutions, and so on, and that the economy is not well-prepared to adopt IT policy (ii) IT places inflation at the heart of monetary policies hampering direct interventions to the economic circumstances that contradicts IT.

A full and strict commitment to IT policy is simply placing inflation as the primary monetary policy and leaving all other indicators as subsidiary not only in the long run but also in the short run. However, practically, central banks do not implement such strict commitments and allows for missing target level in short horizons when economic conditions require other variables to be of primary concern. In fact, some supply side shocks, such as oil price shock, may lead to very costly results in the output level when IT policy is implemented strictly in the short or medium run. On the other hand, short-term flexibilities should never hamper long-term commitments to IT policy. There are no clear sanctions for missing target level but such a fail will destroy the credibility of central banks which highly require to stabilize the economic conditions due to domestic fragilities such as high current account deficits, lack of financial resources and hence requirement of foreign inflows which may generally be attributed to the "non-developed" world. Commitment to IT regime will help improve credibility of central banks and hence more gains can be obtained with less effort in the monetary policy. The importance of IT regime for developing economies is also highlighted in Walsh (2009). He explains that IT improves the macroeconomic performances for developing economies but the performances of IT and non-IT are relatively similar for developed economies.

The scope of this chapter is on Turkey and other emerging economies, a highly debated country group that is characterized with high-growth potential resulting, theoretically from low level of capital, and hence high-marginal productivity, that is, high returns to investment. On the other hand, these economies are generally argued to be lacking in domestic funds to realize their potential. Requirement of financial resources renders them dependent on foreign inflows. Hence, these economies are generally in a competition to attract foreign investors. On the other hand, such openness creates fragilities in the way that abrupt portfolio outflows will have destructive consequences for the domestic economies. At this point, providing and managing credibility to the financial side of the economy is highly important so as to prevent capital outflows due to risk perceptions. Inflation targeting and dedicating policies accordingly can be argued to be a direct contribution to the economics environment through lowering risk perceptions. In this chapter, monetary policy making of inflation-targeting emerging economies will be discussed to observe the proportions of the determinants via decomposing the variation in the policy rate.

There are many studies investigating the effects of IT policy for emerging economies. Mishkin (2004), focusing on two emerging countries, Brazil and Chile, argues that IT, even if it is a complicated issue for emerging economies, can be a very powerful tool to maintain macroeconomic stability, if applied properly. Lin and Ye (2009), using panel data analysis for 13 developing countries that adopt IT, observe that IT has significant impact on lowering inflation and variability in inflation rate. However, the effects are not homogeneous to each economy and that depends on country characteristics such as exchange rate movements, fiscal discipline and the willingness to meet preconditions before adopting the policy. Siregar and Goo (2008) investigate the effectiveness of IT policies adopted by two emerging economies, Indonesia and Thailand, during stable and turbulent years resulting from global economic conditions and examine the commitment to IT policy credibly. Using Markov-switching approach to examine the monetary policy rule for 1990–2008 period, they observe evidence of credible implementation of IT in both economies during stable and turbulent years. They also suggest that both economies have experienced decline in inflation rates during the post-IT period. However, using a panel data analysis for developing countries, Brito and Bystedt (2010) do not find a significant impact of IT on inflation and output growth.

Monetary policies are standardized under Taylor-rule model which formalize how central banks specify interest rate using inflation and output gap. The model can differ according to the monetary rule each central bank defines. Interest rate smoothing mechanism, that is, lagged value of interest rates, changes in exchange rates are generally used in addition to the standardized model. On the other hand, several other economic variables can be included in the monetary rule function depending on the importance central bank gives. Central banks have short-term interest rates as the monetary policy instruments. However, the real side of the economy is directly affected from the long-term interest rates, which are determined in the market through expectations regarding long run, and key interest rates only have indirect effects. The way to increase the power of the link between short-run and long-run interest rates is to increase the credibility of the central bank so that expectations are managed. There is no specific indicator to measure credibility but they can be proxied by governance/institutional variables since credibility is an institutional issue. Considering the importance of credibility for emerging market economies, it will be a more extensive analysis to include a credibility variable to understand the policy decisions of these economies. Accordingly, Mishkin (2004) argues that institutional differences of emerging markets from advanced countries, such as weak fiscal institutions, weak financial institutions including government prudential regulation and supervision, low credibility of monetary institutions, should be taken into account to derive sound theory and policy advice. Similarly, Fraga et al. (2003) explain that IT contributes both to advanced and emerging countries but it is more of a challenge for the latter one due to their volatile macroeconomic environment and weaker institutions and credibility. Hence, it is important to consider institutional factors when analyzing monetary policy of emerging economies.

The empirical literature on monetary policy rule, originating from Taylor (1993), is enormous; however, the evidence on emerging economies is scarce. Empirical findings for emerging markets have mixed results. Frömmel et al. (2011) estimate monetary policy rules for six emerging Central and Eastern European (CEE) economies and find that some CEE countries explicitly switch from defending the peg to targeting inflation while other economies do not. Aizenman and Hutchison (2011) examine the role of real exchange rate and the distinction between commodity and non-commodity exporters under a Taylor-rule model for a panel data of 16 emerging countries. They find clear evidence of a significant and stable response running from inflation to policy interest rates and that non-IT central banks place much less weight on inflation in setting interest rates. Teles and Zaidan (2010) evaluate the validity of Taylor-rule principle for inflation control for 11 emerging countries using threshold unit root test and argue that if a Central Bank wants to stabilize inflation around the target, it should closely follow a long-term more than proportional reaction rule in relation to the expected inflation deviations. Sánchez-Fung (2011) examines whether Taylor-type reaction functions are practical for understanding how monetary authorities in Brazil behave following inflation-targeting adoption and switching to a floating exchange rate regime. He finds that Brazilian Central Bank adjusts overnight interest rate (Selic) in line with the Taylor principle but it does not systematically react to exchange rate developments. Mehrotra and Sánchez-Fung (2011) estimate McCallum and Taylor monetary policy functions for 20 emerging market economies. Taylor monetary policy rule employs for inflation gap, output gap and change in nominal exchange rate, whereas McCallum model regresses monetary base on nominal income gap measure and change in nominal exchange rate. They find that the behavior of the IT economies is better captured with a hybrid McCallum–Taylor rule that regresses interest rates on nominal income gap measure and change in nominal exchange rate. Besides the empirical side of the literature, Taylor-type of monetary policy rules are used as standard formula in papers that develop economic modeling such as New Keynesian DSGE models.

The main objective of this paper is to decompose the weights of the economic fundamentals determining interest rates for Turkey and a panel of emerging economies implementing inflation-targeting policy to compare Turkey to other emerging markets. The relevant empirical technique to apply is variance decomposition after the specification of the simultaneous equation system. VAR is a frequently used technique to obtain variance decomposition. However, there are several criticisms towards VAR models as no theoretical inference is included. In other words, all variables are endogenous, that is, affecting each other. Such criticisms led to the development of structural VAR (SVAR) technique which is derived from standard VAR methodology but including theoretical restrictions to the system so as to identify the model. After the theoretical identification regarding the variables in the simultaneous equation system is determined, short-run and long-run impulse response functions, variance decompositions and historical decompositions are obtained for Turkey. For panel dataset of emerging markets, impulse response functions, variance decompositions are obtained after the determination of panel VAR based on GMM methodology.

The rest of the chapter is organized as follows. Section 2 briefly explains monetary policy in Turkey. Section 3 describes the methodology for SVAR and panel VAR analyses. Section 4 presents the model for interest rate determination and explains the relevant data set. Section 5 is devoted to the empirical findings. Last section concludes the chapter.

2 Instruments of Monetary Policy in Turkey

Turkey is the first country in MENA region adopting explicit IT regime. After decades of high inflation since the late 1970s, Turkish economy experienced unprecedented decline in inflation rate after four-year implicit inflation-targeting regime (2002–2005) and reflected less volatile and fragile economic signs since the explicit inflation-targeting regime of 2006, as depicted in Figs. 1 and 2, for inflation and industrial production, respectively. In Turkey, policy rate was overnight interest rate until May 2010. After that period, one-week repo became the main policy rate. After February 2001, the period of domestic crisis, crawling exchange rate peg regime adopted in 2000 was abandoned and Turkish currency was left to float. The new monetary policy is determined to be inflation-targeting (IT) regime. An implicit form of IT regime was adopted until some economic conditions are satisfied. Public burden was a crucial obstacle to IT regime since risk premium, mainly based on default risk in high-budget deficit economies, put upward pressure on long-term rates (bond rates), exchange rate and hence on inflation expectations. Hence, public issues are at the heart of the economic policy in order to accomplish an active monetary policy. Another impediment against properly working monetary policy is the uninformed and inexperienced public regarding the new monetary policy regime. Within the implicit IT period, fiscal reforms are implemented and communication facilities are prepared in order to achieve the target levels.

Regarding monetary policy in Turkey, there is a plethora of studies since its success in IT regime. Civcir and Akçaglayan (2010) investigate the response of monetary policy to the exchange rate shocks before and after adoption of IT

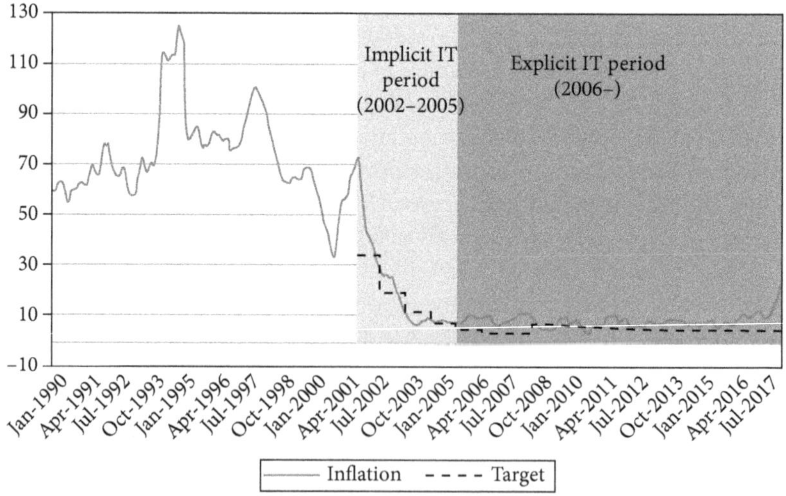

Fig. 1: Inflation data for Turkey (January 2002–September 2018)

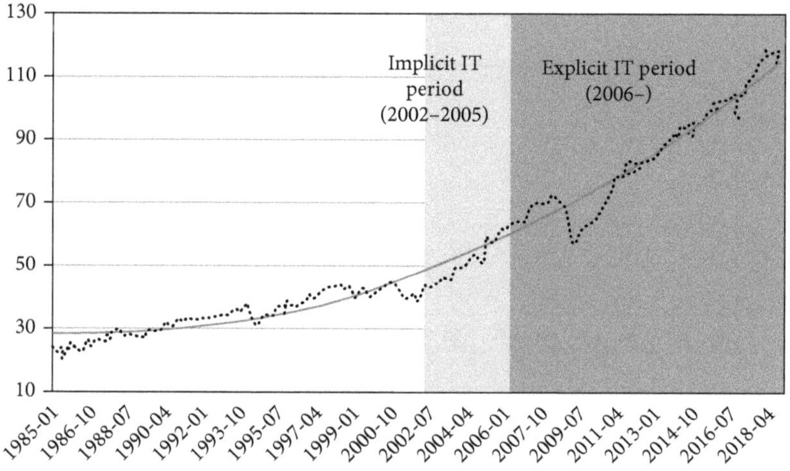

Fig. 2: Industrial production (seasonally adjusted) and its nonlinear trend for Turkey (January 1985–August 2018)

for the monthly period of 1987–2009. Calculating variances decompositions of exchange rate shocks, they show that exchange rate pass-through is strong during whole period. Akyurek et al. (2011), using VAR with structural breaks and rolling VAR and its variance decompositions for the monthly period of 1989–2008, observe that IT regime is effective on Taylor-rule model for Turkey. Güney (2016), examining the role of inflation and output uncertainties on monetary policy for the monthly period of 2002–2014 in Turkey, observes that central bank concentrates mainly on price stability and responds to inflation and growth uncertainties significantly. Gürkaynak et al. (2015) examine the monetary policy in Turkey in the central bank independence period. Using monthly dataset for the period 2003–2014, they observe that there is a break in the Taylor-rule model after 2010. Using three different Taylor rules (one includes inflation rate and percentage deviation of IP from its trend, other one includes inflation rate and annual growth of IP, and the last one includes inflation rate, annual growth of IP and change in USD/TR rate), they assert that the impact of inflation on interest rate declines after 2009, suggesting that the attention Central Bank of Turkey pays declines after the break period.

Another potential determinant of policy rate is as discussed before is credibility which can be proxied using institutional variables such as Kaufmann et al. (2010) governance indicators provided by World Bank. Similar to institutional

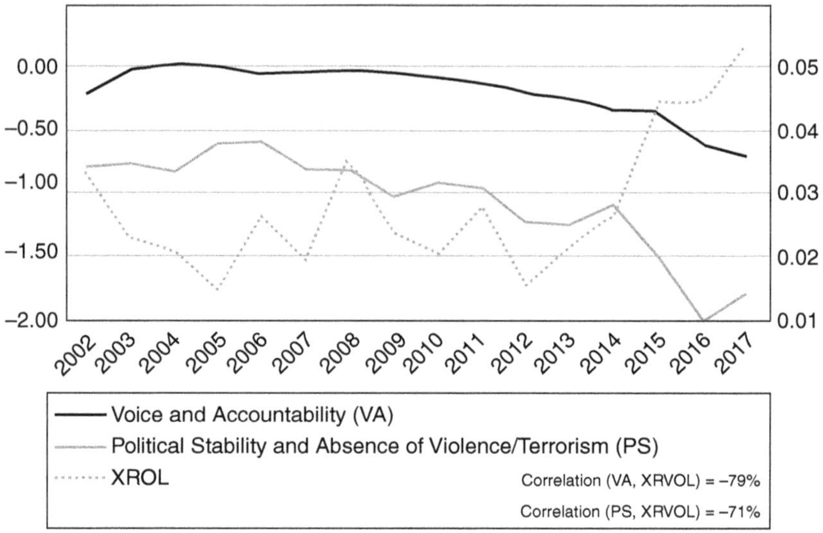

Fig. 3: Proxies for credibility in Turkey (2002–2017). Note: XRVOL is given on the right-hand side axis.

factors, credibility can also be proxied by exchange rate volatility[1] which can easily be argued to be another risk perception concept in Turkey considering its high dependence on foreign currency. In other words, foreign investment inflow or outflows according to the risk environment. In fact, in the given Fig. 3, two crucial and relevant institutional concepts, that is, voice and accountability (VA) and political stability and absence of violence (PS) are observed to be highly correlated[2] with exchange rate volatility (XRVOL), that is, higher than 70 % in absolute value. As this chapter employs monthly data, exchange rate volatility will be used as a proxy for credibility/risk perception.

3 Methodology

3.1 Time Series SVAR Model

The empirical analysis in this study is based on SVAR models proposed by Sims (1986), Bernanke (1986) and Blanchard and Watson (1986). In these models,

1 A basic technique to measure exchange rate volatility is standard deviation.

2 The correlation is negative since a rise in VA or PS is an improvement in the credibility whereas a rise in XRVOL is a deterioration.

parameters are estimated by imposing short-run (contemporaneous) structural restrictions. An alternative methodology is developed by Shapiro and Watson (1988) and Blanchard and Quah (1988) imposing long-run structural restrictions. Differently from standard VAR models, impulse response functions (IRF) and variance decompositions obtained from SVAR methodology have structural inferences.

The methodology for contemporaneous SVAR model is explained below. The standard VAR model for the variables in vectoral form x_t is as follows:

$$Ax_t = C(L)x_t + D\varepsilon_t \tag{1}$$

where $C(L)$ is the lag operator and ε_t is the vector for unobservable variables, that is, errors to the structural equations. Multiplying each side with A^{-1}, the reduced form of this system is obtained.

$$x_t = A^{-1}C(L)x_t + A^{-1}D\varepsilon_t \tag{2}$$

$A^{-1}D\varepsilon_t$ is simply the residuals (e_t) we obtain after running a standard VAR model given that the shocks have temporary effects, e_t has white noise iid process. If shocks have permanent effects, Equation 2 will be written in first differences,

$$\Delta x_t = A^{-1}C(L)\Delta x_1 + A^{-1}D\varepsilon_t \tag{3}$$

Last term in Equations 2 and 3 is the vector of residuals and ε_t is the vector of structural shocks. If A and D are known, the dynamic structure of the model and structural shocks can be calculated from the coefficients of estimated standard VAR. Since these coefficient matrices are unknown, identification is attained by imposing theoretical restrictions. Thereby, the number of unknown structural parameters are reduced to less than or equal to the number of estimated parameters of the variance-covariance matrix of the VAR residuals (Keating, 1992). n(n−1)/2 is the number of theoretical restrictions to achieve full identification where n is the number of variables in the model.

The methodology for long-run SVAR model is explained below. Given the reduced form of this system of the standard VAR model in Equation 2, some arrangements are applied.

$$\left(I - A^{-1}C(L)\right)x_t = A^{-1}D\varepsilon_t$$

$$x_t = \left(I - A^{-1}C(L)\right)^{-1} A^{-1}D\varepsilon_t \tag{4}$$

Equation 4 shows how the structural shocks, ε_t, affect the long-run levels of the variables in the model, that is, $x_t = \left(I - A^{-1}C(L)\right)^{-1} A^{-1}D\varepsilon_t$ is simply the cumulative (long-run) impact of the structural shocks.

Before SVAR model, stationarity of all variables are checked using Augmented Dickey Fuller (ADF) and Phillips-Perron (PP) unit root tests. Both tests have presence of unit root in the null hypothesis. After SVAR estimation, impulse response functions (IRF) and variance decompositions (VARDEC) and historical decompositions are presented. IRFs provide the effect of one standard deviation shock on current and future values of the endogenous variables. VARDEC provides the relative importance of each innovation in the variation of endogenous variables. IRF, VARDEC and historical decompositions are also based on structural factorization.

3.2 Panel VAR Model

Panel VAR methodology is first proposed by Holtz-Eakin et al. (1988). Consider a homogenous panel VAR of order p with panel-specific fixed effects as presented below.

$$Y_{it} = \sum_{j=1}^{p} A_j Y_{it-j} + X_{it} B + u_i + e_{it}$$

where Y_{it} is a vector of endogenous variables, X_{it} vector of exogenous variables, and u_i and e_{it} are vectors of panel-fixed effects and idiosyncratic errors, successively. Using lagged dependent variable in the right-hand side will lead to biasedness even with large number of cross-sectional units. Generalized method of moments (GMM) technique will help obtain consistent estimates with small time period in dynamic panel analysis. In order to control cross-sectional heterogeneity, forward orthogonal deviation[3] (Helmert transformation) is used which is suggested by Arellano and Bover (1995).

After system GMM panel VAR model based on the STATA routine provided by Love and Zicchino (2006), forecast error variance decompositions are also obtained using the STATA routine provided by Abrigo and Love (2015).

Before panel VAR test, the variables are checked whether they are stationary via panel unit root tests. Im et al. (2003, IPS hereafter) is a panel unit root test with heterogeneity assumption in the autoregressive coefficient. Maddala and Wu (1999) propose ADF-Fisher unit root test which is based on bootstrapping procedures disregarding cross-sectional averaging of ADF statistics. Both tests have presence of unit root in the null hypothesis.

---

3 Another method for removing fixed effects is mean-differencing which is commonly used. However, this method will lead to biased estimates.

4 Model and Data

For the simultaneous equation system, Taylor-rule model to examine the determinants of policy rate is given as follows:

$$INT = \alpha + \beta_1 INF + \beta_2 GAP + \beta_3 XRVOL + \delta_1 D_{crisis} + \delta_2 D_{target}$$

4.1 SVAR Model

In the identification of the SVAR model, output gap is assumed to be most exogenous variable and interest rate is assumed to be completely endogenous. Exchange rate volatility is restricted to be affected only from the output gap and inflation is restricted to be affected from output gap and exchange rate. The identification is shown in matrix form (5).

Short-Run SVAR Model:

$$\begin{pmatrix} e_t^{GAP} \\ e_t^{XRVOL} \\ e_t^{INF} \\ e_t^{INT} \end{pmatrix} = \begin{pmatrix} C(1) & & & \\ C(2) & C(3) & & \\ C(4) & C(5) & C(6) & \\ C(7) & C(8) & C(9) & C(10) \end{pmatrix} \cdot \begin{pmatrix} \varepsilon_t^{GAP} \\ \varepsilon_t^{XRVOL} \\ \varepsilon_t^{INF} \\ \varepsilon_t^{INT} \end{pmatrix} \tag{5}$$

Long-run SVAR Model (with the same order in variables):

$$C = \begin{pmatrix} C(1) & 0 & 0 & 0 \\ C(2) & C(5) & 0 & 0 \\ C(3) & C(6) & C(8) & 0 \\ C(4) & C(7) & C(9) & C(10) \end{pmatrix} \tag{6}$$

Inflation data (INF) is monthly percentage changes in CPI. As for policy rates (INF), interbank interest rates are employed for Turkey. Output gap (GAP) is positively defined, that is, actual output minus potential output. The proxy for output gap is selected as industrial production index (IPI) as the data frequency is monthly. Output gap is calculated using HP filter[4] of the natural logarithm of IPI. For a full-fledged model, we incorporate exchange rate volatility (XRVOL)

---

4 There are generally three different options to calculate output gap: (i) linear detrending, (2) nonlinear detrending via Hodrick-Prescott filter, (3) Kalman filtering. Hodrick-Prescott filter is the most common approach.

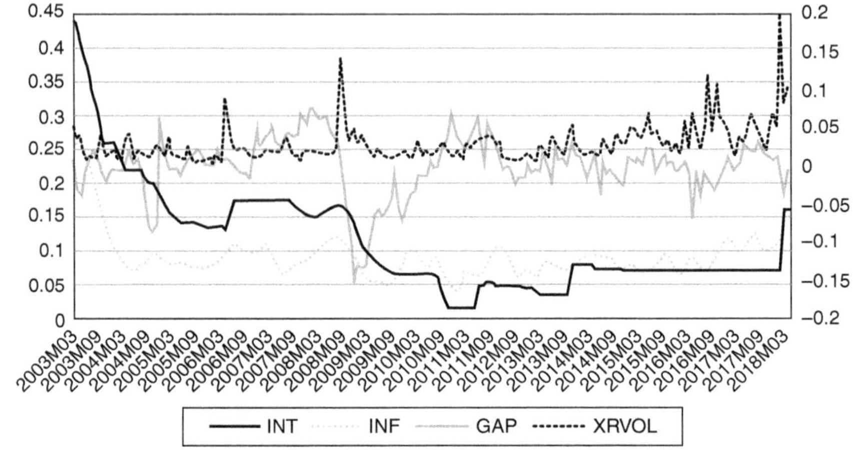

Fig. 4: Dataset for Turkey (January 2003–June 2018). Note: GAP and XRVOL are given on the right-hand side axis.

as a proxy for the risk from financial openness. This may be a major concern for emerging markets as they are generally highly dependent on foreign investment and are argued to be relatively vulnerable. Domestic credibility and portfolio inflows are crucial for the fluctuations in exchange rate. Hence, in determining the policy rate, central banks of emerging markets can be argued to take exchange rate volatility into account. In this study, standard deviation is used as a measurement of exchange rate volatility. Exchange rate is official nominal exchange rate per US dollar. Time graph for the data is given in Fig. 4. SVAR model is applied for Turkey using monthly frequency for the period January 2003[5]–July 2018. Considering the time-length of the model, two dummy variables (D_{target} and D_{crisis}) are employed to capture IT and crisis period (2009).

4.2 Panel VAR Model

Panel VAR model is applied for a group of emerging countries for the period of January 1999–February 2018. Emerging economies selected based on availability of data[6] are Czech Republic, Hungary, Indonesia, Israel, South Korea,

5 The dataset starts by 2003 since the economy is more stable compared to earlier periods.
6 Turkey is not included in the analysis for emerging country group to make an unbiased comparison.

Tab. 1: Inflation Targeting Adoption Dates for Emerging Markets

Country	Formal adoption	Source
Czech Republic	January 1998	Czech National Bank
Hungary	June 2001	Magyar Nemzeti Bank
Indonesia	July 2005	Bank Sentral Republik Indonesia
Israel	June 1997	Bank of Israel
Korea, Republic of	April 1998	Bank of Korea
Mexico	January 2001	Banco de México
Poland	September 1998	Narodowy Bank Polski
South Africa	February 2000	South African Reserve Bank

Note: Hammond (2012) can be checked for detailed and organized information about inflation-targeting countries.

Mexico, Poland and South Africa. Monthly data for interest rate, inflation and industrial production are obtained from OECD databases. Daily exchange rate data are obtained from Bank for International Settlements (BIS) and are transformed into monthly standard deviations. As for policy rates, three-month money market rates are employed for the group of emerging economies. Rest of the variables are the same as in time series model for Turkey. Using an earlier time period than the adoption of inflation-targeting policy, IT dummy variable for emerging markets follows the dates given in Tab. 1.

5 Empirical Findings

5.1 SVAR Model

Before SVAR model, all variables are tested using ADF and PP tests, given in Tab. 4, since SVAR is based on standard VAR model which is assumed to include stationary variables. All variables are observed to be stationary. Crisis and IT dummies are used as exogenous variables in the structural model[7].

Short-run SVAR model for Turkey including GAP, XRVOL, INF and INT, is based on VAR(2), that is, optimal lag is selected as 2 using Schwarz information criterion. Short-run SVAR given in Tab. 6 reflects that INF have positive and

7 A standard OLS analysis is also investigated including crisis and target dummies. The model in Tab. 5 reflects similar results to the previous literature such as Gürkaynak et al. (2015). Besides, crisis dummy is observed to be positively effective and target dummy is negatively effective in the Taylor rule model.

significant[8] impact on INT. Given IRFs in Fig. 6, INF and XRVOL shocks are observed to be positively and significantly affecting INT. Variance decomposition in Tab. 7 reflects that the variation in INT rate is explained by itself mainly with an average ratio of around 70 %. INF is observed to be composing a steady ratio of around 7 % during different periods, whereas XRVOL is observed to be composing a high ratio up to around two-year time horizon but loses it afterwards. Historical decompositions given in Fig. 6 depict that INF shock loses its proportion in the variation of INT after around 2010 whereas XRVOL shock composes relatively high proportion after around 2010 period. GAP is observed to compose a high proportion in the global financial crisis period. Another important observation to highlight is that XRVOL shock moves in the same direction with INT between 2006 and 2015 period whereas it turns into opposite direction after 2017, since during this time XRVOL is rising whereas interest rate is steady.

For the long-run SVAR model, given in Tab. 8 and Tab. 7 all variables are observed to be significant. In the variance decompositions given in Tab. 9, INF is observed to be composing the highest proportion all over the time horizon whereas XRVOL composes relatively higher proportion up to around two-year time horizon but loses it afterwards. In the historical decompositions given in Fig. 8, INF takes the highest proportion during almost all period whereas XRVOL composes high proportions around 2013–2015 period and after 2017 period. GAP composes the highest proportion during global financial crisis.

Models suggest that inflation rate dominates in the decomposition of interest rate variation in the long run whereas exchange rate volatility shows its importance in the short run. In other words, credibility matters in the short-run determination of the policy rate in Turkey whereas the long-run determinant of the policy rate is inflation.

5.2 Panel VAR Model

Tab. 2 provides descriptive statistics of the variables in panel data from eight emerging countries.

Before GMM-based panel VAR model, we conduct IPS and ADF-Fisher panel unit root test which are reported in Tab. 10. The tests suggest that all panel variables are stationary. In GMM-based panel models given in Tab. 11, all variables are in their first lags, that is, t−1. All variables have positive and significant impact on current INT variable. Positive impact of XRVOL highlights the

8 Significant impacts on INT, which is the fourth equation in SVAR model, are shown with bold characters in Tab. 6.

Tab. 2: Panel Dataset Summary Statistics

	INT	INF	GAP	XRVOL
Mean	6.14	4.07	0.00	15.46
Max.	45.50	70.64	0.11	670.34
Min.	0.00	-2.74	−0.23	0.01
Std. Dev.	1.94	5.22	−1.37	6.50
Obs.	1840	1840	1840	1840

importance of credibility for emerging economies. Last but not least, dummy variables suggest consistent results according to the literature. IT dummy has positive impact, whereas crisis dummy has negative impact. The relevant IRFs are given in Fig. 9. Moreover, Tab. 12 suggests that INT itself composes the highest proportion in the variance of INT in the short run as GMM is a dynamic analysis. However, the proportion declines as horizon increases and the proportion of INF rises in higher time horizons.

The empirical findings obtained from panel VAR model for eight emerging countries are consistent to Taylor-rule model. Since the model is based on GMM methodology, it provides dynamic, that is, short run, results. Interest rate is observed to be significantly affected from its lagged value suggesting a smoothing effect as mentioned in the literature. The positive impact of inflation, output gap and exchange rate is consistent to the literature in the way that a rise in inflation rate, a higher actual output than the potential level and a fluctuation in the domestic currency push short-term domestic nominal interest rates upwards. Adoption of IT policy generally suggests a significant and immediate intervention to inflation via interest rates. Hence, a positive impact of IT adoption dummy explains the immediate intervention in the short run. Negative sign of economic crisis dummy is attributed to the desire of central banks to revive the economy when there is crisis.

6 Conclusion

Contributions of IT policy are known globally and many developed and developing countries implement this policy as the main central bank monetary policy rule. Maintaining price stability is very crucial for emerging countries as they are financially fragile. Moreover, credibility seems to be of high importance as the portfolio inflows are generally determined by risk perceptions. Emerging economies have high-growth potential but are generally in need of investment which hampers their capacity to use this potential. These economies attract portfolio investments via relatively higher returns such as interest rates. Hence, fragility creates risk and relatively high interest creates return for the foreign investors. According to the clash between risk and return for the emerging markets, foreign capital outflows or inflows which specifies the fluctuations in exchange rate vis-à-vis US dollar. This study examines Taylor rule for Turkey and emerging countries including inflation, output gap and exchange rate volatility as a measurement for the risk/return perceptions of the foreign investors using VAR methodology.

Turkish economy is at the heart of this study. Moreover, a panel of eight IT-emerging economies is examined. For time series analysis for Turkey, SVAR model is used and the structural IRF, variance decompositions and historical decompositions are observed. Empirical analysis for Turkey suggests that in the short-run models, exchange rate fluctuation is contributing most to the variation in the policy rate after itself; whereas, in the long-run models, inflation is observed to be the main contributor to interest rate. Put it differently, we can mention about a full commitment to IT policy for Turkey for the long run in the way that inflation is the key objectives of the monetary authority. Bernanke and Mishkin (1997) discuss that IT policy is not an ironclad policy rule but rather flexible such that allows even for discretionary monetary policy to accommodate the economy to supply shocks such as oil price shocks. However, they further argue that such a flexibility is possible for short-term targets or there can be an “escape clause” that IT is suspended for some period in the times of adverse economic environment. According to Bernanke and Mishkin (1997, p. 100), “the rationale for treating inflation as the primary goal of monetary policy is clearly strongest when medium- to long-term horizons are considered”. Hence the flexibility of IT occurs in the short run to the variations in exchange rate which suggests that central bank reacts to exchange rate shocks contrary to its so-called single mandate of maintaining price stability. GMM-based panel VAR model—which is a dynamic, that is, short run model—for eight emerging countries (excluding Turkey) suggests that interest rate itself and inflation rate contribute most to the variation in interest rate. This is contrary to the findings for Turkey in the way that in the short run Central Bank of Turkey may give up on the priority of price stability whereas the group of emerging economies do not reflect any flexibility.

Appendix A: Analysis on Turkey (January 2003–July 2018)

Tab. 3: Inflation Targets and Realizations

Years	Target	Realization
2002	35	29.7
2003	20	18.4
2004	12	9.3
2005	8	7.7
2006	5	9.7
2007	4	8.4
2008	4	10.1
2009	7.5	6.5
2010	6.5	6.4
2011	5.5	10.4
2012	5	6.2
2013	5	7.4
2014	5	8.2
2015	5	8.8
2016	5	8.5
2017	5	11.9

Note: Year-end inflation rates calculated as the 12-month change in the CPI are set as the target variable. Explicit IT dates are denoted with gray highlight, the rest are implicit IT dates.

Tab. 4: Unit Root Tests

Variables	ADF	PP
INT	-4.7317	-4.5378
	(0.0001)	(0.0002)
INF	-4.3272	-4.1015
	(0.0005)	(0.0012)
GAP	-4.4740	-4.4616
	(0.0003)	(0.0003)
XRVOL	-4.8806	-8.8611
	(0.0001)	(0.0000)

Note: Augmented Dickey Fuller (ADF) test with constant. Maximum lag is selected as 14 and optimal lag selection is based on Schwarz information criteria. Phillips-Perron (PP) test with constant. Spectral estimation method is Bartlett kernel and automatic bandwidth selection is Newey-West.

Tab. 5: OLS Estimations for Taylor-Rule Model for Turkey

VARIABLES	OLS
INF	1.3348*
	(0.0842)
GAP	0.2124*
	(0.0987)
XRVOL	−0.1744
	(0.1240)
$\mathbf{D}_{crisis}$	0.0553*
	(0.0153)
$\mathbf{D}_{target}$	−0.0996*
	(0.0086)
constant	0.0747*
	(0.0125)
R-square	0.796

Note: Values in parenthesis indicate standard deviations.
(*) indicate significance at 5 %.

Tab. 6: SVAR (Short Run)

	Coefficient	**Std. Error**	**z-Statistic**	**Prob.**
C(2)	−0.0860	0.0760	−1.1320	0.2576
C(4)	−0.0113	0.0281	−0.4020	0.6876
C(5)	0.0621	0.0276	2.2538	0.0242
C(7)	**0.0110**	**0.0280**	**0.3947**	**0.6931**
C(8)	**−0.0117**	**0.0278**	**−0.4200**	**0.6745**
C(9)	**0.2725**	**0.0744**	**3.6648**	**0.0002**
C(1)	0.0219	0.0012	18.9209	0.0000
C(3)	−0.0860	0.0760	−1.1320	0.2576
C(6)	−0.0113	0.0281	−0.4020	0.6876
C(10)	0.0621	0.0276	2.2538	0.0242

Note: VAR model includes two lags after specifying the optimum lag, according to Schwarz information criteria. Log likelihood of the SVAR model is 2067.820.

Tab. 7: Variance Decomposition (Short Run)

Horizon	GAP Shock	XRVOL	INF Shock	INT Shock
1	0.0342	0.0154	6.9208	93.0296
2	0.0255	11.0605	8.3285	80.5855
3	0.2377	14.3020	8.7244	76.7359
4	0.7145	17.8250	8.1866	73.2738
5	1.3234	19.8435	7.4937	71.3394
10	4.4732	21.9376	4.7271	68.8620
20	7.2864	18.7305	3.3867	70.5965
30	0.0342	0.0154	6.9208	93.0296

Note: Structural Factorization

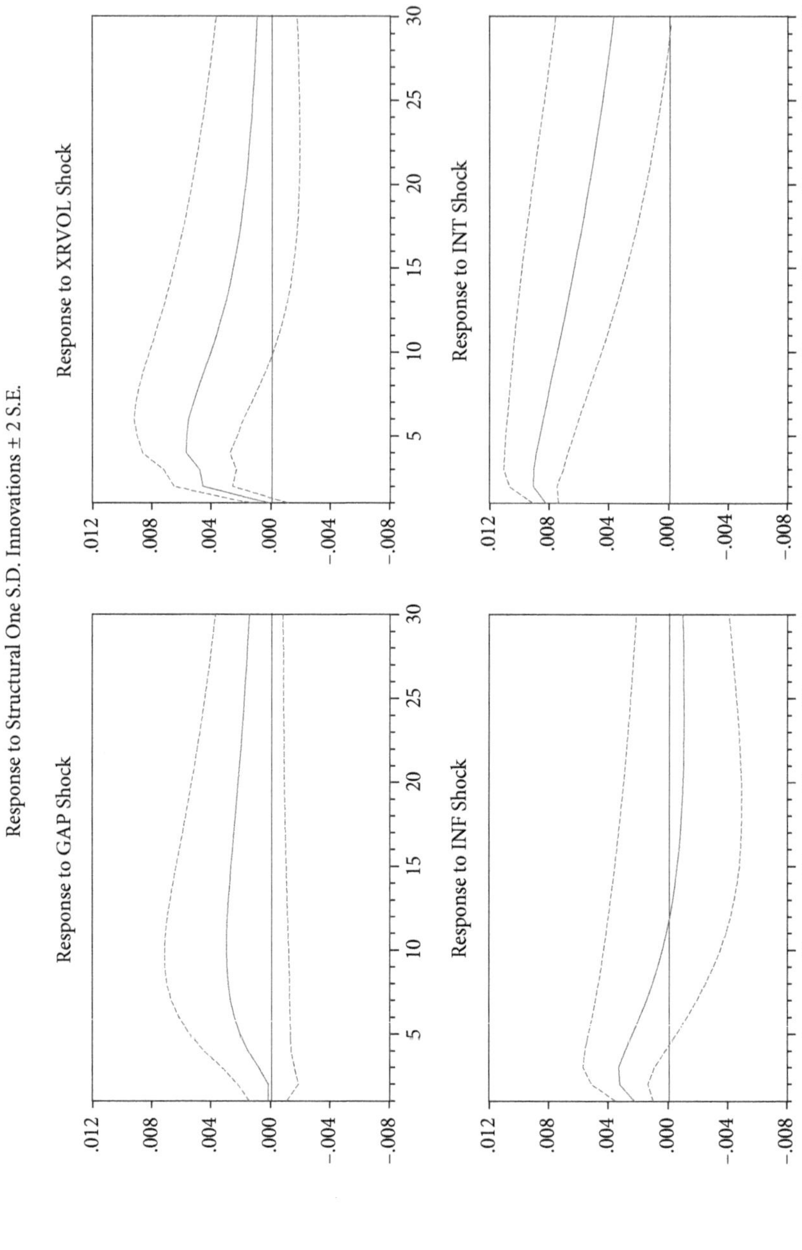

Fig. 5: Responses of INT to structural shocks (short run)

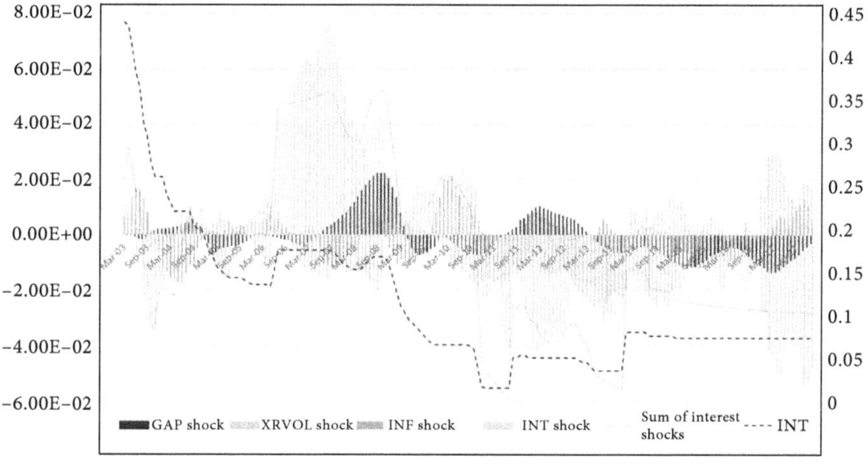

Fig. 6: Historical decomposition (short run) (January 2003–January 2018)

Tab. 8: SVAR (Long Run)

	Coefficient	Std. Error	z-Statistic	Prob.
C(1)	0.0865	0.0046	18.9209	0.0000
C(2)	−0.0297	0.0039	-7.6830	0.0000
C(3)	−0.0172	0.0089	−1.9215	0.0547
C(4)	**0.0602**	**0.0235**	**2.5640**	**0.0103**
C(5)	0.0473	0.0025	18.9209	0.0000
C(6)	0.0805	0.0078	10.3065	0.0000
C(7)	**0.1131**	**0.0225**	**5.0301**	**0.0000**
C(8)	0.0865	0.0046	18.9209	0.0000
C(9)	**0.1864**	**0.0193**	**9.6517**	**0.0000**
C(10)	0.2222	0.0117	18.9209	0.0000

Note: VAR model includes two lags after specifying the optimum lag, according to Schwarz information criteria. Log likelihood of the SVAR model is 2066.541.

Tab. 9: Variance Decomposition (Long Run)

Horizon	GAP Shock	XRVOL	INF Shock	INT Shock
1	0.0412	0.0000	78.3363	21.6225
2	2.1070	8.1394	68.4549	21.2987
3	2.0471	11.4747	65.6442	20.8340
4	1.8264	15.3110	61.7421	21.1205
5	1.5225	17.8757	58.8605	21.7414
10	1.0602	22.3624	50.4624	26.1150
20	2.3928	20.4025	44.1680	33.0367
30	0.0412	0.0000	78.3363	21.6225

Note: Structural Factorization

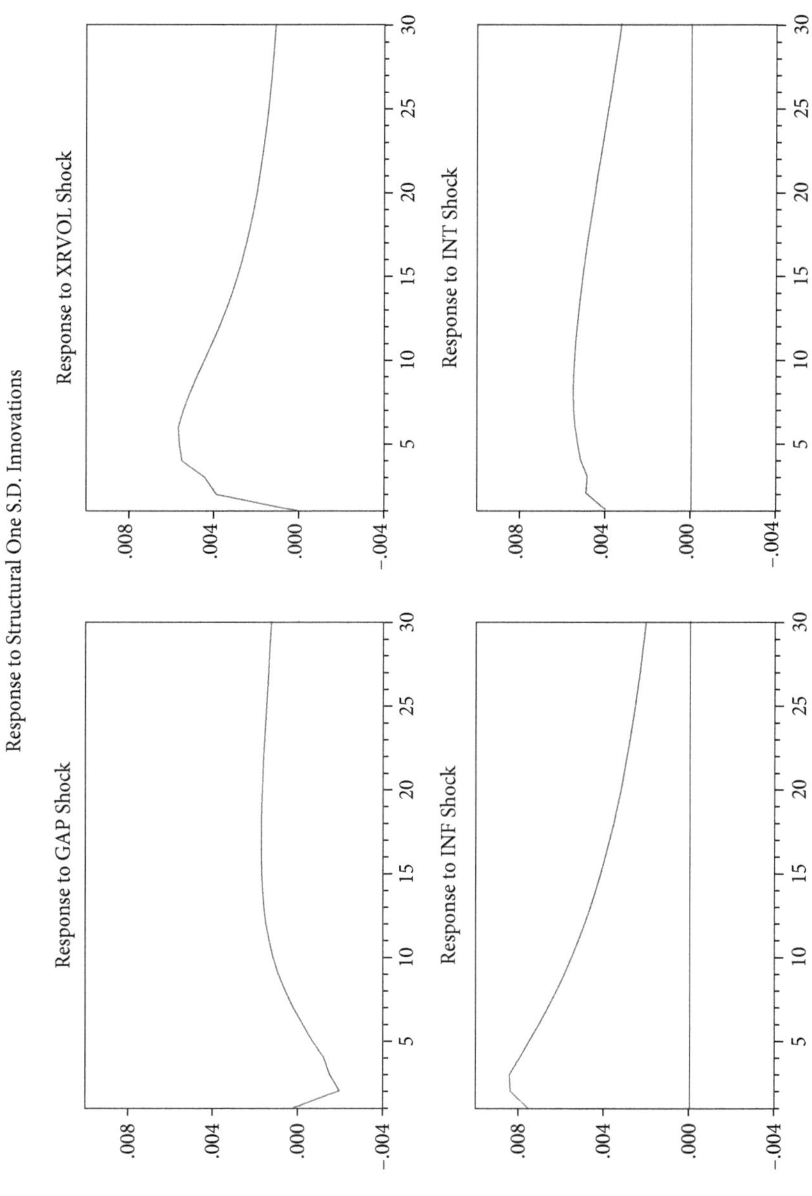

Fig. 7: Responses of INT to structural shocks (long run)

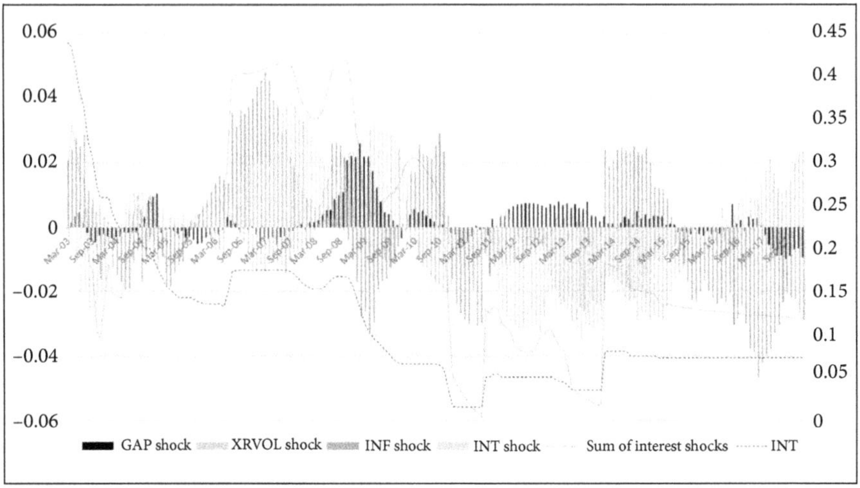

Fig. 8: Historical decomposition (long run)

Appendix B: Panel Model (January 1999 – February 2018)

Tab. 10: Panel Unit Root Test

	Im, Pesaran and Shin W-stat	PP – Fisher Chi-square
INT	-3.8666*	117.512*
	(0.0001)	(0.0000)
INF	-5.0488*	135.171*
	(0.0000)	(0.0000)
GAP	−13.3629*	292.794*
	(0.0000)	(0.0000)
XRVOL	−13.6908*	641.360*
	(0.0000)	(0.0000)

Note: In IPS test, automatic lag length selection based on SIC. In PP test, Newey-West automatic bandwidth selection and Bartlett kernel is used. Tests include individual intercept. Values in parenthesis are p-values. (*) suggests significance at 5 %.

Tab. 11: Panel Estimations

VARIABLES	GMM	FE
INT	0.9763*	
	(0.0056)	
INF	0.0208*	0.6994**
	(0.0063)	(0.0180)
GAP	1.0899*	-2.0507
	(0.3875)	(1.7856)
XRVOL	0.00102*	0.0039**
	(0.0004)	(0.0015)
D_{crisis}	−0.1286*	−0.4345*
	(0.0550)	(0.2560)
D_{target}	0.2071*	-4.1698**
	(0.1054)	(0.2537)

Note: Values in parenthesis indicate standard deviations. Left-hand-side variable is interest rate (INT_t). In GMM model, first-order panel VAR model is used according to Schwarz Info Criteria Number of instruments for GMM model is selected as 4. (*), (**) indicate significance at 10 % and 5 %, successively. In fixed effect model (FE), constant is used. R-square in FE model is 0.71.

Tab. 12: Forecast-error variance decomposition for Panel VAR

Horizon	INT	INF	GAP	XRVOL
1	1	0	0	0
2	0.9935	0.0009	0.0023	0.0033
3	0.9848	0.0028	0.0054	0.0069
4	0.9757	0.0057	0.0086	0.0099
5	0.9667	0.0095	0.0116	0.0122
10	0.9213	0.0378	0.0226	0.0182
20	0.8263	0.1163	0.0358	0.0216
30	0.7412	0.1928	0.0437	0.0223

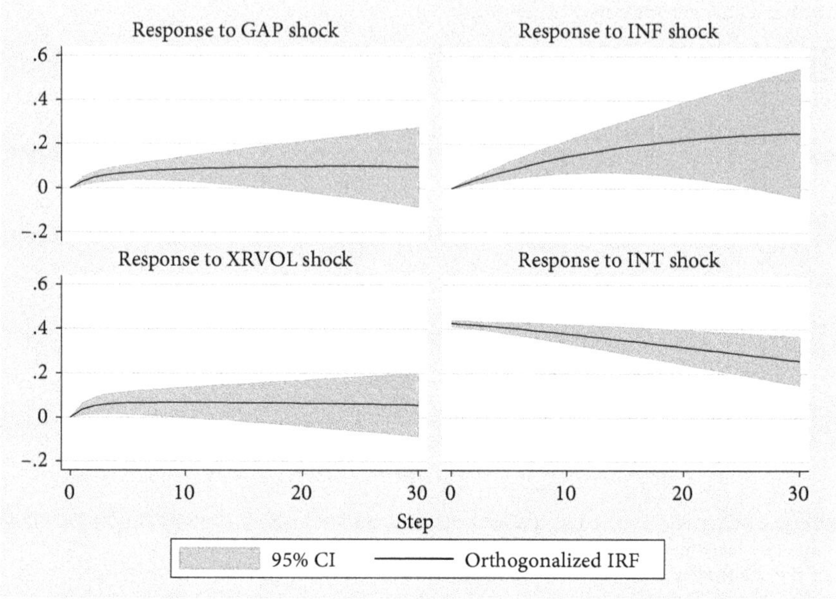

Fig. 9: Responses of interest rate to structural shocks

References

Akyurek, C., Kutan, A. M., and Yilmazkuday, H. (2011). Can inflation targeting regimes be effective in developing countries? The Turkish experience. *Journal of Asian Economics*, 22(5), 343–355.

Aizenman, J., Hutchison, M., & Noy, I. (2011). Inflation targeting and real exchange rates in emerging markets. World Development, 39(5), 712–724.

Arellano, M., and Bover, O. (1995). Another look at the instrumental variable estimation of error-components models. *Journal of Econometrics*, 68 (1), 29–51.

Bernanke, B. S. (1986). Alternative explanations of the money-income correlation. NBER Working Paper, No. 1842. http://www.nber.org/papers/w1842.pdf

Bernanke, B. S., and Mishkin, F. S. (1997). Inflation targeting: A new framework for monetary policy?. National Bureau of Economic Research, No. w5893.

Blanchard, O. J., and M. W. Watson. (1986). Are business cycles all alike?. R. J. Gordon (ed.) *American business cycle: Continuity and change*. Chicago and London: University of Chicago Press, 123–180.

Blanchard, O. J., and Quah, D. (1988). The dynamic effects of aggregate demand and supply disturbances. National Bureau of Economic Research, No. w2737.

Brito, R. D., and Bystedt, B. (2010). Inflation targeting in emerging economies: Panel evidence. *Journal of Development Economics*, 91, 198–210.

Civcir, I., and Akçağlayan, A. (2010). Inflation targeting and the exchange rate: Does it matter in Turkey? *Journal of Policy Modeling*, 32(3), 339–354.

Fraga, A., I. Goldfajn, and A. Minella. (2003). Inflation Targeting in Emerging Market Economies. NBER Working Paper Series 10019.

Frömmel, M., Garabedian, G., and Schobert, F. (2011). "Monetary policy rules in Central and Eastern European Countries: Does the exchange rate matter?" *Journal of Macroeconomics*, 33(4), 807–818.

Güney, P. Ö. (2016). Does the central bank directly respond to output and inflation uncertainties in Turkey? *Central Bank Review*, 16(2), 53–57.

Gürkaynak, R. S., Kantur, Z., Taş, M. A., and Yıldırım, S. (2015). Monetary Policy in Turkey after Central Bank Independence. İktisat İşletme ve Finans, 30 (356), 9–38.

Hammond, G. (2012). State of the Art of Inflation Targeting, Centre for Central Banking Studies Handbook. Bank of England. https://www.bankofengland.co.uk/-/media/boe/files/ccbs/resources/state-of-the-art-inflation-targeting

Holtz-Eakin, D., Newey, W. K., Rosen, H. S. (1988). Estimating vector autoregressions with panel data. *Econometrica*, 56, 1371–1395.

Im, K. S., Pesaran, M. H., and Shin, Y. (2003). Testing for unit roots in heterogeneous panels. *Journal of Econometrics*, 115(1), 53–74.

Kaufmann, Daniel, Kraay, Aart, and Mastruzzi, Massimo. (2010). "The worldwide governance indicators methodology and analytical issues." The World Bank Policy Research Working Paper, No. 5430.

Keating, J. W. (1992). Structural approaches to vector autoregressions. Federal Reserve Bank of St. Louis Review. September/October. http://research.stlouisfed.org/publications/review/92/09/Vector_Sep_Oct1992.pdf

Levin, A., Lin, C. F., and Chu, C. S. J. (2002). Unit root tests in panel data: Asymptotic and finite-sample properties. *Journal of Econometrics*, 108(1), 1–24.

Lin, S., and Ye, H. (2009). Does inflation targeting make a difference in developing countries? *Journal of Development Economics*, 89, 118–123.

Love, I., and Zicchino, L. (2006). Financial development and dynamic investment behavior: Evidence from panel VAR. *The Quarterly Review of Economics and Finance*, 46(2), 190–210.

Maddala, G. S., and Wu, S. (1999). A comparative study of unit root tests with panel data and a new simple test. *Oxford Bulletin of Economics and Statistics*, 61(S1), 631–652.

Mishkin, F. S. (2004). Can inflation targeting work in emerging market countries? NBER Working Paper Series 10646.

Sánchez-Fung, José R. (2011). "Estimating monetary policy reaction functions for emerging market economies: The case of Brazil". *Economic Modelling*, 28, 1730–1738.

Shapiro, M., and Watson, M. (1988). Sources of business cycles fluctuations. *NBER Macroeconomics Annual*, 3, 111–156.

Sims, C.A. (1986). Are forecasting models usable for policy analysis. *Quarterly Review of the Federal Reserve Bank of Minneapolis*, Winter, 2–16.

Siregar, R., and S. Goo. (2008). Inflation targeting policy: The experiences of Indonesia and Thailand. CAMA (Centre for Applied Macroeconomic Analysis in the Australian National University) Working Paper 23.

Taylor, J. B. (1993). Discretion versus policy rules in practice. Carnegie–Rochester Conference Series on Public Policy (December), pp. 195–214.

Teles, V. K., and Zaidan, M. (2010). "Taylor principle and inflation stability in emerging market countries". *Journal of Development Economics*, 91(1), 180–183.

Walsh, Carl E. (2009). "Inflation targeting: What have we learned?" *International Finance*, 12(2),195–233.

Serkan Yeşilyurt and Çağlar Yurtseven

Tourism Response to Domestic Disruptive Events

International Tourism Response to Domestic Disruptive Events: The Case of Turkey

Abstract: In this chapter, we try to investigate the sensitivity of people to the major political and social events in terms of their tourism demand. As a measure of sensitivity, we use the human development index (HDI) by the United Nations Development Programme. For this purpose, the tourism demand from 39 countries (OECD and Other European countries) to Turkey is estimated by using panel data approach for the period between 2000 and 2017. The change in tourist arrivals from each selected country is used as dependent variable and change in relative consumer price index (CPI) and HDI are used as the explanatory variables in order to explain the change in tourism demand to Turkey. With HDI, a dummy variable is used to investigate the effects of disruptive events as the internal problems which are Gezi Park Protest (2013), coup d'état attempt (2016) and the terrorist attacks in major cities of Turkey (2–2013–2016), foreign policy issues as the plane crisis with Russia (2016) on the tourism demand of selected countries. Key contribution of this chapter is to include HDI as a measure of people's sensitivity to such disruptive events. It is found that human development level is a significant variable explaining the change in tourism demand to Turkey in recent years.

Keywords: panel data analysis, human development index, consumer price index, tourism demand, Turkey.

JEL Classification: A12, B23, F14, Z32

1 Introduction

Tourism is one of the key economic sources for many countries, including Turkey. Turkey attracts many tourists from different countries due to its cultural sites, beaches and many other features. Combining Europe and Asia, Turkey has a unique position that fuses different climate, geography and culture elements making it a natural destination for tourism. Turkey has various climate types in its different regions. The Black Sea region experiences a temperate rainy climate, the Central Anatolian region a continental, and the south a partially subtropical Mediterranean climate, respectably. From west to east, there are also considerable differences and contrasting climatic regions. In the Marmara and the Aegean regions, hot summers and mild winters are the norm, and in Eastern Anatolia it is common to experience extremes of temperature where the winters are long with heavy snowfall.

Having this variation in climatic conditions, the flora and fauna of Turkey are correspondingly diverse. The flora varies from those of lush forests, that of the wild steppes to typical Aegean and Mediterranean vegetation. Turkey has nearly 10,000 species, hundreds of which are endemic to Turkey. Turkey is on the migratory routes of birds and there are a number of areas which are the natural habitat for many different species, including many rare ones.

Turkey is an attractive destination for international tourists who are interested in historical sightseeing. Turkey due to its presence on the migration routes of the tribes, who settled in Anatolia, has been home to many tribes. Hittites, Phrygians, Lydians, Ions civilizations, the Roman, Byzantine, Seljuk and Ottoman empires have traces including numerous underground and above-ground assets. The history of humanity has continuously merged and accumulated, from that of the earliest settlements to contemporary Turkey today.

Therefore, investigating the tourism demand of Turkey is important to understand the factors which have positive and negative impact on tourist arrivals. This study can also be used as guide for both Turkey and other countries to understand some new factors that might affect the tourism demand. Moreover, correct policy implementations, considering this study's findings, can increase tourism demand in Turkey and in the countries which have similar tourism characteristics to Turkey.

Tourism in Turkey can be examined in two periods; before 1963 and planned period starting with the 1963 plan. The planned period can be examined in two sub-groups as the state-led years until 1983 and the liberal period after 1983. In this chapter, we focus on volatile term of the liberal period, namely 2000–2017. In addition to above-mentioned huge advantages of the Turkish tourism, we should remember the frequently stated weaknesses of tourism in Turkey as well. First of all, infrastructure and sectors related to tourism do not respond to the rapidly evolving tourism industry's needs. There are deficiencies in the energy and health sectors. Large-scale hotel investment in the rural area which does not match with the natural purity of the regions is another problem. Many strategic decisions regarding the tourism industry are given instantaneously without enough academic research. Actually, development plans carried out by the Ministry of Development of the Republic of Turkey are prepared periodically for tourism sector as well. In most of the recent reports, which were prepared with the opinion of the government, sector representatives and universities, Turkey's threats about tourism have been itemized as below:

a) Negative publications in national and international media,
b) External threats from geopolitical position,
c) The fact that international travel organizers dominate the market and adversely affect the efficiency of the Turkish tourism sector,
d) The policies of the European Union to encourage the movements of the intra-Union tourism,
e) The lack of necessary coordination between the public institutions.

Previous literature on the tourism demand to Turkey focuses on the economical and geographical factors to explain the change in tourism demand. This chapter contributes to the literature by adding a political-social dimension to tourism demand estimations. Human development index (HDI) is used to explain the change in the tourism demand of the selected countries as a proxy of sensitivity of people to major political-social events.

The analysis has been based on 39 countries, a sample from 5 country groups; OECD Europe (22), OECD Other (7), Other European (10), all OECD (29) and all countries (39). The analysis is made for the period between 2000 and 2017, which Turkey has the highest number of tourists in its history and experienced a decrease since 2013.

Random effects and fixed effects models are used in the analysis. For the tourism demand of Turkey, stated hypotheses are as follows:

- Internal and external political and social issues of Turkey will have negative impact on tourism demand of countries to Turkey.
- Higher HDI implies a bigger response to such disruptive events in terms of the change in the tourism demand.

2 International Tourism to Turkey

The annual number of foreign visitors arriving in Turkey has increased from 15 million in 2000 to 38 million in 2017. A total of 38.6 million foreign tourist arrivals were recorded in Turkey in 2017. This represented a recovery from the year 2016 in which a travel ban is enacted to tourists from Russia to Turkey following a steady rise in the previous ten years. Including citizens residing abroad, the number of inbound arrivals in Turkey has also recovered in 2017.

Turkey attracts tourists from many different countries. However, it mostly attracts tourists from European countries. From Fig. 2 and Tab. 1, 2 and 3, it is seen that from 2000 to 2017, more than half of the tourists come from European countries. Moreover, 55.33 % of the tourist arrivals are from OECD countries (average of last 18 years). Besides that, OECD Europe countries also have a

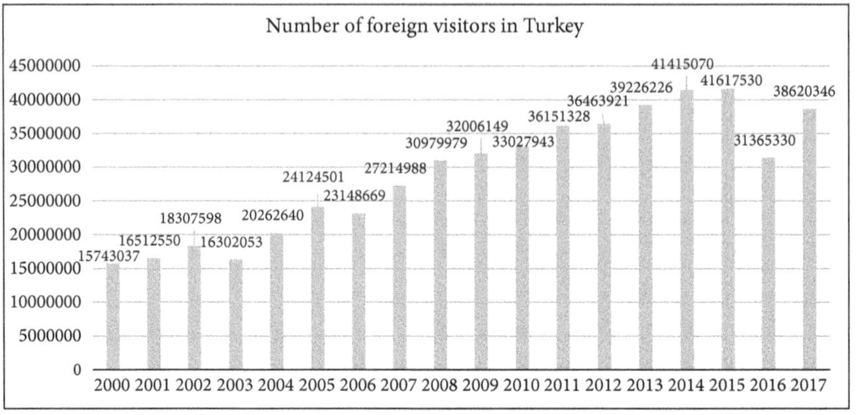

Fig. 1: Number of foreign visitors arriving in Turkey from 2000 to 2017.
Source: Turkish Statistical Institute (TUIK)

significant share in total number of tourists between 2000 and 2017. The tourism demand to Turkey has a decreasing trend for OECD Europe, OECD other and other European country groups since 2013 (see Figs. 1 and 2).

There are many metrics that affect the tourism revenues of countries. One of the most important determinants is the duration of stay. Turkey has provided different type of tourism opportunities for its guests from beach tourism to cultural and religious tourism. When purpose of visit of tourists in 2017 is investigated, entertainment and culture has the highest share, more than 50 %. On the other hand, visiting relatives and/or friends, shopping and business conferences also have significant rates (TURKSTAT, 2018). In Tab. 4, average number of overnights between 2000 and 2017 can be seen from the Turkish Ministry of Culture and Tourism data. It is seen that number of overnights constantly decrease until 2012 but after 2012, there is a trend of stability between 2013 and 2015 with 5.7 overnights and increase afterwards. From 2003 to 2016, there is 8.1 % decrease in average number of overnights.

In Tab. 5, top 10 countries in terms of the tourist arrivals (selected from OECD Europe, OECD Others and Other European Countries) is given for 2014–2017. Data is retrieved from Turkish Statistical Institute. It is clearly seen from the table that except for USA, all top countries in terms of the tourist arrivals are from Europe.[1]

1 We used three countries group in this study; OECD Europe (22 countries), OECD Other (10 countries) and Other Europe countries (7 countries). This classification is done by TURKSTAT.

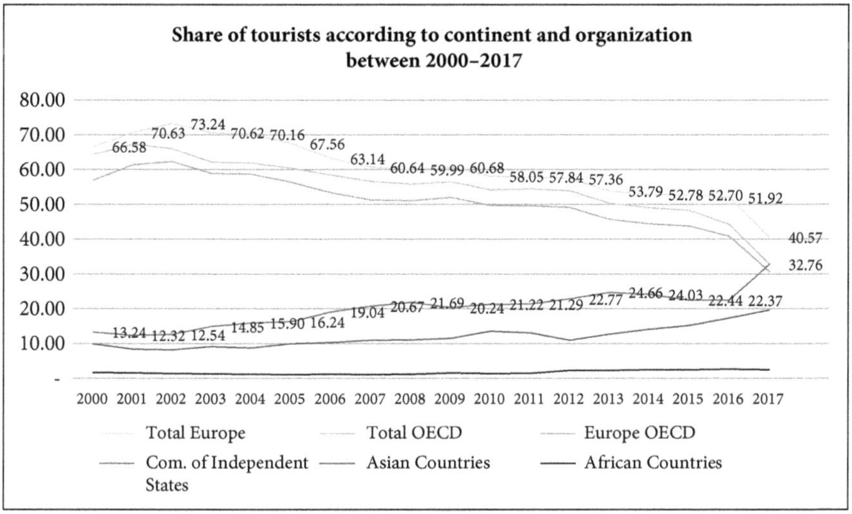

Fig. 2: Share of tourist according to continent and organization between 2000 and 2017. Source: TURKSTAT, http://www.tuik.gov.tr/PreTablo.do?alt_id=1072 Visiting time, November 22, 2018

Tab. 1: Number of tourists according to continent and organization (2000–2005)

Country groups	2000	2001	2002	2003	2004	2005
OECD Countries (Europe)	5929299	7122708	8245884	8209668	10304978	11903177
Other European countries	1013327	1084897	1457681	1646995	2006416	2369796
OECD Countries (other)	774556	696870	497243	458240	561092	851671
Com. of ındependent states	1380731	1431190	1661767	2072103	2790003	3431601
East Asian Countries	34137	39706	43818	42295	51131	63943
Southeast Asian Count.	41828	40131	39382	36094	46156	61650
South Asian Countries	404012	351641	453803	546244	673878	1008432
West Asian Countries	621530	613571	623552	726944	856235	1085045
African Countries	172545	181301	185295	174114	198278	233266
American Countries	44441	46047	28655	29301	40577	93394
Ocean Countries	790	269	477	281	351	428
Haimatlos	10957	11578	10619	14126	19289	22483
Citizens total	5314884	4892641	5059422	5817368	7097473	8045085
Number of tourist total	**10428153**	**11619909**	**13248176**	**13956405**	**17548384**	**21124886**

Tab. 2: Number of tourists according to continent and organization (cont.) (2006–2011) (Turkstat,2018)

2006	2007	2008	2009	2010	2011	2012
10562927	11955580	13424264	14051895	14209364	15599564	15583736
1952075	2198075	2374360	2377986	2412354	2595476	2646012
1001935	1232127	1271170	1234670	1293272	1499625	1541518
3772925	4824943	5713180	5480640	6075484	6695501	7236582
75311	92806	92717	98661	108013	134639	161054
67087	89532	104874	124208	120487	184917	201217
934560	1144936	1228729	1488876	1986910	2004059	1330050
1094623	1406223	1664789	1609965	1887040	2088314	2147531
233148	258148	312096	426119	377300	445487	713399
105748	118005	127117	157651	135902	181617	185300
207	171	246	183	2870	359	4694
19287	20365	23135	26260	23208	26518	31739
8167369	8854788	9690814	10242183	10921427	11592653	11731463
19819833	**23340911**	**26336677**	**27077114**	**28632204**	**31456076**	**31782832**

Tab. 3: Number of tourists according to continent and organization (cont.) (2012–2017). (Turkstat,2018)http://www.tuik.gov.tr/PreTablo.do?alt_id=1072Visiting time, November 22, 2018

2013	2014	2015	2016	2017
15954808	16376814	15870330	10352977	9927582
2823049	3066220	3231773	2808773	3220760
1604399	1670819	1628522	851248	688545
8607486	8850923	8134242	5670686	10618403
197065	273396	388726	233896	332825
221087	260962	266339	187876	263241
1356997	1797290	1941867	1860354	2733843
3055786	3377008	3563993	2505651	3593001
807484	888107	885887	666727	794254
245961	228035	278140	175025	182847
475	672	377	553	437
35501	47654	54436	38447	54296
12474218	12768914	13617038	13443961	14444990
34910098	**36837900**	**36244632**	**25352213**	**32410034**

Tab. 4: Average number of overnights between 2003 and 2017

Years	Number of overnights
2003	6.6
2004	6.5
2005	6.5
2006	6.4
2007	6.2
2008	6.2
2009	6.1
2010	6
2011	5.9
2012	5.6
2013	5.7
2014	5.7
2015	5.7
2016	5.9
2017	6.1

Tab. 5: Top 10 countries in terms of the tourist arrivals for 2014–2017 (Million)

Nationality	2014	Nationality	2015	Nationality	2016	Nationality	2017
Germany	5250036	**Germany**	5580792	**Germany**	3890074	**Germany**	3584653
United Kingdom	2600360	**United Kingdom**	2512139	**United Kingdom**	1711481	**Bulgaria**	1852867
Bulgaria	1693591	**Bulgaria**	1821480	**Bulgaria**	1690766	**United Kingdom**	1658715
Netherlands	1303730	**Netherlands**	1232487	**Netherlands**	906336	**Netherlands**	799006
France	1037152	**France**	847259	**Greece**	593150	**Greece**	623705
Greece	830841	**United States**	798787	**France**	555151	**France**	578524
United States	784917	**Greece**	755414	**United States**	459493	**Romania**	423868
Italy	697360	**Sweden**	624649	**Belgium**	413614	**Belgium**	419998
Sweden	667551	**Belgium**	617406	**Romania**	357473	**United States**	329257
Belgium	660857	**Italy**	507897	**Denmark**	329618	**Poland**	296120

Tab. 6: Touristic facilities and statistics. Source: TURSAB

Tourism Investment Licensed				Tourism Operation Licensed		
Years	**Facilities**	**Rooms**	**Beds**	**Facilities**	**Rooms**	**Beds**
2000	1824	156367	325168	1300	113452	243794
2001	1980	175499	364779	1240	107262	230248
2002	2124	190327	396148	1138	102972	222876
2003	2240	202339	420697	1130	111894	242603
2004	2357	217664	454290	1151	118883	259424
2005	2412	231123	483330	1039	128005	278255
2006	2475	241702	508632	869	123326	274687
2007	2514	251987	532262	776	112541	254191
2008	2566	268633	567470	772	113487	258287
2009	2625	289383	608765	754	103119	231456
2010	2647	299621	629465	877	114771	252984
2011	2783	319319	668829	922	122364	267900
2012	2870	336447	706019	960	126592	273877
2013	2982	357440	749299	1056	139928	301862
2014	3131	384454	807316	1117	145648	309556
2015	3309	404462	850089	1125	146162	314194
2016	3641	426981	899881	1135	144162	312912
2017	3771	446228	935286	1051	122228	263033

Over the last two decades, Turkey has made significant investments on infra and super structure. This also includes transport infrastructure such as modernization of airports, motorways and railroads as well as construction of the new ones. To understand the investments in tourism, in Tab. 6 the number of facilities, rooms and beds are given for the period between 2000 and 2017. This special data is retrieved from Association of Turkish Travel Agency (TURSAB). It is clearly seen that tourism continues to be an attractive sector for investors in Turkey with an upward trend in the investments since 2000.

Main indicators of Turkish tourism between 2003 and 2017 are given in Tab. 7. Tourism revenue in Turkey has increased from 2003 to 2014 (expect 2006, 2010, 2015 and 2016) gradually. There is a slight decrease in 2015 and sharp decrease in 2016 and again an increase in 2017. Initial insights from the year 2018 also show us an upward change (over 35 million tourist visited Turkey in 10 months).[2]

2 35.571,419 tourist visited Turkey between January 2018 and October 2018. Source TURKSTAT.

Tab. 7: Tourism revenue and average expenditure per capita between 2003 and 2017. Source: Turkish Statistical Institute (TUIK)

Years	Tourism Revenue(1000$)	Number of Visitors	Average Expenditure ($)	Share in GDP
2003	13 854 866	16 302 053	850	4.4
2004	17 076 606	20 262 640	843	4.2
2005	20 322 112	24 124 501	842	4.1
2006	18 593 951	23 148 669	803	3.4
2007	20 942 500	27 214 988	770	3.1
2008	25 415 067	30 979 979	820	3.3
2009	25 064 482	32 006 149	783	3.9
2010	24 930 997	33 027 943	755	3.2
2011	28 115 692	36 151 328	778	3.4
2012	29 007 003	36 463 921	795	3.3
2013	32 310 424	39 226 226	824	3.4
2014	34 305 904	41 415 070	828	3.7
2015	31 464 777	41 617 530	756	3.7
2016	22 107 440	31 365 330	705	2.6
2017	26 283 656	38 620 346	681	3.1

The share of tourism revenues in GDP follows a decreasing trend. The average expenditure per capita become lowest in 2016 and it follows a decreasing trend as well. Even though there is no decrease in the number of visitors except 2016, tourism revenue increases at a slower rate and average expenditure per person has actually decreased. These statistics actually are very important for the sector and policy makers have to understand the reasons behind this phenomenon to come up with suggestions that can increase the importance of tourism for the Turkish economy.

3 Literature Review

It is very difficult to measure the effects of foreign policy issues of a country on its tourism demand. Hence, similar studies in the literature mainly focus on terrorism. Most of the papers in the literature divide the time path of a country's tourism as before the terrorist attack and after the terrorist attack and try to measure the effect of terrorism on tourism. In this study, we chose 2013 as the beginning year of disruptive political, social and security issues Turkey has experienced.

Vivero (2008) analyzed the impact of terrorist activity on international tourist flows. He estimated a cross-sectional gravity equation for tourism from the G-7 countries to a sample of 134 destinations over the period 2001–2003. He concluded that both domestic victims and international attacks are relevant factors when foreign tourists make their choice and the impact of terrorism is more severe in developing countries.

Saha and Yap (2014) examined the effects of political instability and terrorism on tourism separately. They found out that the effect of political instability on tourism is far more severe than the effects of one-off terrorist attacks. In addition, they put out that terrorist attacks increase tourism demand for those low- to moderate-political-risk countries. However, countries that experience high levels of political risk witness significant reductions in their tourism businesses.

Fidansoy (2016) pointed out the other explanatory variables such as seasonal factors,migration and competing destinations in his study. These are explanatory variables importance of which are obvious but not used so common in the literature. For the income, GDP or GNP is the most commonly used variables. Relative prices depend on CPI of both origin and destination country and exchange rate. Transportation cost mainly measured as the price of air travel. However, this is not an effective way to measure transportation costs.

Ajogbeje, Adeniyi and Folarin (2017) gauge the influence of terrorism shocks on the tourism sector specifically on the one hand and broadly the response of some key macroeconomic variables on the other hand. They found a negative response of tourism revenues to terrorist incidents over the long haul as well as adverse effects on other key macroeconomic variables.

Buigut (2018) and Buigut and Amendah (2016) used dynamic panel model to compare the effect of terrorism on developed and emerging country demand for tourism in Kenya. He concluded that intensity of terror attack measured by fatalities significantly reduces tourist arrivals from developed countries but not from emerging countries.

Liu and Pratt (2017) quantify the relationship between terrorism and tourism in 95 different countries and territories using international tourism demand models. After controlling for income, we find there is no long-run effect of terrorism on international tourism demand and the short-run effect is quite limited from a global perspective using panel data models. Only 9 countries out of the 95 show a long-run impact of terrorism on tourism and 25 countries out of the 95 show a short-run impact using time series models, implying that international tourism is resilient to terrorism.

Sönmez (1998) after a thorough literature concluded that based on the availability and the applicability of information, tourists are pretty much on their own; individuals must make their own decisions and proceed accordingly.

Santana-Gallego, RossellÃ-Nadal, and Fourie, (2016) examined the effect of terrorism, crime and corruption on tourist arrivals for 171 countries for the period 1995–2013. Their findings show that terrorism and crime have a negative effect on tourist arrivals but that corruption has no effect. They also found out that crime and corruption in the destination country have a negative effect on inbound tourism but that instability in the origin country has no clear effect on tourist departures.

Ivanov, Gavrilina, Webster, and Ralko (2017) collected data via a self-administered questionnaire completed by 102 hotel managers and 73 travel agency managers in Ukraine. The findings confirm previous research results that political instability leads to negative impacts on the tourism industry of a country – decreased revenues, plummeting numbers of tourists and overnights, and increased costs.

On the tourism demand determination side there is a huge literature and explanatory variables used generally don't change much over time.

Lim (1997) makes the analysis out of 100 published articles on used explanatory variables to explain change in tourism demand. The first study covers the years between 1961 and 1994, 56 of them uses annual data and 5 of them uses monthly data. Out of these, 56 articles that use annual data, number of observations vary between 5 and 28 and frequencies vary between 1 and 6.

Lim (1997) defines a general model, which the dependent variable is the tourism demand and the explanatory variables are income of origin country, transportation costs, relative prices, exchange rates and qualitative factors for destination country. For the model, only log-linear single equations are used in 56 articles. As for the dependent variable, which is the tourism demand, there are different alternatives. In 51 articles, number of tourist arrivals and/or departures are used which is followed by tourism expenditures and/or receipts in 49 articles. For the explanatory variables, income is the most frequently used variable in 84 articles which is followed by relative prices (73 articles), transportation costs (55 articles), and exchange rates (25 articles).

4 Data and Model

In this study, we investigate the sensitivity of people to major political and social events in terms of their tourism demand. As a measure of sensitivity, we use the HDI by the The United Nations Development Programme. In the analysis, the dependent variable is the number of tourists, which is the most common dependent variable when estimating the international tourism demand of a country taken from TURKSTAT database. Lim (1997) states that in 51 out of 100 articles about international tourism demand, number of incoming tourist is used as the dependent variable. Only difference is that we chose the change in the number of tourists as the dependent variable. We used two explanatory variables and one dummy variable in the panel data analysis.

The explanatory variables are change in relative consumer price index (CPI) taken from OECD database, and HDI dummy interaction which is the main contribution of the paper taken from UNDP database. In the existing literature, there are many explanatory factors that are used to explain the change in tourism demand of any country. However, HDI is used for the first time in this study in order to measure the sensitivity of different countries to major political and social events in the outbound country. As an additional control variable, we chose relative CPI (relative to Turkey) which is used frequently as a powerful explanatory variable in the literature (Lim 1997).

As we try to find out the effects of domestic and international political issues on tourism demand in Turkey, we use a dummy variable for the years 2013–2016, which indicates a time of the domestic and international issues which attract significant international media coverage. The first example can be given as Gezi Protest. Then continues with tragic plane crises, coup d'état and terrorist attacks in major cities.

In the panel data analysis, fixed effect model and random effect model are used.[3] In sum, change in tourism demand of country (TDC) is the dependent variable while change in relative CPI, and HDI are independent variables.[4]

To have a better grasp of the issue, the dataset of all variables are divided into five parts named as (1) OECD (32 countries), (2) OECD Europe (22 countries), (3) OECD other (10 countries), and (4) Other European (7 countries). The analysis is done for (5) all countries (39 countries) as well. The tourism demand from these groups to Turkey is estimated by using panel data approach for 39 countries for the period between 2000 and 2017. In total, 732 observations are used in the analysis. The list of countries is given in appendix.

Tab. 8 presents the descriptive analysis of 39 countries. It is observed that average value of TD (number of tourists coming from country "i" to Turkey), CPI and HDI are 390452, 95.07 and 0.85 with the standard deviation of 747915, 14.44 and 0.08, respectively.[5]

---

3 Hausman test assist in selecting the appropriate model for selection between fixed and random effect model.

4 All the variables are in logarithm form. TD is from country "i" to Turkey.

5 All descriptive statistics are in raw levels.

Tab. 8: Descriptive statistics of all countries. Source: Author's calculation

39 countries			
	TD	**CPI**	**HDI**
Mean	390451.8	95.06607	0.847533
Median	134754	98.22473	0.869
Maximum	5580792	138.6655	0.953
Minimum	1275	19.75769	0.442
Std. Dev.	747914.6	14.43536	0.082929

Tab. 9: Descriptive statistics OECD Europe countries. Source: Author's calculation

OECD Europe			
	TD	**CPI**	**HDI**
Mean	544408	95.94128	0.877402
Median	251691.5	98.0407	0.8845
Maximum	5580792	121.957	0.953
Minimum	1275	54.73185	0.764
Std. Dev.	923386	11.7121	0.04106

Tab. 10: Descriptive statistics OECD other countries. Source: Author's calculation 3

OECD other			
	TD	**CPI**	**HDI**
Mean	153631.1	96.66871	0.873254
Median	93279.5	100	0.8945
Maximum	798787	130.1978	0.939
Minimum	10249	63.31281	0.702
Std. Dev.	189663.8	12.49131	0.059316

Tab. 9 describes the statistics of the OECD Europe group. It is found that the average value of TD, CPI and HDI are 544408, 95.94 and 0.88 with the dispersion rate of 923386, 11.71 and 0.041, respectively.

Tab. 10 shows that OECD other countries has the average value of TD, CPI and HDI are 153631.1, 96.67 and 0.87 along with the standard deviation of 189664, 12.50 and 0.06, respectively.

The average value of TD, CPI, and HDI are for other European countries are 217523, 92.02 and 0.76 with the standard dispersion rate of 402486.7, 19.79, and 0.11 respectively (see Tab. 11).

Tab. 11: Descriptive statistics other European countries. Source: Author's calculation 4

Other European			
	TD	**CPI**	**HDI**
Mean	217522.7	92.01875	0.763817
Median	61815.5	97.15184	0.789
Maximum	1852867	138.6655	0.896
Minimum	4047	19.75769	0.442
Std. Dev.	402486.7	19.78771	0.106151

Tab. 12: Descriptive statistics OECD total. Source: Author's calculation 5

OECD Total			
	TD	**CPI**	**HDI**
Mean	450082.5	96.11687	0.8764
Median	186801	98.39608	0.888
Maximum	5580792	130.1978	0.953
Minimum	1275	54.73185	0.702
Std. Dev.	826488.8	11.89672	0.046103

In Tab. 12, we see that TD, CPI and HDI of OECD total countries are 450083, 96.12, and 0.88 with the standard deviation of 826489, 11.90 and 0.05, respectively.

The following five equations are estimated:

$$(\textbf{Model 1})$$
$$\left(\boldsymbol{TDC\ OECD\ Europe}_{i,t}\right) = \boldsymbol{B}_0 + \boldsymbol{B}_1\left(\boldsymbol{CPI}_{i,t}\right) + \boldsymbol{B}_3\left(\boldsymbol{HDI}_{i,t}\right) + \boldsymbol{B}_4\ \boldsymbol{dum}2013 + \boldsymbol{u}_{i,t}$$

$$(\textbf{Model 2})$$
$$\left(\boldsymbol{TDC\ OECD\ Other\ Countries}_{i,t}\right) = \boldsymbol{B}_0 + \boldsymbol{B}_1\left(\boldsymbol{CPI}_{i,t}\right) + \boldsymbol{B}_3\left(\boldsymbol{HDI}_{i,t}\right) + \boldsymbol{B}_4\ \boldsymbol{dum}2013 + \boldsymbol{u}_{i,t}$$

$$(\textbf{Model 3})$$
$$\left(\boldsymbol{TDC\ OECD\ Countries}_{i,t}\right) = \boldsymbol{B}_0 + \boldsymbol{B}_1\left(\boldsymbol{CPI}_{i,t}\right) + \boldsymbol{B}_3\left(\boldsymbol{HDI}_{i,t}\right) + \boldsymbol{B}_4\ \boldsymbol{dum}2013 + \boldsymbol{u}_{i,t}$$

$$(\textbf{Model 4})$$
$$\left(\boldsymbol{TDC\ Other\ European}_{i,t}\right) = \boldsymbol{B}_0 + \boldsymbol{B}_1\left(\boldsymbol{CPI}_{i,t}\right) + \boldsymbol{B}_3\left(\boldsymbol{HDI}_{i,t}\right) + \boldsymbol{B}_4\ \boldsymbol{dum}2013 + \boldsymbol{u}_{i,t}$$

$$(\textbf{Model 5})$$
$$\left(\boldsymbol{TDC\ All\ Countries}_{i,t}\right)=\boldsymbol{B}_0+\boldsymbol{B}_1\left(\boldsymbol{CPI}_{i,t}\right)+\boldsymbol{B}_3\left(\boldsymbol{HDI}_{i,t}\right)+\boldsymbol{B}_4\ \boldsymbol{dum}2013+\boldsymbol{u}_{i,t}$$

The definitions of variables are as follows:

$\boldsymbol{TDC\ OECD\ Europe}_{i,t}$= Change in the number of tourist arrivals to Turkey from OECD Europe country "i" in year "t"
$\boldsymbol{TDC\ OECD\ Other\ Countries}_{i,t}$= Change in number of tourist arrivals to Turkey from OECD other country "i" in year "t"
$\boldsymbol{TDC\ OECD\ Countries}_{i,t}$: Change in the number of tourist arrivals to Turkey from OECD country "i" in year "t"
$\boldsymbol{TDC\ Other\ European}_{i,t}$: Change in the number of tourist arrivals to Turkey from Other European country "i" in year "t"
$\boldsymbol{TDC\ All\ Countries}_{i,t}$: Change in the number of tourist arrivals to Turkey from country "i" (from the group all 39 countries)
$\boldsymbol{dum}2013$: Year dummy. 1 for 2013–2014–2015–2016 and 0 for other years.
$\boldsymbol{CPI}_{i,t}$: Change in Consumer Price Index ratios. CPI $\text{Country}_{i,t}$/CPI Turkey_t
$\boldsymbol{HDI}_{i,t}$: An interaction term: Human development index in year "t"*dum2013

5 Results

First of all, Tab. 13 presents the results of Hausman test for the selected panel data. Based on the results, Hausman test suggests the use of the random effect model for all 39 countries and OECD other countries group whereas it suggests to use fixed effect model for the remaining groups.

In the following tables (14–18), we present the estimation results as suggested by the above-mentioned Hausman test.[6] This section examines the influence of change in relative CPI and especially HDI on tourism demand change with the help of a dummy variable (DUM) which tries to consider the effects of the major events as Gezi park protest, tragic plane crises, conflict between Russia and Turkey, coup d'état attempt and major terrorist attacks on the various places of Turkey on tourism activities (TDC) for 2013–2016.

Based on the results, we found out positive signs for CPI and HDI and a negative sign for DUM. (There is only one exception, the negative sign of CPI for other European countries.) It clearly indicates that when the country's relative price level increases according to Turkey, the country send more tourists to

6 Alternative estimation results are given in the appendix part. Robust results are provided.

Tab. 13: Hausman test. Source: Author's calculation

Series	Group	P-value	Decision
1	All 39 countries	1.000	Random Effect Model
2	OECD Europe	0.019	Fixed Effect Model
3	OECD Others	1.000	Random Effect Model
4	Other Europe	0.000	Fixed Effect Model
5	OECD total	0.041	Fixed Effect Model

Tab. 14: Model results of all countries. Source: Author's calculation 7

39 countries					
Variable	**Coefficient**	**Std. Error**	**t-Statistic**	**Prob.**	**Model**
CPI	0.51	0.14	3.73	0.00	Random Effect Model
HDI	9.88	0.85	11.57	0.00	
DUM2013	−0.16	0.04	-4.17	0.00	
C	11.19	0.78	14.44	0.00	

Tab. 15: Model results OECD Europe countries. Source: Author's calculation 8

OECD Europe					
Variable	**Coefficient**	**Std. Error**	**t-Statistic**	**Prob.**	**Model**
CPI	1.55	0.27	5.81	0.00	Fixed Effect Model
HDI	9.32	1.51	6.16	0.00	
DUM2013	−0.32	0.05	-6.35	0.00	
C	6.43	1.38	4.68	0.00	

Tab. 16: Model results of OECD other countries. Source: Author's calculation 9

OECD others					
Variable	**Coefficient**	**Std. Error**	**t-Statistic**	**Prob.**	**Model**
CPI	1.33	0.54	2.47	0.01	Random Effect Model
HDI	10.83	3.24	3.34	0.00	
DUM2013	−0.28	0.10	-2.80	0.01	
C	6.82	2.85	2.39	0.02	

Tab. 17: Model results of other European countries. Source: Author's calculation 10

Other Europe					
Variable	**Coefficient**	**Std. Error**	**t-Statistic**	**Prob.**	**Model**
CPI	−0.16	0.17	−0.92	0.36	Fixed Effect Model
HDI	10.94	1.23	8.90	0.00	
DUM2013	−0.08	0.08	−1.02	0.31	
C	15.10	1.05	14.32	0.00	

Tab. 18: Model results of all OECD countries. Source: Author's calculation 11

OECD total					
Variable	**Coefficient**	**Std. Error**	**t-Statistic**	**Prob.**	**Model**
CPI	1.50	0.24	6.16	0.00	Fixed Effect Model
HDI	9.70	1.41	6.86	0.00	
DUM2013	−0.31	0.04	-6.89	0.00	
C	6.53	1.26	5.18	0.00	

Turkey. More importantly, the positive sign of the interaction term HDI tells us that if a country has a higher HDI score, it is more responsive to the disruptive political and social events.

6 Policy Recommendation

Tourism demand to Turkey has been examined several times in the literature. However, many articles are relatively old and do not cover the recent Turkish political and social issues. Turkey recently experienced a loss in tourism volume. In the literature, there aren't any articles, which investigate the effects of the recent social and political issues on the tourism demand to Turkey. We did this by having HDI as a measure of sensitiveness of people to major disruptive events. The results of the study saying that higher human development level increases the sensitiveness of tourists to major disruptive events can be used in practice to find the determinants of tourism more precisely for Turkey and for other similar countries.

Turkey has been considered to be one of the most attractive destinations because of affordable prices and variety of options available for tourists. Turkey will also remain as one of the major global tourism markets and is recovering slowly from the downfall of tourism sector since 2013, especially 2016. The market continues to face a challenging outlook considering the diplomatic and internal political issues, geopolitical tensions and terrorist attacks.

Regional instability including war in Syria, tension between the Gulf countries, political friction between EU (particularly Germany) and Turkey and terrorism in general remain as main concerns of the industry. The stable relations with the NATO partners and stability in the borders are important metrics for tourism.

Tourism industry's direct contribution to GDP has a decreasing trend since 2014. It was 34.5 billion in 2014 but it was 26.1 billion in 2017 (Tourism Market Overview, 2018). The reason of this decreasing trend can be explained by decreasing average expenditure of tourists. The loss in the average tourist expenditure is much larger than the loss in the number of incoming tourists to Turkey in the time period 2013–2016.

When we remember the findings of our analysis saying that countries which have higher human development level are more prone to disruptive events, the decrease in average expenditure of tourists becomes more understandable. Countries with higher development index are also the countries which have higher GDP per capita.

As a result, country image in these high HDI countries for tourism revenue-related considerations is very important. Preventing political and social events to keep tourism revenue high as a policy suggestion is obviously unrealistic. However, Ministry of Tourism should make image improvement work in countries which has high HDI. In addition, opposition parties, the media, and civil society when using their democratic rights of criticism should remember the negative externalities that can be created through exaggerated negative image of Turkey. An exaggerated negative image of Turkey affects high HDI negatively, which are also mostly high income countries more in their tourism destination decisions. This can cause a decrease in tourism demand, average tourist expenditure and tourism revenue just because of an exaggerated negative country image.

Appendix

1 List of Countries

OECD Countries (Europe)	OECD Countries (other)	Other European countries
Austria	Australia	Estonia
Ireland	Canada	Latvia
United Kingdom	Japan	Lithuania
Belgium	Korea	Albania
Czech Republic	Mexico	Bulgaria

OECD Countries (Europe)	OECD Countries (other)	Other European countries
Denmark	New Zealand	Croatia
Finland	United States	Macedonia
France		Romania
Germany		Serbia
Greece		Slovenia
Hungary		
Iceland		
Italy		
Luxembourg		
Netherlands		
Norway		
Poland		
Portugal		
Slovakia		
Spain		
Sweden		
Switzerland		

2 Alternative Model Results

39 countries					
Variable	**Coefficient**	**Std. Error**	**t-Statistic**	**Prob.**	**Model**
LNCPI	0.51	0.14	3.73	0.00	Random Effect Model
LNHDI	9.88	0.85	11.57	0.00	
DUM	-0.16	0.04	-4.17	0.00	
C	11.19	0.78	14.44	0.00	
OECD Europe					
Variable	**Coefficient**	**Std. Error**	**t-Statistic**	**Prob.**	**Model**
LNCPI	1.55	0.27	5.81	0.00	Fixed Effect Model
LNHDI	9.32	1.51	6.16	0.00	
DUM	-0.32	0.05	-6.35	0.00	
C	6.43	1.38	4.68	0.00	

(*continued on next page*)

OECD others					
Variable	**Coefficient**	**Std. Error**	**t-Statistic**	**Prob.**	**Model**
LNCPI	1.33	0.54	2.47	0.01	Random
LNHDI	10.83	3.24	3.34	0.00	Effect
DUM	-0.28	0.10	-2.80	0.01	Model
C	6.82	2.85	2.39	0.02	

Other Europe					
Variable	**Coefficient**	**Std. Error**	**t-Statistic**	**Prob.**	**Model**
LNCPI	-0.16	0.17	-0.92	0.36	Fixed
LNHDI	10.94	1.23	8.90	0.00	Effect
DUM	-0.08	0.08	-1.02	0.31	Model
C	15.10	1.05	14.32	0.00	

OECD total					
Variable	**Coefficient**	**Std. Error**	**t-Statistic**	**Prob.**	**Model**
LNCPI	1.50	0.24	6.16	0.00	Fixed
LNHDI	9.70	1.41	6.86	0.00	Effect
DUM	-0.31	0.04	-6.89	0.00	Model
C	6.53	1.26	5.18	0.00	

References

Ajogbeje, K., Adeniyi, O., & Folarin, O. (2017). The effect of terrorism on tourism development in Nigeria: A note. *Tourism Economics*, 23(8), 1673–1678.

Buigut, S. (2018). Effect of terrorism on demand for tourism in Kenya: A comparative analysis. *Tourism and Hospitality Research*, 18(1), 28–37.

Buigut, S., & Amendah, D. D. (2016). Effect of terrorism on demand for tourism in Kenya. *Tourism Economics*, 22(5), 928–938.

Fidanboy, K., (2016). Demand for Turkey as tourist destination. Master thesis. Charles University, Faculty of social sciences, ınstitute of economic studies.

Ivanov, S., Gavrilina, M., Webster, C., & Ralko, V. (2017). Impacts of political instability on the tourism industry in Ukraine. *Journal of Policy Research in Tourism, Leisure and Events*, 9(1), 100–127.

Llorca-Vivero, R. (2008). Terrorism and international tourism: New evidence. *Defence and Peace Economics*, 19(2), 169–188.

Lim, C. (1997): Review of International Tourism Demand Models. *Annals of Tourism Research*, 24(4), 835–849.

Liu, A., & Pratt, S. (2017). Tourism's vulnerability and resilience to terrorism. *Tourism Management*, 60, 404–417.

Saha, S., & Yap, G. (2014). The moderation effects of political instability and terrorism on tourism development: A cross-country panel analysis. *Journal of Travel Research*, 53(4), 509–521.

Santana-Gallego, M., RossellÃ-Nadal, J., & Fourie, J. (2016). The effects of terrorism, crime and corruption on tourism. Economic Research Southern Africa (ERSA), 1–28.

Sönmez, S. F. (1998). Tourism, terrorism, and political instability. *Annals of Tourism Research*, 25(2), 416–456.

Tourism Market Overview, Turkey, Istanbul, 2018.

List of Figures

List of Tables

www.ingramcontent.com/pod-product-compliance
Ingram Content Group UK Ltd.
Pitfield, Milton Keynes, MK11 3LW, UK
UKHW020152290926
15471UKWH00005B/837

9 783631 782798